PRAISE

Veiled Honor gives us a glimpse into an American's encounter with the radically changing Arab world, particularly Saudi Arabia, before and after 9/11. From the shock of seeing how women (and non-Muslims) are treated to the fears and suspicions she and we all have come to feel regarding that part of the world, the author paints a sobering picture of the problems and challenges facing the Arab world today as it struggles with the forces of both modernity and radical Islam.

At the same time, Ms. Ross challenges us in the West to respond to the radicalization of the Arab world and to explore how we might prod those problematic segments to adopt enlightened views of life, liberty, religion, and freedom without imposing our culture on them or striking at their dignity and religious values.

Clearly, the world is going to be more and more split between the forces of radicalism emanating mainly from the Islamic world on the one hand and the voices of moderation arising from the rest of the world – among Christians, Jews, and Muslims.

Veiled Honor gives us a remarkable insight into the evolving Arab world and the challenges we in the West face in dealing with it. You need to read it!

Rabbi Yechiel Eckstein, President
International Fellowship of Christians and Jews

Veiled Honor is a must read for every American. It contains powerful information that could change your views of world events. Mary Laurel Ross has chronicled the significant occasions of her life by connecting them in a time line with events taking place on the world's stage, resulting in a fascinating multi-layered book.

For the military family there is obvious relevance in *Veiled Honor*. Written from the perspective of an educator and the wife of a career military officer, the book defines the struggles and challenges of the military family as an exciting adventure well worth the effort required.

The history enthusiast will enjoy reading the chronology of Middle Eastern conflicts, the role Saudi Arabia played in them, the irony of dubious alliances, and the resultant impact on all our lives. The author provides an intelligent analysis of those conflicts and gives ample documentation to support her conclusions.

Advocates for women's rights and religious freedom will be challenged by the shocking descriptions of life for females living under the strictest interpretation of Islamic law. The author speaks honestly and candidly about Muslim cultures in the Middle East and specifically in Saudi Arabia where she was given a revealing view from inside the restricted life of Saudi women. Few non-Muslims have had the experiences she writes about.

And finally, *Veiled Honor* takes the reader on a journey down the path leading to the attack on America of 9-11 by giving context to the events and personalities involved in the deadly terrorist act. You will be intrigued by the connection between major players who plotted the destruction of America.

The book is meticulously researched and richly detailed. It is both credible and relevant. As a pilot who flew in Desert Shield in late 1990 and spent time in Persian Gulf states including Saudi Arabia, I can attest to the accuracy of her writing. Reading the author's description of Khamis Mushayt, for example, was like landing, once again, in that remote air station. It was described exactly as I remembered.

I became acquainted with Mary Laurel Ross over forty years ago when her husband and I attended Air Force Flight School together. That she so quickly became friends with persons of diametrically opposed cultures is totally consistent with her friendly, outgoing, and gentle personality and of no surprise to me. Reading her book was like sitting down with old friends for a most enjoyable evening of stimulating conversation, provocative thought, and nostalgic reminiscing.

Lt. Colonel Randall Hurst, USAFR (Ret)

Veiled Honor is a riveting, incredibly powerful revelation of the Muslim mind and the interplay of Muslim history and religion. The author's firsthand experience gives her a compelling grasp of the subservient role of women and gives this book an incomparable picture of Muslim life. My gratitude for being privileged to read the manuscript is beyond measure.

Florence J. Edwards
Editorial Board, *The Voice*
Educator, Glendale Unified School District, CA

Events of the past in the Middle East have had significant impact on events in the present and the future, both in the Middle East and in many other parts of the world. In this book, Mary Laurel Ross has set her experiences of life in the Middle East in the context of many of those historical events, providing insight that will be helpful to military or civilians who anticipate living there in the future.

Veiled Honor is also a very readable addition to the libraries of those who would just like a brief refresher on Middle-eastern history and culture.

Colonel David Massey, USAF (Ret)

John and Janet,

Wishing you all the
best always — Love.

from your cousin, neighbor
and friend.

Mary Laurel Ross

VEILED

HONOR

BY

MARY LAUREL ROSS

Father's Press, LLC
Lee's Summit, MO

Cover photograph by Ryan M. Walsh
Modeled by Anitta Vrancea

Grateful acknowledgement is made for permission to reprint
excerpts from the following previously published material:
The Kingdom: Arabia and the House of Sa'ud, copyright 1981
by Robert Lacey, reprinted by permission of Houghton Mifflin
Harcourt Publishing Company.
The New King James Version, copyright 1979, 1980, 1982 by
Thomas Nelson, Inc. Used by permission. All rights reserved.
Sixty Minutes: Power to the People (Women Speak Out in
Saudi Arabia) reprinted by permission of CBS News Archives

The author Mary Laurel Ross can be contacted at:

marylaurelross@gmail.com

ISBN: 978-0-9824982-4-8

Father's Press, LLC
Lee's Summit, MO
(816) 600-6288
www.fatherspress.com
E-Mail: fatherspress@yahoo.com

DEDICATION

Veiled Honor is dedicated to those
Who long for freedom,
To those who are finally free,
And to those who make freedom possible.

ACKNOWLEDGMENTS

I would like to acknowledge the assistance of loving family members and dear friends who have been ceaseless in their encouragement, prolific in their suggestions, and gentle in their critiques of *Veiled Honor*. I am particularly grateful to the cover model Anitta Vrancea and photographer Ryan Walsh for their compelling, creative contributions. My gratitude extends to my attorney, Robert Digby of Digby Law Offices, P.C. for his immensely valuable legal advice and to my publisher, Mike Smitley of Father's Press, LLC, whose enthusiasm is contagious. Finally, I am indebted to my young Arabian friends Ahmed and Khalid who opened their homes and culture to me in the most unanticipated ways and in doing so made the writing of *Veiled Honor* possible.

To protect the identity and privacy of persons whose stories are included in *Veiled Honor*, many of their names have been changed.

VEILED

HONOR

CONTENTS

Introduction

HONOR REQUIRED

HONOR CONFLICTED

HONOR AVENGED

INTRODUCTION

From the moment the airliner landed in Jeddah, Saudi Arabia, I knew I was embarking on an adventure unlike any I had ever experienced. My husband's military career as a fighter pilot had taken us to assignments in multiple states, including three years in America's last frontier, Alaska, and in travel to European and Asian countries. In rural Germany I had stayed in the local *gasthaus* where livestock was stabled beneath the raised floor. I had relished the quaint charm of French and Swiss country sides that had changed little since World War II. I had marveled at the incredible gold temples in Bangkok, Thailand, and toured one of the world's great rivers, the mighty Mekong, where residents lived in shanties extending over the water's edge. But the Kingdom of Saudi Arabia, exotic and disarming, was a world apart from any place I had ever been.

Wanting to share the incredible experience, I began writing lengthy letters to friends and relatives; there was so much to tell, so much to describe. I wondered if the daunting length of my communications would rebuff my intended readers, resulting in quick disposal of my narratives. Would others find the extreme veiling of women, the rule of the religious police who wielded cane poles, the mournful sound coming from multiple minarets calling the faithful to daily prayers, and the seventh-century souqs of the desert Kingdom as fascinating as I did? Would my readers cringe at the reality of public beheadings for crimes against Islamic law?

As an American, I had taken for granted the freedoms guaranteed by our Constitution until I saw the incredible contrast between our rule of law and that of Shari'a, as enforced in the country that is the birthplace of Islam. I had assumed that all people recognize the value of our way of life, but I had not been in the Kingdom long when I realized we were not envied for our freedoms. Rather, we were scorned by the country's religious leaders because of them.

Soon after our arrival in the Kingdom, I had a chance encounter with two young Saudi men who would befriend my family in the most unexpected ways. Ahmed and Khalid became enthusiastic guides who opened the guarded Islamic state to my family. I was able to meet Arabian women and participate in family celebrations that were normally closed to Westerners. The young men, eager to convince me that Islam is the religion that most honors women, answered my questions with surprising candor. My new Arabian friends who spoke the same language as did the Prophet Mohammed found it inconceivable that anyone would choose not to become a Muslim. "Islam is the fastest growing religion in the world," Ahmed never tired of telling me.

After my return to the States, I learned that my mother-in-law had kept and bound my letters. A lovely gesture, I thought. I had no idea how useful those saved pages would later become in the writing of *Veiled Honor.* Meanwhile, I resumed my teaching career and accepted occasional invitations to speak about Saudi Arabia to various groups: university cultural diversity classes, women's meetings, and social events. My friends and co-workers were eager listeners of my Saudi Arabian anecdotes, and at times they suggested that I should write a book. I did not take their promptings seriously, though there were few publications about life for women in the Islamic state.

And then America was attacked. The world changed on that horrific September day. Suddenly, the Kingdom in which I had lived and my husband had advised was no longer merely an exotic Middle-Eastern country from whom we purchased oil. Osama bin Laden, the world's most wanted man dead or alive, was from Saudi Arabia, as were fifteen of the nineteen terrorists who struck America with deliberate murderous intent. Still, I only briefly considered writing about life in the Islamic state. I had a full-time teaching contract and a beautiful grandson; my days were full.

A chance visit from a college friend provided the impetus I needed. My friend, a teaching principal of a middle school in California, told me he kept my letters from Arabia and for twenty years had used them as a primary source in his social studies instruction. He insisted that since 9-11 the letters had profoundly increased in relevance. Those writings from half way around the globe were providing students a glimpse into a culture that produced men willing to die in a holy war against America. Finally convinced that my experience of living in an Islamic state should be shared with a wider audience and aware that most Americans have no idea how different our culture is from those in much of the Middle East, Asia, and Africa, I began forming *Veiled Honor.*

I am indebted to my mother-in-law who had the foresight to save my letters and to my friend who persuaded me of their value. It is my hope that the resultant book will prove enlightening and worthy of the confidence placed in me by all those who encouraged me to finally put memories to pen.

I invite my readers to share my journey into the Islamic state that had long been America's best friend among Arab nations. Considered a moderate state politically, Saudi Arabia is not moderate in its adherence to the religion that governs every aspect of life in the desert kingdom named for the family of Sa'ud. Even the national flag bears witness to the union between religion and government. Inscribed with the first tenet of Islam, the flag of Saudi Arabia declares: *There is no god but Allah and Mohammed is his messenger.*

PART ONE
HONOR REQUIRED

1
UNDER THE VEIL OF ISLAM

The cumbrous airliner shuddered as it descended into the humid and oppressively hot midnight air. Lights on the ground below, distorted by the moisture-laden atmosphere, danced eerily as we crossed the Red Sea and moved ever closer to brightly marked parallel runways that appeared to be floating in the black abyss of the Arabian desert. All evidence of alcoholic beverage service forbidden even in the airspace above the Islamic state had disappeared. Speaking in Arabic, flight attendants were preparing hundreds of travel-weary passengers for arrival in the country that is both the birthplace of Islam and guardian of the religion's two holiest shrines.

On board, nervous yet excited with anticipation, I busied myself with my two young sons, unaware at first of the remarkable transformation quietly taking place in the cabin. Coiffed hair and faces with elaborate makeup were being wrapped in thick, shapeless, black veils. Feminine features and alluring eyes believed to be suggestive, even blatantly sexual, had to be concealed and protected from the view of men. Designer fashions disappeared under black *abayas* that covered all but a few inches of skirted hemlines extending below the wearers' ankles. Western clothing suitable at departure in Frankfurt, Germany, was no longer acceptable.

We were about to land in Jeddah, customs port of entry and first in country stop on the way to our new home in Riyadh, the capital city of Saudi Arabia. It was nearly two decades before the attack on America of September 11, 2001, and long before I heard the name of the Saudi Arabian terrorist Osama bin Laden.

The initial shock was palpable as we, surrounded by silent, black-draped forms, moved off the airliner and down the Jetway stairs onto the hot tarmac. We had entered a fascinating but strange world in which the culture, religion, and government were totally interwoven under the veil of Islam. Life in the Kingdom of Saudi Arabia would prove to be intriguingly exotic but far more disconcerting than any I could have imagined.

Arabian women veil, we had been told. An interesting but harmless cultural practice in some parts of the Middle East, I reasoned. I had watched belly dancers, veiled and scantily clothed, as they gyrated to the music of flutes and stringed instruments. I had envisioned Arabian women of books and movies who wore thin veils, while laughing, seductive eyes were peeking through jeweled openings. I remembered the Biblical account of Abraham's son Isaac whose bride, Rebecca, her virginal honor intact, wore a veil to meet her new husband. The veil – the bridal veil – added to the mystery, allure, and romance of that first meeting of the ancient couple from whom would come the people of Israel. I thought I knew about veils.

I could not have been more mistaken. The only distinguishing feature beneath all the layers of black gauze was the protruding edge of an occasional eyeglass frame. The draped, shapeless masses leaving the airplane and being guided onto the terminal bus were neither laughing nor seductive. The women, not merely veiled but bagged in black, were both obscured and diminished. They spoke quietly only to one another or to their male escorts who handled all matters of entry for them.

The heat was suffocating. As a native Arizonan I was accustomed to hot summer nights, but this sweltering midnight was unlike any I had ever experienced. I wondered how the women could endure the heat with multiple layers of black gauze encasing their heads and black capes enveloping their bodies head to toe, even to fingertips.

At once I felt sympathy for the voiceless women I did not know – women who were being herded, directed, and spoken for by male relatives responsible for them. The women around me were being controlled in a way I had never before witnessed.

Gradually a vague uneasiness began to pull at my senses replacing the initial rush of sympathy. It was not fear. There was no apparent danger lurking in the unfamiliar surroundings. My uneasiness grew, however, like waves of nausea until I recognized the feeling to be that of unaccustomed oppression.

Oppression, borne not of race or nationality, encumbered these Arabian women solely on the basis of their gender.

Was this the cultural difference I had expected and for which I had prepared, or was there a much deeper chasm with the West, one that cuts to the very core of our values and beliefs about liberty and gender, about life and death, and most of all about honor? I was to learn that the rights Americans treasure were considered evil, even satanic, by many in this Islamic state. We were not envied for our freedoms of speech, the press, and religion; we were scorned because of them. I would also learn that honor, particularly the honor of men, was defined very differently than in any way I had ever known.

I had read books and watched televised films, including a documentary on Saudi Arabia, in preparation for our move to this Middle-Eastern state. The United States Air Force had sent both my husband and me to an extensive cultural training course, followed by a trip to the Pentagon for briefings. With all my accumulated knowledge, I thought I was well prepared for arrival in the Kingdom of Saudi Arabia. Incredibly, most of the books I read and films I watched were banned in the Islamic state where they were considered heretical and slanderous, both to Islam and to the House of Sa'ud, the Saudi Arabian Royal Family.

*   *   *

As were most Americans, I was stunned when terrorists struck America with deliberate murderous intent. Upon learning, however, that fifteen of the nineteen hijacking terrorists were from Saudi Arabia, I was not surprised. Those men, fervent followers of radical Islam, would have been babies when I lived in the Kingdom. Had I visited the homes or shared tea with the mothers of any of those young men who would years later desire most of all to kill Americans?

Was this Islamic state whose religious beliefs totally dictate societal rules and governmental policies really a breeding ground for terrorism against any who would choose to live differently?

Had my Arabian friends and guides, Ahmed and Khalid, become teachers of radical Islam and hatred for the West? Had Ahmed's fervor led him to do as he vowed he would to prevent the encroachment of Western freedoms into his beloved kingdom?

"I would fight to the death…" He had told me.

2
FESTERING HUMILIATION

The sunsets in Arizona are spectacular. The last of the sun's rays breaking through multiple layers of dust present themselves in brilliant bursts of scarlet, flaming orange streaks with bands of purple and golden shadows against a canvas of blue. At the turn of the century, homesteaders rushed to this beautiful but arid land, then a territory, to claim a piece of the raw desert on which to build homes. Eventually, tractors and plows used in the small farming community where I grew up contributed their share of dust to create the incredible display of color every evening before darkness descended upon the desert state.

Hardworking, patriotic, and God-fearing, the farming families seemed scarcely aware of events taking place in the Middle East and the festering humiliation that would have profound effect on all our lives. Our small town doctor and one of the local shop keepers were of Middle-Eastern descent. I neither knew nor cared whether they were Arab or Jewish. In fact, I didn't know there was a difference. My father had said, "Jews and Arabs are the same. They are like brothers who fight all the time."

My father had moved by himself from North Dakota in his mid-twenties. A determined, single young man with a strong work ethic, he cleared bottom land and cultivated a small farm near the Gila River. A man of great physical strength, my father's definition of honor had nothing to do with wealth, status, appearance, education, or religion. For him, a man of honor was one whose word was his bond. Written contracts were not necessary. He respected men whose work was honest, men who provided for their families and were faithful to them. My father had no use for pretentiousness or false piety. He scoffed at those who wore fancy suits and jiggled coins in their pockets. "A man who brags about money," he said, "is only pretending he has any."

My mother's family, devastated in the dust bowl, left Oklahoma in the 1930s and sought a livelihood in Arizona where she and my father met and married. Our family grew with a new birth about every eighteen months until my mother had given life to ten children in all.

World War II ended when I was two years old. My uncles returned from the battlefields of Europe and Asia, married their sweethearts and resumed their lives becoming copper miners in Arizona and roughnecks in California oil fields. The United States economy was, once again, flourishing. Prosperity returned to Americans who had endured the Great Depression, the crash of the stock market, a devastating drought, and two world wars.

The original homestead was sold a year later, and my family moved to a much larger farm. Products of the American farmer were in demand. We sold milk to dairies and cotton to the local gins. My brothers grew melons, which were regularly pilfered from the field by local teen-agers on late night dares, and sold them roadside in front of our farm. My mother's plump chickens and turkeys were famous throughout our rural community. Roasted or fried, they graced holiday and Sunday dinner tables all across the valley.

A small woman in stature only, my mother could catch a chicken, kill, clean, and dress it for a waiting customer in mere minutes. The poultry, so fresh it had been cackling only minutes before, cooked up tastier than any purchased from a market ever could. The pockets of her splattered and feather covered apron bulged with payment for her labors every Saturday, her busiest day of the week. Later that evening, the same small fingers that had deftly wrung the necks of countless chickens crocheted lovely table scarves from the most delicate of threads.

Our nearest neighbors were the *zanjero* for the Roosevelt Irrigation District and his pleasant-natured wife whom he affectionately called "Babe." The irrigation district, for which he supervised the distribution of water to farmers, provided them a comfortable home and about twenty acres of farm land. A large citrus grove filled their back yard. My siblings and I, walking the quarter mile barefoot, made regular trips down the dirt road to fill our gunny sacks with the fresh fruit they generously allowed us to pick. Dragging the bulging sacks home and spilling fruit along the way, we passed the home of the only black family I knew as a child.

The zanjero had a hired man to manage the farming of his land. Slim and his wife, Belle, lived with their many children in a small ramshackle cabin midway between our farm and the zanjero's home. We passed their little house, its blackened stovepipe belching gray puffs from the wood that provided their only heat, on every trip to pick fruit or to watch television with our neighbors.

Though Slim and Belle had children the same ages as some in our family, we never played together. In the days before desegregation, it would have been unthinkable, even in Arizona, for white children to play with black children.

I was too young then to know about past slavery in America or that the horrid practice would not end in Saudi Arabia, the birthplace of the Prophet Mohammed, until the 1960s, a hundred years after it ended in the United States. Third-World laborers replaced official slavery in that Middle-Eastern state. Many observers said there was little difference!

*   *   *

The State of Israel was founded in 1948 when I was five years old. The United Nations had partitioned Palestine, still under British mandate, into an Arab state and a Jewish state, though the holy city of Jerusalem, the capital of ancient Israel, remained part of Jordan. President Harry Truman announced America's recognition of the State of Israel within minutes of its formation.

Prince Faisal bin Abdul Aziz was head of the Saudi Arabian delegation to the United Nations General Assembly at the time. Outraged, both by the creation of the State of Israel and America's immediate recognition of it, Prince Faisal felt betrayed. "Break off all links with America at once," he reportedly urged his father, King Abdul Aziz ibn Sa'ud. The old king ignored his son's counsel and continued to court friendship with the United States. Prince Faisal, who later became king of Saudi Arabia, "and his militant younger brothers felt humiliated."

During the next year and a half, conflicts flared between the newly formed Israel and its Arab neighbors: Syria, Egypt, Jordan, and Lebanon, with token support from Saudi Arabia. Israel's territory increased by about one third during these conflicts; the festering humiliation and growing hostility of neighboring Arab States compounded accordingly.

* * *

There were no major cities near our rural home. Trips to Phoenix were rare and required an entire day if we were to have time to shop, eat at the Woolworth's lunch counter, purchase hot cashews for the trip home, and return before nightfall. As a result, my family used the treasured Sears and Roebuck catalog for all our school clothing. Even Santa Claus came from the catalog, though we were convinced the jolly old elf somehow found his way into our farmhouse, despite the absence of a chimney.

After countless hours of pouring through dog-eared pages of the catalog, selections were finally made, circled and check marked, crossed out and prioritized. My father carefully listed the dresses – five for each of his six daughters – blue jeans and shirts for my brothers, numerous packages of underwear and socks, and a pair of shoes for each of us on the multi-page order. My mother, using her sewing tape measure, determined the correct clothing size for her many children. We then took turns placing our right foot on the catalog's diagram with its size markings to select appropriate shoe sizes.

Once the bulging envelope containing all our intriguing selections was placed in the mail, our anticipation grew by the hour until we could scarcely endure the wait. We calculated again and again the necessary number of days before we could expect delivery but hoped, nonetheless, that it would miraculously come sooner.

When finally our order arrived, Mr. Miller, the Rural Free Delivery mailman, knowing we were dying with eagerness and that we needed to have a wheelbarrow roadside, began honking his automobile's horn well before reaching our farm. We could hear his notice of impending delivery, but all we could see as he approached was a cloud of dust as he sped our precious parcel to us. He was greeted roadside by a passel of eager, barefoot, and sun-tanned youngsters of progressive stair-step heights waiting to transport the enormous box back to our house.

Our father was immediately summoned from his work in the fields, for he alone as master of the home was allowed to open the box and check ordered items off the invoice, determining if dreaded substitutions had been made. Only then could we each begin the most arduous of tasks – deciding what to wear on the first day of school!

Ordering school clothing from a catalog would again be a necessity decades later when I lived in Saudi Arabia. Local markets offered only Middle-Eastern styles, and shopping excursions were limited; women were neither allowed to leave their homes unescorted nor to drive in that Islamic state.

* * *

My birth family did not have a television set – those early Philcos with tiny screens fixed in enormous cases. Newspapers were not delivered to our rural address, but our radio with its scratchy static brought the world into our old farmhouse. We listened to Margaret Truman, the President's daughter, sing. My mother's favorite radio soap opera, which she never missed as she worked in the home, was "Stella Dallas." Every weekend we looked forward to listening to "The Grand Ole' Opry," "The Shadow," and "Gunsmoke."

My father, an avid listener of news, was politically opinionated, and we were all persuaded by his interpretation of world conflicts and the leaders who were embroiled in them. There was never any doubt about whom he supported for political office; one of my brothers born in the late 1930s is named Franklin Delano! I can remember the presidency of

Harry Truman, but the first presidential election I remember was that of Dwight Eisenhower. My father supported the Army General and war hero enthusiastically, just as he had supported F.D.R. National events such as the Democratic and Republican Nominating Conventions were never missed by my family. In those days the party nominee was not chosen, or so we believed, until delegate votes were cast at the convention. My entire family gathered around the radio listening intently as the forty-eight states were called one by one and votes were cast. My father kept tally of the roll call on the back of a used envelope. Our old farmhouse reverberated with cheers when delegates announced their votes for Ike at the Republican Nominating Convention.

It was during the Eisenhower presidency that Soviet leader Nikita Khrushchev interrupted a speech at the United Nations by pounding his shoe on his desk and making his ominous threat against America, saying, "We will bury you!" We had no doubt he meant to do just that!

We feared polio and we feared Communism. We and everyone we knew were far more concerned about the threat of Communism than tension in the Middle East. Our schools practiced civil defense alerts as regularly as fire drills. We all understood that the Soviet Union as it spread like a cancer across Eastern Europe was the greatest threat to all freedom-loving people.

Following World War II, country after country had fallen under the domination of the totalitarian empire – the Communist regime that insisted faith in God undermined the authority of the state. When Latvia fell to the Soviet Union, several families escaped their homeland and clutched freedom to their breasts in our community. The blond daughters became my classmates and quickly learned English. In time, even the adults became thoroughly "Americanized."

We came to know a family from Hungary who had been secreted out of their homeland by hiding with their baby daughters in a small merchant ship under the cloak of darkness.

Their desire for freedom from Soviet domination outweighed their terror at the possibility of being caught and punished.

The Hungarian family, knowing their loved ones were certain to face harsh interrogation after their disappearance and fearful of retaliation against their relatives, chose to keep their plan of escape totally secret. Their families were safer if none had answers to the certain questioning that would follow. It was years before our friends could get word of their safe escape to their families and decades before they would again see any of their relatives. In the meantime, they treasured every day of freedom in the "Land of the free and home of the brave."

Life changed dramatically for Americans in the years following the end of World War II, though wars had, of course, not ended. My uncle, the youngest of my mother's eight brothers, was serving in the Korean War; my husband would serve in Vietnam; years later my son served under President Clinton as part of the U.S. Army's First Cavalry Division in Bosnia, and my former students have served in Afghanistan and Iraq.

By the mid 1950s, tiny-screened television sets with black and white images were bringing enticing commercials into homes all across our great land. Innovative home appliances of every imaginable kind were being introduced to homemakers. Long before the advent of "plastic," as we know it today, major retailers began to promote the purchase of their goods on credit, allowing families to fill their homes with luxuries they could not have dreamed of during the long years of war rationing and economic depression. Housewives traded in their wringer washers for automatic ones. White Frigidaires replaced old ice boxes. Portable electric sewing machines in convenient plastic carrying cases – though the machines were far too heavy to carry – were favored over treadle models. Gleaming chrome and Formica dinette sets found center stage in American homes, taking the place of solid oak, maple, and hickory tables that had served generations so faithfully. We discarded our huge solid oak pedestal dining table, choosing instead a new fashionable set made of steel frames and padded vinyl seats!

In the 1950s, men, including my father, were delegated master of the home. It was a perception encouraged by television commercials in which women were always meticulously groomed in crisp white aprons and high-heeled shoes while scrubbing bathrooms, by popular programming such as "Father Knows Best," and by tips published in the "The Good Wife's Guide," a magazine for women:

> Over the cooler months of the year, you should prepare and light a fire for him to unwind by...After all, catering for his comfort will provide you with immense personal satisfaction.
>
> Let him talk first – remember, his topics of conversation are more important than yours.
>
> Don't complain if he's late home for dinner or even if he stays out all night. Count this as minor compared to what he might have gone through that day.
>
> Remember, he is the master of the house and as such will always exercise his will with fairness and truthfulness. You have no right to question him.

More than half a century later, Arabian men in the cultural practices inherent in Islamic law remain unquestionably masters of their homes in ways American wives can barely fathom. Veiled and isolated in *harems*, women in Saudi Arabia are subject to the same restrictions that have governed females for centuries. As in other polygamist cultures, many live with limited health care or education and without a voice in a system devised by men. An Arabian man's honor is tied to his property: his gold and his harem. His culture provides him the ability to be master of both.

*   *   *

When Israel and Egypt fought in 1956 over shipping rights in the Suez Canal, I was in the eighth grade. If I heard news of the conflict, I paid no attention to it. The dread disease polio had afflicted a number of my classmates and left them in iron lungs or wheel chairs. The promising new vaccine developed by Jonas Salk, the race with the Soviets to put a satellite into orbit, and the cutest boy in school, Ronnie Watkins, were of much more interest to me than events in the Middle East.

The 1956 War lasted less than a week and resulted in Israel seizing the Gaza Strip, which had been Egyptian-controlled and used by Arab guerillas for raids into southern Israel. Israel also claimed nearly all of the Sinai Peninsula, producing intense Arab humiliation. The war ended with a United Nations General Assembly Resolution of ceasefire and the call for Israeli withdrawal from Egyptian territories.

Two years before the Suez-Sinai War, the Egyptian Foreign Minister Muhammad Salah al-Din had proclaimed, "The Arab people will not be embarrassed to declare: We shall not be satisfied except by the final obliteration of Israel from the map of the Middle East." A year later, Egypt's President Gamal Abdel Nasser began importing military weapons from the Soviet Union. In addition to those arms, he unleashed an unconventional weapon against Israel. The Egyptian President announced, "Egypt has decided to dispatch her heroes, the disciples of Pharaoh and the sons of Islam and they will cleanse the land of Palestine…There will be no peace on Israel's border because we demand vengeance, and vengeance is Israel's death." Egypt's "heroes," her "disciples of Pharaoh and the sons of Islam," the Arab guerillas who conducted raids into Southern Israel were the *Fedayeen,* Islamic militants.

The Middle East was being divided, as was much of Europe, between states aligned either with the United States or the Soviet Union. While Egypt was receiving military aid from the USSR, the Communist state we all feared, Saudi Arabia, having formed a friendship with the United States, was allowing American oil companies to pump "black gold" from the Arabian desert.

Saudi Arabia's King Abdul Aziz ibn Sa'ud had rejected overtures from the Soviet Union largely because of the Kremlin's god-less belief. A deeply religious Muslim, Abdul Aziz reasoned that the Soviet Union or any nation that did not believe in a Supreme Being could not be trusted.

But life in America had never been better, and we paid little attention to the political posturing taking place in the Middle East. In the year following the latest Middle-Eastern war, the iconic 1957 Chevrolet was a prized vehicle destined to become a revered classic. A young man named Elvis was redefining popular music and would come to be known as "The King." Bob's Big Boy was a double-deck hamburger, girls wore poodle skirts, and boys combed their hair into ducktails.

While Americans were vacationing in Disneyland and listening to "rock and roll," the Soviet Union launched the world's first artificial satellite, dubbed "Sputnik." Within a month, the USSR tested an intercontinental ballistic missile armed with a nuclear warhead. Our Communist enemy had the capability of launching a weapon of mass destruction that could reach the United States in thirty minutes!

That chilling realization terrified American leaders at the highest levels of government, resulting in a frantic race to outer space and the implementation of a three-pronged defensive program of mutually assured destruction or M.A.D. The threat of retaliatory obliteration would prove to be an effective deterrence against the USSR for the next three decades.

It was in the year of America's heightened awareness of the Soviet nuclear threat that Osama bin Laden was born – a Saudi Arabian whose organization of terrorism would seek to end freedom and bring catastrophic destruction to the United States just as the leader of the Soviet Union Nikita Khrushchev had threatened. However, unlike the Communist state that sought to rule as a god-less socialist society, Osama bin Laden's radical views were fueled precisely by the religion that governed his life.

Osama bin Laden is a son of Muhammad Awad bin Laden, a Yemen-born construction magnate who gained favor with the Royal Family and amassed his fortune in Saudi Arabia.

Osama's Syrian mother, described as a stunningly beautiful woman, was reportedly the least favorite of Laden's ten or eleven wives. Muhammad bin Laden had, in fact, already divorced and replaced her before Osama's birth in 1957. I, too, would one day live in the city of Osama's birth, though I would not hear his name or know of his jihadist organization of terrorism, *Al Qaeda*, until the next century.

* * *

In 1958 my parents sold the family farm and we eagerly moved to town, a community with a population of less than two thousand. We purchased a brand-new tract home for fourteen thousand dollars – a whopping twenty-six thousand, we marveled, if all of the interest were allowed to accumulate over the life of the mortgage!

At the same time, Saudi Arabians, for the most part, still lived in Bedouin tents woven of black goat hair or in mud huts. The tremendous wealth that came from oil discovered in the Arabian sand two decades earlier had primarily enriched the Royal Family and would not bring significant change to the lives of the general populace for another twenty years.

A new home was not our only purchase that year. A shiny Edsel station-wagon sat in our driveway. We were immensely proud of that new automobile – turquoise and white in color with its distinctive grill. We couldn't fathom why we were the only ones to purchase the car named for Henry Ford's son!

Saudi Arabians did not buy the Edsel either or, for that matter, any other of Henry Ford's automobiles. The Arab Boycott, an economic jihad, was instituted after the formation of the State of Israel in 1948 and included a ban of the Ford Motor Company.

American life was uncomplicated in the years of prosperity following World War II. During the 1950s and 1960s, the plague of street drugs had not yet reached into our culture. Even alcohol use was unusual among my peers. Rumors circulated of an occasional beer party on the desert, usually when someone's older sibling acquired a six-pack or two. Sex was generally reserved for marriage. "My mother would kill me," was the standard safety net, which meant, "It would break my mother's heart if I were pregnant."

An occasional classmate did leave school for a year to live with an aunt or other relative out of state and everyone suspected why. Neither pregnant girls nor unmarried young mothers were allowed to continue their public educations. Girls who had been popular cheer-leaders or prom princesses were suddenly excluded from high school. The young fathers, however, remained in classes and were captains of sports teams. Their educations and social lives were undeterred.

Common to our moral training was the view that teen-aged boys had little control of their raging hormones. Responsibility for restraint, therefore, fell upon the girls they dated. I bristled even then at the inequity of that double standard – that males received a hormonal pass on responsibility.

Little did I know that in Arab countries of the Middle East, not only was the same double standard prevalent, it was carried to the extreme and it did not end after adolescence. Unmarried girls who were believed to no longer be virgins were not merely excluded from attending school; they became victims of honor killings. Spilling their "tainted" blood inexplicably restored the requisite honor to men of their birth families and to the culture as a whole.

*　　*　　*

College, which had long been reserved for the privileged, was becoming a reality for middle-class American boys and girls alike. My oldest brother was one of the first from our community to receive an academic scholarship and to attend college. In time it was my turn, and university provided me a wide-eyed exposure to a broad cultural diversity. I had professors whose accents I had difficulty understanding and classes that were several times larger than those in the high school from which I had come. I had friends from Europe, Asia, Africa, and even a roommate from Mississippi! Jewish dorm mates prepared special foods and ate their meals in their rooms. I attended a wedding reception with a Buddhist friend and tasted my first authentic Japanese delicacies. My friend who was from India and practiced Hindu asked me to check her use of English in college papers.

Living in a dormitory was much like summer church camp, I thought. We had defined study hours, a curfew, and a strict house mom. Of course the young men were not allowed past the parlor. Individual rooms had neither a telephone nor a television. Fortunate students owned a portable typewriter; for the unquestionably fortunate, it was an electric one. In the years before spin-off products made possible by space exploration, no one dreamed of digital watches, calculators, cell phones, personal computers, or Blackberries.

The sixties was a time of violent upheaval for America. John F. Kennedy, the first Catholic to be elected President of the United States, was both inaugurated and assassinated during my college years. Our nation collectively grieved. The escalating war in Vietnam divided us for the next decade as we lost more than 58,000 of our young men. We had vigorous national debate. The Civil Rights movement, led by Dr. Martin Luther King, Jr., confronted long held prejudices and injustices. We had both freedom marches and race riots. The lines of discrimination separating religion, race, and nationality were beginning to blur.

It was a decade of changed attitudes and forgiving spirits. Only twenty years earlier, allied fighter pilots had flown Spitfires and P-51 Mustangs in aerial combat against the Luftwaffe. Now, several of my college friends dated and married German military pilots who were stationed for flight training at United States Air Force bases. An American friend of mine was casually dating a Chinese student. She unexpectedly announced her impending marriage in our junior year because his visa was about to expire, and he would be deported unless he was married to an American. Cross-racial dating, though still unusual, was becoming more accepted as well.

At university I knew two handsome males who were both engineering students and Muslims. Mohammed and Shah were from Iran, the country once known as Persia. The dark, swarthy young men were affable, dressed as any American student would, seemed to have money to burn, and were eager to date. Meeting American girls was most likely the prime motivation for those Islamic young men attending our Baptist student activities.

Mohammed and Shah were particularly persistent in asking my roommate and me out, though we were comfortable with them in group activities only. Perhaps our reluctance to date them was the result of their frequent calls to our lobby phone or the way they showed up unexpectedly in the dormitory parlor. Their insistence that we should date them gave us an uneasy feeling – a sense of apprehension that their expectations were different from ours.

Did I detect an assumption from them that we were available or even loose? Had I been warned that Middle-Eastern men think all American women are "easy"? Most certainly I had unacknowledged, unrecognized prejudices born of cultural stereotyping that shaped my attitudes and developed cautions far more than I realized.

*   *   *

Years later another young Muslim, Khalid Sheikh Mohammed, attended a Baptist college in Murfreesboro, North Carolina. Khalid, the son of an *Imam*, an Islamic cleric of the *Shi'a* sect, was studying engineering at the small college.

His family had left their native Pakistan and moved to Kuwait when he was a child. The wealthy Kuwaitis treated the Pakistani family as second class citizens, and Khalid struggled to find his place while learning both Islamic fervor and resentment borne of humiliation.

The humiliation and feelings of isolation Khalid experienced as a child in Kuwait only intensified during his college years in America. He and fellow Muslim students at the Baptist College removed their shoes and left them outside their doors while performing daily prayers facing Mecca. Other students, in typical college pranks, took the shoes of the praying men and tossed them into the campus lake.

In 1983 the engineering student who was the son of a Shi'a cleric answered the call for jihad. It was a call for Muslim men from around the world to join the fight – the holy war in Afghanistan – against the Soviet invaders and ultimately against all "enemies of Islam." Khalid Sheikh Mohammed would become the engineer of 9-11.

*   *   *

Lyndon Johnson was President of the United States, and I was finishing my second year teaching first graders in 1967 when on June fifth the Israeli-Egyptian Six Day War began. This was my first real awareness of the tremendous strife in the Middle East. I remember coworkers who were older and far more experienced than I discussing the war. They said, as many Americans have in subsequent conflicts, "It's all about oil." I was only beginning to learn that it was far more about religion, about humiliation, about a culture of honor, and about land considered holy.

In church I had studied the Biblical history of the Children of Israel and the importance of Judaism as the foundation of Christianity. The Israel of my Bible under the rule of King David had made Jerusalem its capital city. Later under the rule of David's son Solomon, the first Jewish temple was built on Mount Moriah, the very site of Abraham's obedience a thousand years earlier in being willing to offer his son Isaac in sacrifice.

The capital city of ancient Israel is significant for Christians as well. It was in the Jewish temple that Jesus was circumcised and later confounded the scribes with his teachings. Much of his ministry took place in Jerusalem, as did both his crucifixion and resurrection.

Jerusalem was conquered by Muslims in the seventh century, and in the year 687 A.D. the Islamic Dome of the Rock was erected in the very place where Solomon's temple had stood. An adjoining mosque was subsequently built and together they form an Islamic compound known as *Al Haram Al Sharif*, which covers one-fifth of Jerusalem's land space.

Jerusalem, important to both Jews and Christians, became the third holiest site in Islam.

The holy city was still part of Jordan in 1967 when Egypt's President Gamal Abdel Nasser waged a jihad, a holy war, against Israel. President Nasser, angered by the creation of the Jewish state and humiliated by the Arab defeat in 1956 when Israel triumphed over Egypt in the Suez-Sinai War, had vowed to avenge the loss of Arab lands.

I listened to news reports and heard for the first time that when a Muslim leader verbally calls for a jihad, his followers are impassioned with a religious fervor that far exceeds patriotism. I learned that an oral call for jihad does not, in fact, require the conflict to be a holy war. Just speaking the words makes it become one. The power of an Islamic leader's words on Arab listeners and their acceptance of those words as absolute truth is a phenomenon Americans, who question and debate every issue, can little understand.

Egyptian President Nasser, in calling for a jihad against Israel, proclaimed a holy war in the name of Islam, in the name of the Prophet Mohammed, and in the name of Allah. There was no greater sacrifice than to die for Allah. Young Muslim men impassioned with religious fervor were not only willing to die in a jihad against Israel; they believed Paradise would be their reward.

Israel was surrounded by an alliance of Arab nations ready to attack. On June 5, 1967, the Jewish state began preemptive air strikes against Egyptian, Jordanian, Iraqi, and Syrian airfields. In only six days, Israel forced the Arab armies into retreat and seized land that came to be known as the "occupied territories." The Sinai Peninsula, the Gaza Strip, the West Bank of Jordan, including the city of Jerusalem, and the Golan Heights all came under Israeli control.

Egypt was the brunt of blistering ridicule for its crushing defeat. Typical jokes at the time posed questions such as, "How do you recognize an Egyptian tank?" Answers mocked Egypt's rapid retreat in the face of Israel's pre-emptive strikes. "An Egyptian tank has only back-up lights." President Nasser and the Arab world, after calling for a holy war in the name of

Allah, were humiliated yet again. Not only had Israel driven Arab militaries back, it had conquered additional lands, including the holy city of Jerusalem, and it had done so in just six days!

That defeat and resultant humiliation produced terrorists throughout the Arab world who would one day call for jihad against all "enemies of Islam." Radical clerics demanded the death of Jews and promised a victorious return of Mohammed's army. While the hateful rhetoric was initially directed at Israel, America would soon be included in the call for death to the "Infidel."

* * *

Muslim cleric Abdullah Azzam had lived much of his life in Saudi Arabia where he taught in the *madrasahs*, the religious schools, and in mosques. The radical cleric saw his Palestinian hometown come under Israeli occupation during the 1967 Six Day War. Enraged and humiliated, Azzam vowed to reclaim the lost land and his peoples' honor. It was he who years later in Afghanistan, after calling for Muslims from around the world to join in the fight against the Soviet invaders, formed an international jihad network to fight the "Infidels," the "enemies of Islam." The organization was named Al Qaeda and was funded by Osama bin Laden.

* * *

When my first son was born in 1970, Richard Nixon was president, America was fighting a war in Vietnam – a proxy war with the Soviet Union – and President Gamal Abdel Nasser of Egypt died. Anwar Sadat became the new president of the Arab state. As Egypt's leader, he vowed to fight Israel and reclaim the occupied territory that had been lost in the Six Day War.

In 1972 President Sadat publicly stated that Egypt was committed to going to war with Israel and that his nation was prepared to sacrifice one million Egyptian soldiers! There could be no greater sacrifice for Islamic jihadists than to die in an effort to obliterate the State of Israel.

With money provided by Saudi Arabia, Egypt began a concentrated effort to build up its forces; it received airplanes, tanks, missiles, and various other forms of weaponry from the Soviet Union. America's greatest threat following World War II was clearly supporting Arab nations in their quarrel with our ally Israel, while Saudi Arabia, using proceeds from oil purchased by the West, funded many of those military procurements.

Unused weapons supplied by the Soviet Union were stockpiled in Egypt and in an incredible twist would one day be brokered by Americans for use in Afghanistan against the very government of their origin. Further, Saudi Arabia, the financier of weapons acquired by Egypt, would align with America in the common goal of defeating the Soviet Union, matching dollar for dollar America's support of the *Mujahadeen* in Afghanistan.

The United States of America, because of our support for Israel, our expanding economy's growing dependence on oil, and our containment policy to prevent the spread of totalitarian Communist domination, had become inexorably linked to the Middle East, specifically to Saudi Arabia, a region of the world that was festering with humiliation.

3

AN EMERGING THREAT

"We were coming out of a spin today when I realized he still didn't understand horizon." Air Force instructor pilots swapped stories about their Iranian students who with rudimentary English were often late in understanding key references as basic as horizon and how to use them to orient their aircraft in flight. The Shah of Iran, ruling hereditary monarch, sent the best and brightest Iranian young men to bases in America for flight training from the United States Air Force.

Critical communication was difficult with the Iranian flight students due to their limited knowledge of English. Idioms were particularly confusing. The problems created by language barriers were exacerbated by their culturally ingrained sense of pride or "saving face." It was humiliating for them to indicate they didn't understand a command or concept. Their pride made the men unlikely to ask for help or even clarification of training procedures in the aircraft they were learning to fly. Further, they were unwilling to admit error in judgment during flight. To do so would have brought dishonor to these proud Middle-Eastern men.

Even worse, to fail in flight training and return to Iran without military flight wings would have resulted in great humiliation for their families and, it was rumored, probable death to the failed student pilots. Humiliation, we were to learn, was the "most powerful driving force" in the Middle East. Death was more honorable and always preferable to embarrassment or humiliation. Honor killings were, after all, well, honorable.

"If Allah wants me to die, I die!" the Iranian men said with a shrug of the shoulder. All of life's circumstances and ultimately death were controlled by Allah. Personal choices were of little consequence. *Masha'allah.* Allah's will was the guiding principle of their lives. An airplane crash resulting in death would surely be Allah's will; it could never be caused by their error.

I shuddered at their fatalistic approach to life in general and to learning to fly military aircraft in particular. It was clearly not the philosophy an instructor pilot or his wife could comfortably accept in a student pilot!

My husband had many Iranian flight students during his tenure as an instructor pilot, and two of them became particularly close to us. Mohammed and Hajji often visited our home and played with our baby son. They shared our meals and occasionally cooked traditional Iranian dinners for us. We respected their Muslim food and drink restrictions and their need to have a prayer rug with them for regular prayers facing Mecca.

Proud men, Mohammed and Hajji were eager to become part of the Iranian Air Force. So appreciative were they of my husband teaching them to fly their first military jet, they presented me with Iranian jewelry and hand painted picture frames and vases with intricate designs similar to those in Persian rugs. They spoke often of the Shah of Iran. It was obvious they held him in highest regard.

"He is doing much to make our country better," Hajji told us.

*   *   *

1973 brought tremendous change to the United States. Some of it was long overdue and welcomed with rejoicing, while other developments wreaked havoc in our government and on our economy. Americans long held and tortured in prison camps in and around Hanoi were finally released and returned home. The prisons' names given by the captured U.S. servicemen who suffered in them reflected the awful truth: the facilities were administered in the totally inhumane fashion so common to Communist regimes. "Dogpatch" and "Heartbreak" both saw many more U.S. prisoners of war enter their gates than ever lived to leave them. Books with titles such as *The Passing of the Night* and *Six Years in Hell* detailed the unspeakable horrors those men endured in service to our nation.

President Nixon, re-elected only a year earlier, was embroiled in the Watergate investigation. Vice President Spiro

Agnew resigned after pleading no contest to tax evasion charges, and Congressman Gerald Ford replaced him. "Mash" and "The Waltons" were popular television shows that provided needed respite from nightly reports of crisis in the Executive Branch, while Middle-Eastern oil-producing nations were threatening an embargo; it was an action akin to an economic jihad against America.

My husband returned from his year-long combat tour in Vietnam, we moved to Alaska, and in October I gave birth to our second son. In his new military assignment, my husband flew air defense alert missions over the Bering Strait, the first line of defense of America against the nuclear-equipped long-range Soviet bomber fleet. His alert status and frequent rapid deployments provided me daily awareness of the danger we faced, but I wondered how many Americans were even aware of the ominous Soviet nuclear threat lurking at our northern border.

Television programming in Alaska was limited and came to us from the lower forty-eight via sea-going barge on a two week delay. Hearty, independent Alaskans cared little about what happened "outside." We heard more about the Iditarod, the annual dog-sled race from Anchorage to Nome, winter fur carnivals, and the rescue of climbers on Denali than we heard about the Middle East.

Current news was available by radio, but with a toddler and an infant I had limited time to listen to reports of the latest Middle-Eastern war fought from October 6 to October 26. Egypt and Syria had launched an attack against Israel on the holiest day of the Jewish calendar. Known as the Yom Kippur War, the Ramadhan War, the October War, and the 1973 Arab-Israeli War, it covered a period of time that came to be recognized as the "Two weeks that changed the world."

Saudi Arabia was now ruled by King Faisal bin Abdul Aziz. As prince and head of the Saudi Arabian delegation to the United Nations General Assembly, Faisal had, years earlier, urged his father to break all ties with the United States after the establishment of the State of Israel. He had been humiliated when his father, King Abdul Aziz ibn Sa'ud, ignored his counsel. Now the ruling monarch, King Faisal continued to sell oil to America while at the same time providing funds for Egypt's purchase of weaponry from the Soviet Union – weaponry meant to "bloody Israel" and force its defeat.

Humiliated by the 1967 loss to Israel, Egyptian President Anwar Sadat and neighboring Syria sought during the Yom Kippur War to regain lost territories and restore their national and cultural honor. President Sadat "set into motion a plan to recapture the Suez Canal and wipe out the humiliation of the six day war...Sadat's goal was to cross the Suez, bloody the Israeli army, recapture the Canal and as much of the Sinai as possible." Initially, Arab armies made significant advances against Israel, but with America's backing, the Jewish state was able once again to defeat her enemies.

Saudi Arabia's King Faisal was furious with the United States over our support of Israel during the 1973 War and, as a result, was first to announce an oil embargo against America. Oil producing nations in the Middle East decreased production and forced a steady rise in the price of crude, causing America to face its first fuel shortage since World War II. Never again were we to see the price of oil at two dollars a barrel!

Ironically, as Arab hatred for Israel grew, the 1973 War contributed to an unexpected peace between Israel and its long-standing enemy Egypt. Arab nations had been humiliated in prior conflicts with Israel, particularly the Six Day War of 1967. Early in the Yom Kippur War, however, Arab armies celebrated a string of victories, somewhat assuaging the humiliation of earlier defeats.

The "psychological vindication" of the Arab world that early victories produced paved the way for a peace process normalizing relations between Egypt and Israel. Egypt, the first Arab nation to recognize the State of Israel, in March 1979 entered into a peace agreement at Camp David. President Jimmy Carter witnessed the signing of the agreement by Egyptian President Anwar Sadat and Israeli Prime Minister Menachem Begin. With that peace, "Egypt began to leave the sphere of Soviet influence."

The signing of the Camp David Accords was hailed as a major diplomatic accomplishment. It was to establish President Carter's legacy as a Middle East peace-broker. However, the peace agreement infuriated Muslim zealots, leading to the assassination of the Egyptian President who signed it. In 1981 as Anwar Sadat saluted troops during an annual military parade, one that celebrated the Arab string of victories during the Yom Kippur War, a group of men in military uniforms rushed the reviewing stands and unleashed a barrage of machine gun fire and grenades. With the death of the Egyptian President who had made peace with Israel, moderate Islam began to take a back seat to more radical views. Following the Camp David Accords, radical Islamists planned terrorist attacks both within Israel and in America.

* * *

Ramzi Yousef, a young man of Pakistani descent, though he had lived much of his life in Kuwait, was angered by the peace agreement between Israel and Egypt. He began forming plans meant to punish Israel and restore his peoples' honor. Fourteen years after the Camp David Accords, Ramzi Yousef built and planted a bomb of cyanide gas in the World Trade Center in New York. His expressed intent was to kill as many Jews as possible and to bring carnage of Biblical proportion to America.

Ramzi Yousef, a nephew of Khalid Sheikh Mohammed, the engineer of 9-11, received permission to carry out the 1993 terrorist act against America from Sheikh Omar Abdel Rahman, a cleric of the Al Farouq Mosque in Brooklyn, New York. The Islamic connection to his terrorist act was undeniable.

* * *

The Camp David Accords angered some in Israel, as well. An underground movement resisted the return of any occupied land to Palestinians. Reportedly, some Israelis plotted destruction of the Dome of the Rock, the third holiest place in Islam, which sits on the Temple Mount, the site of Solomon's temple in Jerusalem.

While Israel's claim to Jerusalem was, in part, "We were here first," the Arab claim was, "We are here now." According to Islamic teachings, the Prophet Mohammed made a mystic night journey flying on a white, winged horse-like creature from Mecca in Arabia to the Temple Mount in Jerusalem. There, Islam teaches, he came face to face with Abraham, Moses, and Jesus.

Led by the Angel Gabriel, Mohammed was taken to the pinnacle of the rock where a ladder bathed in golden light was suspended for him. Climbing the alternating gold and silver steps, Mohammed ascended through the seven heavens for a personal meeting with Allah who instructed him in the religion of Islam. Following that meeting and before the morning light of dawn, the Prophet of Allah was flown back to Mecca on the same winged steed known as *El Buraq* or "Lightning."

Jerusalem was captured by the Muslim Caliph Umar in 638, six years after the Prophet Mohammed's death. Later in that century, the conquering Muslims desired to build a "more spectacular edifice" than the existing Christian structure the Church of the Holy Sepulcher, which had been commissioned three hundred years earlier by Helena, mother of the Roman Emperor Constantine. "The site chosen [for the Islamic Dome of the Rock] was the very same rock where previously stood the Jupiter temple of the Romans and before that, the [twice built] temple of the Jews."

The Dome of the Rock was meant to proclaim the supremacy of Islam, to commemorate the miraculous night journey of its prophet, and to ensure that Muslim converts would not be persuaded to accept Judaism or Christianity. The *Al-Aqsa Mosque* was subsequently built adjacent to the Dome of the Rock as a place for Muslims to offer their prayers to Allah.

* * *

My husband's former flight students Hajji and Mohammed had both returned to Iran and were serving in the Iranian Air Force. We continued to receive letters from them – letters filled with appreciation and warmest regards to our family. The correspondence continued until Iran fell in 1979 to Islamic extremists who called for the overthrow of the Shah.

The Shah of Iran, Muhammad Reza Pahlavi, had led his moderate Muslim nation to strong economic growth and modernization. The growing middle class in Iran enjoyed purchasing goods from Europe and America and was copying the West in matters of style and practice. Young Persian women not only dressed in fashionable clothing, they attended university and accepted positions alongside men in the work force. The Shah had appointed women as ministers, or cabinet secretaries, in his government. There were even a few Christian missionaries serving in Iran, which was a predominantly Muslim nation.

"He is doing much to make our country better," our friend Hajji had said of the Shah of Iran.

With its ties to the West and to the United States in particular, Iran, the best non-Jewish friend America had in the Middle East, was a welcomed balance to the several countries in the region that continued to receive military aid from our Communist enemy the Soviet Union. However, the Shah used the secret police, the *Savak,* to control the country. Dissidents were imprisoned and tortured. The Iranian monarch was reviled by his critics as a brutal dictator and a "Puppet of America." Fueled by the exiled Islamic leader the Ayatollah Khomeini, opposition grew against the Shah until Iran was close to civil war.

During his exile in both Iraq and France, the Ayatollah Khomeini continued to send taped messages of revolution into Iran. He called for an end to the Shah's rule in order to establish a *Caliphate,* a government ruled by Islamic law, in the nation that until 1935 had been known as Persia. The Islamic revolution and the call for a Caliphate gave political voice to the religion of the Prophet Mohammed. It was a voice for radical Islamic jihad and the reclaiming of dominance that in earlier centuries had been held by Muslim armies as they marched across Asia, Europe, and Africa.

The Ayatollah Khomeini practiced *Shi'a* Islam – a different sect than the *Sunni* Islam of the Shah. Sunni Islam, observed by about eighty-five percent of Muslims world-wide, provides that Muslim leaders be chosen by community consensus. Shi'a Islam, the minority sect, believes that Muslim leaders must be descendants of Ali ibn Abu Talib, a cousin of the Prophet Mohammed.

Mohammed's parents both died when he was a very young child. His uncle Abu Talib, assuming the role of protector, brought the orphaned boy into his home. Years later, a son Ali was born to Abu Talib. (*ibn* means "the son of" and *Abu* means "the father of." Ali *ibn Abu* Talib means Ali, *the son of the father of* Talib.) Ali was only ten years old when the older Mohammed began teaching his religious revelation that was said to be from the Angel Gabriel. Though still a child, the boy cousin was an eager student of the prayers and precepts Mohammed taught him. Ali was second only to the Prophet's wife Khadijah in converting to Islam.

Ali became Mohammed's son-in-law as well when he married the Prophet's daughter Fatimah. She produced two sons for her husband, and the boys, Hasan and Hussein, were said to be the joy of their grandfather, the self-proclaimed messenger of Allah. Mohammed's wife Khadijah had given birth to two sons and four daughters, but both sons died in infancy, leaving the Prophet in the unenviable position of being a father of girls.

After Mohammed's death, his followers disagreed about who would become the leader of Muslims in his stead. Most believed the religious leader should be chosen by consensus. After all, Mohammed had a number of close associates from whom to choose – associates who shared the views, teachings, and lifestyle of the Prophet. But others among the Muslims insisted that only Ali, the cousin and son-in-law of Mohammed and closest male relative, should succeed him.

The majority view prevailed, and Abu Bakr (*the father of* Bakr) was selected as Mohammed's successor to be the first Islamic *Caliph* after the Prophet. Abu Bakr had been an early convert to Islam and remained a close associate of Mohammed's. In fact, he became father-in-law to Mohammed after his young daughter Aisha became one of the Prophet's wives.

A smaller portion of the followers of Islam remained adamant that the successor should have been Ali. Eventually Ali did become the fourth Caliph in the year 656 after his predecessor was assassinated. He was considered the first *Imam* or male descendant of the Prophet to rule Islam. (Ali was, of course, a relative not a descendant.) The religion continued to be rife with dissent, conflict, and struggle for control, leading to Ali's assassination five years later in the town of Kufa in present-day Iraq. The followers of Ali were known at *Shi'at Ali* or Partisans of Ali, and throughout history they have remained the minority sect of Islam.

As Partisans of Ali, Shi'a Muslims consider him their first "legitimate" Islamic ruler after the Prophet. Ali's two sons by his wife Fatimah, Hasan and Hussein, became the second and third Imams, respectively. In the year 680, Hussein who was then the third Imam led his army in battle against a much more powerful army of the ruling Muslim "illegitimate" Sunni Caliph in Karbala, Iraq. But the battle did not go well for the Shi'a warriors. Hussein, the son of Ali and grandson of the Prophet Mohammed, was beheaded and the bodies of his massacred army were mutilated.

Hussein's "martyrdom" greatly intensified the split between Sunni and Shi'a Muslims. It made Karbala a place of tremendous religious significance for the Shi'a who commemorate Hussein's death with self-flagellation and grieving in recognition of the pain he and his family suffered. "A popular Shi'a saying proclaims that, 'A single tear shed for Hussein washes away a hundred sins.'"

Shi'a Muslims believe that Ali's wife Fatimah was Mohammed's only daughter, rather than the youngest of four, making Ali ibn Abu Talib the Prophet's sole son-in-law and only rightful successor. Fatimah was also the mother of a martyred son, Hussein. As the only daughter of the Prophet, the wife of Ali the "legitimate" Imam, and the mother of a martyred son, Fatimah is held in highest esteem by Shi'a who consider her the Muslim counterpart to the Christian Mary, mother of Jesus. One of Fatimah's names given by the Shi'a is *Maryam al-Kubra,* which means "the greater Mary."

Throughout history, each Islamic sect continued to have its own religious leader: Sunnis chose Caliphs by consensus, while Shi'a designated Imams who were male descendants of the Prophet. The line of Imams followed Ali's blood line until the death of the eleventh one, Hassan al-Askari, in 873. His son, Muhammad al-Mahdi, would have become the twelfth Imam, but he mysteriously disappeared during his father's funeral, leaving only representatives not descendants of Mohammed to succeed him.

Shi'a Muslims look forward to the return of the twelfth Imam whom they believe to be in hiding since the unexplained disappearance of Muhammad al-Mahdi. Known as "The Mahdi," the twelfth Imam is perceived as a kind of messiah who will bring the entire world under the rule of Islamic law. Many believe The Mahdi will not only share the name of their prophet, he will even physically resemble Mohammed.

The most fervent of Shi'a believe they can hasten the coming of the twelfth Imam, the messianic-like Mahdi, by ridding the world of all evil in their midst. Willing to sacrifice millions in an apocalypse that would result in world-wide Islamic rule, many Shi'a Muslims are convinced it is their duty to kill "Infidels" who oppose their mission for Allah.

The Ayatollah Khomeini, in fomenting the Islamic Revolution in Iran, used the martyrdom of Hussein the son of Ali and grandson of the Prophet Mohammed to rally his faithful in the fight against the Iranian monarchy and to catalyze political action in his favor. His radical view of Islam called for Muslims to rise up and destroy all evil in the world in order to clear the way for the establishment of a true Islamic state, one that would in time be ruled by a descendant of the Prophet Mohammed. The murderous revolution that ensued resulted in the deaths of countless Iranians.

America, under the leadership of President Jimmy Carter, according to Robert Lacey in *The Kingdom*:

> "...seemed to hope it could get out of
> fighting any more Vietnams by transforming
> the human race into a more moral category

of animal, and in Iran this confused idealism had both encouraged opposition to the Shah and fatally undermined the man whom America had installed and maintained for twenty-five years as her best non-Jewish friend in the Middle East."

Ironically, the Ayatollah Khomeini's revolution in Iran had nothing to do with human rights or ending the abuses of the Shah. Those ideals were merely pretexts used in the rhetoric of the revolution to destroy the monarchy and establish an Islamic state in its place.

The Shah left Iran on January 16, 1979, reportedly at the urging of President Carter. Two weeks after the Shah's departure, the Ayatollah Khomeini returned to Iran. Critics of the President have said, "Carter threw the Shah under the bus while spreading a welcome mat for the Ayatollah!"

Within weeks, Khomeini declared the country an Islamic Republic. The new constitution required that every aspect of society and government be decided by strict Islamic rule. There would be no division between church and state. The country was to be totally controlled by the dictates of Islam under *Shari'a*, the social code of Islam considered "the straight path," which governs every action in life. Terrorism groups, among them *Hamas* and *Hezbollah*, were given birth by Iran after its fall to radical Islam.

We watched televised coverage of crowds of Shi'a Muslims chanting and performing self-flagellations in the streets of Tehran. Their clothes were bloody from self-inflicted beatings with chains as they celebrated the return of Shi'a rule and commemorated the martyrdom of Hussein, the grandson of their prophet.

My young sons asked if such a revolution, an Islamic revolution, could happen to us in America. "Never!" I replied. How could I have known in 1979 that radical Islam's war against America had begun with the fall of Iran, and twenty-two years later, radical Islamists, most of whom were from Saudi

Arabia, would attack America in the worst terrorism attack in history?

"If only we had stood firmly with the Shah," my husband had said at the time of Iran's Islamic revolution. "It was a mistake to let Iran fall."

*　　*　　*

Iranians demonstrated in vain against their new Islamic government. Dissenters protested the strict laws, the loss of freedoms, and the severe dress code for women. However, the Ayatollah had already begun the purging. Anyone who was loyal to the Shah or had worked in his government or voiced dissent to Islamic law was executed. The human rights violations of the Shah paled in the wake of the Ayatollah's murderous revolution.

We have no doubt that former flight students Mohammed and Hajji, as members of the Shah's Iranian Air Force, were brutally killed as the Islamic government replaced the Shah's regime, and his movement toward modernization and friendship with America ended.

"They are dead," my husband said of Hajji and Mohammed. "They were too loyal to the Shah to have survived." Sadly, I knew he was correct.

The American Embassy in Tehran was overtaken by radical Islamists, most of whom were students, in November 1979. Of the sixty-six hostages taken, sixty of them were Americans. Twelve of the hostages were released in late November, but those remaining were held captive for 444 days, despite a failed American attempt to rescue them.

The Shah, the "Puppet of America," had been driven to exile. But why, I wondered, was the United States Embassy in Iran attacked? In the newly proclaimed Islamic Republic, how had the United States become an "enemy of Islam"? America, above all, valued freedom of religion. But according to the radical belief of the Ayatollah, freedom of religion was an anathema. Only Islam was allowed, and anyone who did not practice his strict interpretation of the laws of Mohammed was both an "Infidel" and an "enemy of Islam."

The Americans held hostage in Iran were released just before President Carter handed the keys of government to the newly elected American president. I was attending a military officers' wives coffee on that winter day. We watched the televised inauguration of President Ronald Reagan and heard a simultaneous newscast announce that the airplane carrying the hostages had left Tehran. It was January 20, 1981. Saudi Arabia's perception of America as its ally during this tumultuous period diminished dramatically. America's "confused idealism" under President Carter that had "fatally undermined" the Shah also prevented Crown Prince Fahd of Saudi Arabia from supporting the Camp David Accords, the peace agreement between Israel and Egypt. Though Prince Fahd had long been a friend to America, "he had finally to agree with his brothers that an America that could not save the Shah could not save the Al Sa'ud [the Royal Family of Saudi Arabia] either." America had failed in its military attempt to rescue the hostages held in Iran. What good would America be in saving Arabian oil fields if they were attacked? The consensus of Prince Fahd and his brothers was that "President Carter was more likely to wring his hands and talk of human rights than to send in the marines…"

*　*　*

The fall of Iran from a pro-west regime to a radical Islamic state provided the first glimpse most of us in America had of the religion that is prominent in the Middle East. The armies of Mohammed had once used the sword to spread his religion across much of Europe, Asia, and Africa. Now, centuries later, we witnessed the resurgence of Islam as a political force. Freedoms in Iran were replaced with an unrelenting enforcement of Islamic law in the name of Allah.

My Jewish-born Christian Pastor shook his head sadly, commenting that the murderous revolution in Iran was being done in the name of Abraham, the first Patriarch of Judaism and the Father of Faith to Christians. I soon learned that while Islam does claim its beginning in Abraham, it is not of the same lineage as for Christians and Jews. Instead of descendants from

Abraham's son Isaac, the "Son of the Promise," according to Genesis, the first book of the Bible, Islam claims lineage through Ishmael, Abraham's son by Hagar, who was an Egyptian slave.

I learned that God promised a son to Abraham and Sarah, even in their old age. His descendants would be numbered as the stars of the sky. Through this promised son's lineage, according to the Bible, the entire world would be blessed.

In an act of faith and obedience, Abraham had been willing to sacrifice his "only son, Isaac" on Mount Moriah in response to God's testing. A thousand years later, the Jewish Temple was erected on Mount Moriah, and a thousand years after that, the crucifixion of Jesus took place on nearby Golgotha. While Isaac's lineage leads to the Jewish people and ultimately to the birth of Jesus Christ, Ishmael's lineage leads to many of the Arab people, to Islam, and to Allah.

According to Islam, the sacrificial experience of Abraham was not with Isaac; it was with Ishmael, Abraham's son by Sarah's handmaiden, Hagar. Ishmael was conceived when Sarah doubted God would give her a child in her old age and offered her slave to her husband for the purpose of producing a son. The Koran teaches that Abraham's offering of Ishmael took place, not on Mount Moriah, but in Mecca, Saudi Arabia.

Twenty-six centuries after Abraham, the Prophet Mohammed was born in Mecca. The culture in which he lived was one of pagan, tribal polytheism. Each tribe and, in fact, each family had its own idols or gods. Allah was one of hundreds of gods worshipped. However, Allah was not considered a supreme god, a personal god, or one who involved himself in human matters.

The Prophet Mohammed, after learning of *Elohim* the God of the Bible and of Abraham the first Patriarch of Judaism, declared the first tenet of Islam:

There is no god but Allah, and Mohammed is his messenger.

*   *   *

America and her allies had fought the spread of
Communism all of my life. The Soviet Union for thirty years
had posed the greatest threat to freedom, and it would continue
to do so for another decade. Deterrence was our best defense
against the Great Bear of the North; a strong military and an
advanced nuclear defense system kept the Soviets at bay. Their
leaders knew that any attack on America would result in a
massive counter attack with the potential of obliterating their
cities. The Kremlin understood and responded to deterrence.
Committed to a state, not an ideology, the Socialist Republic
was brutal, but it was not suicidal.

By 1979 a new threat was emerging. It was a threat that
would, in time, replace that of the Soviet Union as the greatest
danger we faced. America, the friend of Israel, had inexplicably
become an "enemy of Islam," resulting in unprecedented acts of
terrorism against our nation.

Unlike the Soviets, radical Islamists *are* suicidal. Deterrence
would prove ineffective against jihadists who serve an ideology
for which death is a noble act that ensures Paradise. Egyptian
President Sadat had been willing to sacrifice a million young
men in his jihad against Israel. Their deaths would not have
been for the good of the Egyptian state but, rather, for an
ideology in service to Allah.

"If Allah wants me to die, I die," the Iranian flight students
had said, their shoulders shrugged. Osama bin Laden would
later proclaim, "We love death. The United States loves life.
That is the big difference between us."

In 1979 Israel and Egypt signed the Camp David Accords.
The Jewish Underground resisted the return of any occupied
lands to Palestinians, while Islamic jihadists sought the
destruction of Israel and the killing of Jews both in the Jewish
state and in America.

In 1979 Iran became an Islamic Republic. With the
revolution, the religion of Mohammed gained a political voice
that emboldened its challenge of the West. Radical students
stormed the United States Embassy in Tehran, and Americans
were held hostage for more than a year without retribution from
our government. In the thirty years since, we have not had an

embassy in Tehran nor do we have normal diplomatic relations with the country that was once our best non-Jewish ally in the Middle East. The Islamic government of Iran continues its state sponsored terrorism and its desire to develop nuclear weapons. Its leaders have repeatedly vowed to destroy Israel.

The ultimate goal of ruling Shi'a Ayatollahs in Iran is to bring the entire world under the dictates of Islamic law. While awaiting the return of the messianic-like descendant of the Prophet Mohammed, religious leaders proclaim the first tenet of Islam to the absolute exclusion of all other religions.

In 1979 Saddam Hussein, a Sunni Muslim, was named President of Iraq. The following year his army invaded Iran, the new Islamic Republic, in a costly war financed largely by Saudi Arabia and Kuwait. The Iraqi President, furious after Kuwait's refusal to forgive his ten billion dollar war debt, a decade later attacked that benefactor nation with the intent of taking control of the world's largest oil reserves. America and her allies marked "a line in the sand" against Iraq, ending its occupation of Kuwait, though the dictator known as "The Butcher of Baghdad" continued to rule with murderous brutality until the fall of Baghdad in April 2003.

In 1979 Idi Amin, the ruthless dictator of the African nation Uganda, was overthrown. "The Butcher of Uganda" was responsible for the murder (including that of one of his wives who was found dismembered) and disappearance of as many as 500,000 persons during his reign of terror. Complicit in the Palestinian hijacking of an Air France Airliner, Amin held about one hundred Israeli passengers hostage at the Entebbe Airport in Uganda. On July 4, 1976, (the bi-centennial of America) Israeli commandos rescued the hostages – a personal defeat that deeply humiliated the dictator. (Two hostages were shot during the rescue and one was inadvertently left behind – a British-Israeli grandmother who was later brutally executed.)

After being deposed, Idi Amin who was a convert to Islam fled the country with his four wives, thirty mistresses, and twenty of his forty-three children. He was granted sanctuary in Jeddah, Saudi Arabia, where he lived until his death in 2003. The Saudi Arabian Royal Family who granted him safety and a government stipend was widely criticized for not allowing the international community to bring "The Butcher of Uganda" to justice.

Criticism of Saudi Arabia was not limited to outside voices. Dissidents within the Kingdom protested the Royal Family, claiming it was not adhering to Islamic law and was, therefore, not suitable to rule the birthplace of Islam or to protect its holiest shrines. King Faisal had been assassinated four years earlier. Now the reign of King Khalid and Crown Prince Fahd was threatened by those who called for a stricter enforcement of Shari'a.

Saudi Arabia practiced Salafism, which is often referred to as Wahhabism. It is an interpretation of Islam that places great value in the traditions of the patriarchs. The austere lifestyle of the Prophet Mohammed and his closest associates was revered and considered "the straight path." Modernization to a traditionalist represented a departure from the teachings and example of the Messenger of Allah.

By 1979 the Royal Family of Saudi Arabia had begun using its tremendous oil wealth to modernize the desert kingdom. King Khalid authorized the construction of the nation's first hospitals; wealthy Saudis were engaging in big business endeavors, and foreign laborers were hired to do the work Saudis, themselves, would never do. However, traditionalists opposed any changes in the Kingdom. New high-rise buildings and the influx of foreigners, many of whom were regarded as "Infidels," constituted unacceptable threats to the seventh century culture of the Islamic state.

Could an Islamic revolution, I wondered, overthrow the House of Sa'ud, the Royal Family of Saudi Arabia? Radicals voiced their opposition to the government, but no one could have predicted the shocking focus of their protests.

In an unimaginable attack, armed dissidents seized the Grand Mosque in Mecca, Saudi Arabia. From a loud speaker, one normally used for prayers, a voice proclaimed the return of the messianic-like Mahdi, declaring that he would both cleanse Arabia of its corruptions and spread justice to the entire world.

One hundred twenty-seven Saudi Arabian soldiers were killed and nearly five hundred injured as they fought to reclaim the shrine revered by Muslims worldwide as the holiest place on earth.

King Khalid was said to have been deeply grieved, both by the loss of life and injury to Saudi young men and by the inconceivable violence that had desecrated the Grand Mosque. As monarch of Saudi Arabia, he had the ultimate responsibility of protecting its most revered shrines. Under his watch, the Grand Mosque in Mecca, meant to be a place of reverence and submission to Allah, had become the site of bloodshed and death.

As reports of the violent capture of the Grand Mosque reached the outside world, Iran's Ayatollah Khomeini capitalized on the occasion to further fuel hatred for America and Israel. Knowing that as an Islamic leader the veracity of his words would not be questioned, he announced that it was Americans and Zionists who had "defiled Islam's most sacred shrine" in Mecca. In response to his fallacious report, an angry mob attacked the American Embassy in Pakistan, killing two United States Marines. To much of the Muslim world for whom honor was more important than truth, America was not only the friend of Israel; we had become an "enemy of Islam."

The Ayatollah's poisonous rhetoric resulted in additional uprisings against the Royal Family of Saudi Arabia. The eastern provinces of the Kingdom were inhabited primarily by Shi'a Muslims who by virtue of their allegiance to Ali more identified with the Ayatollah of Iran than with the House of Sa'ud. They were religiously separated from the pious Wahhabi Saudis.

These "Partisans of Ali," who numbered in the 200,000s, worked in the oil fields of Arabia but shared little of the wealth of the Kingdom. The Islamic revolution in Iran, in which Shi'a Muslims had gained governmental control, had encouraged the Arabian Shi'a to fight for freedom from the "tyranny oppressing them." Their pilgrimages to shrines in Iraq in remembrance of the deaths of Ali and his son Hussein only furthered their discontent with the Sunni Royal Family who ruled the

Kingdom. The division between Sunni and Shi'a Muslims was growing ever wider in the birthplace of Islam.

* * *

While the world's attention was focused on Middle-Eastern turmoil and the American hostages being held in Iran, the Great Bear of the North, the Soviet Union, quietly prepared to conquer yet another sovereign nation. On Christmas Eve 1979, Soviet troops in a massive show of force rolled into Kabul, Afghanistan.

Americans, observing one of the most important days in Christianity, gave little heed to the latest Soviet incursion, though it was an invasion that would forever change our lives. The Soviet Union had unwittingly set in motion events that would mark the beginning of the end for the Communist empire and, at the same time, provide impetus for a well-organized and funded network of Islamic jihad emerging as the new threat to America: Al Qaeda.

One can only wonder if Moscow's unmitigated gall to invade Afghanistan was the direct result of America's decision not to support the Shah against the Islamic Revolution in Iran. In November Islamic radicals had stormed the United States Embassy in Tehran, and Americans were taken hostage without any reprisal from our government. Our president seemed to do little more than "wring his hands and talk of human rights" while Americans held by religious extremists languished in captivity. One month later, Soviet troops invaded Afghanistan. The American response under President Carter was merely to boycott the 1980 Olympics in Moscow!

The USSR's invasion of Afghanistan showed the Communist regime to be totally bereft of humanity, despite President Carter's emphasis on human rights. Soviet soldiers were barbaric killing machines in a country that was still primitive by world standards. Entire villages of defenseless Afghans were savaged by Soviet troops. Powerful helicopters flew overhead, killing everyone on the ground. Pregnant women were bayoneted, piles of bodies were burned, and children were maimed by explosives tied to toys, food, and clothing. An estimated 1.3 million Afghans died during the Soviet war.

Though many Americans would have had difficulty finding Afghanistan on a map and had little interest in the latest Communist invasion, other than from nightly news reports, Muslims around the world were called upon to support an Islamic jihad, a holy war, by going to Afghanistan to fight with their Muslim brothers, the religious warlords the Mujahadeen, against the Soviet invaders.

The former engineering student at the Baptist College in North Carolina, Khalid Sheikh Mohammed, heard and responded to the call for Muslim men to join the fight in Afghanistan against the Soviet "Infidels." He traveled to Pakistan and began working in refugee camps. It was there that he met Osama bin Laden and, in time, became part of "The Base," an organization of Islamic jihad against all "enemies of Islam."

Osama bin Laden, the seventeenth or twenty-fifth son of about fifty-seven children fathered by Muhammad Awad bin Laden, had experienced a growing isolation from his family as early as 1978. Osama's father died in the 1970s when the boy was thirteen, and it has been reported in televised and written biographical reports that Osama's Syrian mother was Laden's least favorite of his ten or eleven wives. The uncertainty of the number of wives or the birth order of his sons indicates the lack of importance given to them in the Saudi culture.

Under Islamic law, men in Saudi Arabia are allowed four wives. Muhammad Awad bin Laden upheld the law by keeping three wives in a somewhat permanent status, while changing the fourth one as frequently as desired. He continued to financially support a divorced wife and her children, but they did not have the same position within the family that others enjoyed. Osama bin Laden was born after his father had already divorced his mother, resulting in his diminished status within the family.

Subjected to taunts and ridicule from his half siblings, Osama was jeeringly called "the son of the slave woman" in obvious scorn. It is no wonder he experienced growing isolation from his family. Perhaps he identified with Ishmael, Abraham's son of the Bible. Also "the son of the slave woman," Ishmael with his mother had been isolated and separated from Abraham's family. Muslims believe Hagar and Ishmael who were exiled to Arabia found refuge in Mecca, the holiest city in Islam. Osama bin Laden would find his own refuge of sorts in Pakistan and Afghanistan.

Schooled in the Islamic madrasahs and mosques of Saudi Arabia, Osama bin Laden had been drifting toward religious extremism. An association with members of the local Muslim Brotherhood fueled his inner crisis. A radical group, the Muslim Brotherhood surely exploited the demoralizing incongruity between Saudi Arabia's rapid modernization, made possible by the discovery of oil, and the revered seventh century traditions of the Prophet Mohammed that formed the basis of Islamic law.

Osama bin Laden's decision to leave Saudi Arabia and answer the call to join in the Afghan "holy war" was influenced by Prince Turki, the son of Faisal and grandson of Abdul Aziz ibn Sa'ud. King Faisal had been the first to announce an oil embargo against America. He had been angered and humiliated by the establishment of the State of Israel in 1948 and our nation's support of Israel during the 1973 Yom Kippur War. His son Prince Turki was Director General of the General Intelligence Directorate, the Kingdom's main foreign intelligence service, from 1977 to 2001. (Prince Turki bin Faisal bin Abdul Aziz who was educated at Georgetown University became the Saudi Arabian Ambassador to the United States in 2005.)

Infuriated by the Soviet invasion of Afghanistan, a Muslim country, Osama bin Laden sought counsel from Prince Turki who encouraged him to use his immense financial assets to aid the Afghan resistance. Following Prince Turki's advice, the twenty-four year old Saudi Arabian traveled to Pakistan. There he financed refugee camps and hospitals for the Afghan war-wounded. He was nicknamed "Samaritan" for his relief efforts. It was in Pakistan that Osama bin Laden met Khalid Sheikh Mohammed, the engineer of 9-11, and began a working relationship with Abdullah Azzam.

Muslim cleric Abdullah Azzam's Palestinian hometown was part of the land conquered by the Israelis during the Six Day War in 1967. Stung by the humiliation of that defeat and enraged with increasing hatred for Israel and for all who support her, Azzam's extremist fervor grew.

When the Soviet Union invaded Afghanistan, Azzam was the first to call for a world-wide network of jihadists who would fight for Islamic causes including the defeat of the Soviet Union and the destruction of Israel. Abdullah Azzam and Osama bin Laden became partners in the creation of the jihad network that established terrorism cells around the world for the recruitment of Muslim men. The organization came to be known as "The Base for Islamic Jihad" or Al Qaeda.

Responding to the call, Muslim volunteers came to Pakistan and Afghanistan to join the Afghan "freedom-fighters." Additionally, the Mujahadeen were backed by Pakistan and, more importantly, by Saudi Arabia and the United States of America. In 1983 King Fahd bin Abdul Aziz of Saudi Arabia pledged to match dollar for dollar the financial aid provided to Afghanistan by America. Saudi Arabia had allied with America in the common goal of defeating the Soviet Union.

In an effort not to directly confront the Soviet Union, America initially sought to provide weapons to the Mujahadeen in Afghanistan that could not be traced back to our government. Egypt had a huge stockpile of aging weapons from the Soviet Union purchased a decade earlier with money supplied by Saudi Arabia. Now our tenuous ally, Egypt was persuaded to provide those armaments to the Afghan rebels through the conduit of Pakistan. Soviet-made weapons originally meant to "bloody Israel" were now to be used *against* Soviet troops in Afghanistan!

The out-dated weapons were no match, however, for the superior air power of the USSR and did little more than frustrate the Communist leaders, creating a lengthy and expensive war that was draining the Soviet economy. To be victorious over the well-trained and equipped Soviet troops, Afghan rebels needed more up-to-date defenses.

In 1986 President Reagan unilaterally decided to supply the Mujahadeen with the single most important weapon necessary to defeat the Soviet Union. Armed with Stinger-shoulder-fired-missiles, the Afghan rebels were able to shoot down the helicopters of the Soviet Union. America, in its support of the Mujahadeen, was fighting another proxy war with the Soviet Union, this time in Afghanistan.

*   *   *

1979 was a year of profound implications for the Islamic world and for the United States of America. It was the year of the Camp David Accords – a peace treaty that infuriated radicals. It was the year of Iran's Islamic Revolution, which ended friendship with America. It was the year Saddam Hussein became president of Iraq. It was the year of the attack on Islam's holiest site, the Grand Mosque in Mecca, Saudi Arabia. It was the year of the Soviet Union's invasion of Afghanistan and America's support for the Mujahadeen, the Afghan rebels. It was the year a new threat to America emerged – radical Islamic terrorism.

Three years later my husband accepted an assignment to the Kingdom of Saudi Arabia where he would be an advisor to the Royal Saudi Air Force. He would work in their military headquarters – the Saudi equivalent of our Pentagon. Our two sons and I were allowed to accompany him. Housing, transportation, schooling, and vacations would all be provided by the Kingdom of Saudi Arabia. The cost to the Saudi Arabian government to have my husband in the country as a senior military advisor and our family accompanying him was reportedly at least $200,000 each year.

Our relatives reacted to the news of our new assignment with shock.

"Where in the world is Saudi Arabia?"

"Is it safe to live in the Middle East?"

"But what about terrorism?"

"Why in the name of heaven would you want to go there?"

We answered that the Kingdom was safe. After all, there was more terrorism in Italy than in Saudi Arabia; we would not be afraid to live in Italy. Furthermore, an act of terrorism had been reported in Tucson, Arizona, where an attorney had opened his mailbox to find a poisonous snake placed inside!

How glib I was and how naïve. Like most Americans at the time, I had no idea of the looming terrorism threat to America. The hard truth is that radical Islamic terrorism cells were actively being established in cities all across the United States; Tucson, Arizona, so close to my childhood home, was already the site of numerous terrorism cells. Among the many groups in the 1980s were The Islamic Center of Tucson with ties to Al Qaeda, the Al Bunyan Islamic Information Center in Tucson with ties to Ramzi Yousef, the terrorist who planted a bomb in the World Trade Center in 1993, and the Islamic Association for Palestine, a Hamas group that used Tucson as the base for its Information Office.

* * *

Before leaving the States, my husband and I met both Prince Abdullah who served in the Saudi Arabian Air Force and his brother Prince Fayed. Prince Abdullah was celebrating completion of advanced fighter pilot training conducted by the United States Air Force. We were invited to attend his graduation party.

Numerous bodyguards, swarthy men who were heavily armed and wearing black suits and dark sunglasses even indoors, were positioned around the room, by the doorways, and outside. Black limousines were parked near the entry; their engines and air-conditioners were running, while drivers waited at the ready for the partying princes.

"Are they really at risk?" I incredulously asked my husband. I wondered why so much security was needed for the princes. After all, who had ever heard of them? Surprised I was so unaware of the implications of a Saudi Arabian member of the Royal Family having received advanced flight training in the F-15, my husband answered.

"Of course they are at risk. In the hands of their country's enemies, Prince Abdullah with his knowledge of flight tactics in one of the most advanced fighter aircraft in the world would become a hostage of immeasurable value."

My musings were interrupted by the dashing princes as they approached us in greeting. We were welcomed warmly, my husband and I, with handshakes and a kiss on each cheek. Dark and mustached, the brother princes who looked little like one another wore expensive designer suits and Italian leather shoes. Prince Abdullah whose graduation we were celebrating was the far more gregarious of the two.

I had thought I should dress conservatively for a party given by a member of the Royal Family of an Islamic state. My modest attire turned out to be unnecessary; the celebration hosted by Prince Abdullah was anything but conservative. In addition to other military officers and their wives, there was a bevy of young women in attendance who had obviously not attended the same cultural briefings as I! Short skirts and plunging necklines were their attire of choice.

A lavish buffet was spread for all to enjoy, along with an open bar. A mixture of American rock and swing beckoned couples onto the dance floor. Entertainment was provided by two exotic belly dancers gyrating to Middle-Eastern rhythms.

Ironically, a similar party with men and women attending, alcohol, dancing, and female entertainment *never* would have been permitted inside the Kingdom – the kingdom that was ruled under Islamic law by the princes' uncle King Fahd and established as an Islamic State by their grandfather King Abdul Aziz ibn Sa'ud.

Prince Abdullah was celebrating his success with an exuberant freedom to indulge in drink and dancing. He clearly enjoyed his party. Not only did he dance with the many female guests, as the evening wore on he joined the gyrations of the belly dancers, making a challenge of not spilling his drink as he mimicked their hip movements.

I spent much of the evening visiting with Prince Fayed who because of a throat problem talked in a husky whisper. We sat together on an overstuffed sofa just beyond the noise of the revelry. I asked him how he liked Arizona's desert, which can be quite lovely with mountains on all sides, saguaro forests, and wild flowers. He answered with a dismissive wave of his hand and a toss of his head. "Phew," he said. "It is nothing."

I learned that he raised prized white camels, and though he disparaged Arizona's desert, he loved Las Vegas. He told me he had spent the last two weeks there and had left reluctantly to attend his brother's graduation. But Monte Carlo, he said, was far better than any place in America. He asked about my family but did not share anything about his. He said he was certain I would like his country. At the end of the evening I received another princely kiss on each cheek.

My husband had occasional contact with Prince Abdullah in the Royal Saudi Air Force, but we never saw Prince Fayed in the Kingdom. We did see a number of white dromedaries competing in the annual camel races. Perhaps some of them belonged to him.

We welcomed the adventure of living in a foreign culture, an international school for our sons, and the generous travel opportunities afforded us. We were well aware of the value to the United States of having close ties with a moderate Arab nation.

The Kingdom of Saudi Arabia was purchasing the world's most advanced fighter aircraft from the United States, and their military pilots received flight instruction at our Air Force bases. Furthermore, the United States Congress, after much debate as well as vociferous opposition from Israel, had recently approved the delivery of surveillance aircraft to Saudi Arabia. The E-3A, Airborne Warning and Control System planes known by the acronym AWACS were now being flown over the desert kingdom with the assistance of United States Air Force flight crews. Saudi Arabia, rich in oil revenue, needed to build a military defense and was happy to pay for the most advanced armament as well as the advice of the finest armed forces in the world, the United States Military.

What irony, I thought. We, Christians who were avid supporters of Israel, who had built a military career fighting Communism, were leaving the United States to live in and advise an Arab nation, an Islamic state, a state that refused to recognize the existence of the Jewish State of Israel.

4
MUTAWA'S RAISED CANE

The King Abdul Aziz International Airport, named for the first monarch of Saudi Arabia, the Bedouin warrior who had united the land of Mohammed as an Islamic State, had opened only the year before. In earlier days, the old king had not allowed any plane to land in his kingdom without his personal approval. Visitors passed through tents and were sometimes offered a small cup of hot, sweetened tea before continuing their journey across the stark desert that he named for the family of his father, the Sa'ud. Arrival in Saudi Arabia had changed during the intervening years, but we, too, entered the country only with the approval of the Royal Family, the sons of the now deceased King Abdul Aziz ibn Sa'ud.

The bus transporting us from the airliner to the terminals felt more like a cattle car than an airport shuttle. The eerie black-draped forms and we had been herded through long, slow moving lines and finally onto the bus. As we approached our terminal, one of three that accommodated travelers, we could see the distinctive Hajj Terminal Building. Resembling a gigantic white Bedouin tent, the massive Hajj Terminal is one of the world's largest tensile buildings. Designed with two hundred-ten cone shaped canopies, it covers over one hundred acres of ground space and can serve up to 80,000 pilgrims at a time. The Hajj Terminal is open only during the pilgrimage season and is used exclusively by *Hajjis* performing their annual religious trek to Mecca. The South terminal was reserved for Saudia Airlines, the national carrier. We were transported to the North terminal, which accommodated all other airlines allowed to enter the country.

Inside, the terminal was teeming with people in the traditional garb of their home countries. With brightly turbaned heads and dressed in gray or brown robes or in colorful jumpsuits, laborers from Yemen, Pakistan, Bangladesh, Korea, the Philippines, and various African states were crowding into lines of entry to the Kingdom. Personal space and queues were ignored as men pressed forward without regard to others who were ahead of them. Old men, their faces wrinkled and weathered by years in the sun, and young men barely beyond adolescence had entered the Kingdom on employment contracts to perform the necessary tasks of an oil rich but still developing country.

Hot and humid, the midnight air was filled with the pungent aroma of spices and cardamom coffee, of nervous sweat and stale urine, of clothes and sandals too long worn. Old men chewed sticks, a Middle-Eastern form of tooth brushes. Sleeping men lay on the floor, prayer rugs rolled under their heads for pillows. Others squatted in small groups sharing the hot, bitter coffee made over portable hot plates. The glaring lights, the crowded room, the odors, and the noisy clatter of diverse languages were head-spinning.

The terminal was dramatically different from the one in Frankfurt, Germany, from which we had departed only seven hours earlier. There were no food or drink vendors, no book or newsstands, no gift shops, and certainly no duty-free shops. I was wearing my loose fitting, long sleeved, ankle-length dress but couldn't escape the stares of men unaccustomed to seeing a Western woman's face. My adventurous sons who were always eager to wander and explore new places were content to stay close to us. Though they had not slept for hours, they were wide-eyed at the unusual sights, sounds, and scents.

The Saudi officials were stern and thorough as they checked our red diplomatic passports. There was no "Welcome to Saudi Arabia" spoken. We were clearly outsiders, and every effort was made to show the scrutiny under which we were being allowed into their country. Tourists were not permitted in Saudi Arabia and neither were journalists or missionaries. Visas had to be for specific employment at the government's authorization. Jews and anyone whose passport had an Israeli visa stamp were denied entry into the Kingdom.

All of our suitcases were opened and searched with a deliberate show of authority. Items were entirely removed – lifted and examined – as though our clothing held some threat to the security of the country. We had been told that anything packed within under-garments would be less scrutinized in customs inspections. I was not certain I could discern that difference.

Aware of the long list of forbidden objects including books or magazines with women pictured on the covers, alcohol, pork products, and weapons, we cleared customs without incident. Bibles, religious symbols, or anything that represented either Judaism or Christianity were also prohibited. Our Bibles were shipped to us within our household goods that came through the United States Embassy and, therefore, did not go through customs inspections. This was one of many benefits afforded us that many expatriate families did not have.

The Royal Family was not subject to customs inspections. Rumors circulated, primarily by multi-national nurses who staffed the relatively new hospitals, that returning princes brought illegal drugs and alcohol back to their young sisters. Treatment for drug addiction and alcoholism was rumored to be common in the hospitals of the Royal Family.

*   *   *

Continuing our flight east from Jeddah into the center of Saudi Arabia, we could see the glow of burnished copper along the horizon – the promise of a coming day. The sun had not yet broken through the cover of night when we landed in Riyadh and were driven to our compound.

Our bodies weary and our eyes burning with want of sleep, we had just arrived in our apartment when we heard the first prayer call of the day. Male voices chanting in Arabic and coming from multiple minarets in close proximity overlapped one another as they called the faithful to begin the day in worship of Allah. It was impossible not to hear the call to prayer. Even with windows closed and air-conditioners running, the melodic, yet mournful sound filled every Arabian morning. We never learned to sleep through it.

Prayer, five times a day and lasting about twenty minutes each time, is one of the five tenets of Islam. The daily prayers begin before sunrise. They continue at midday, at four in the afternoon, at sunset, and shortly before midnight. Muslims must wash before praying lest their prayers are wasted, and they must face the holiest shrine in Islam, the Ka'aba in the Grand Mosque in Mecca, which is toward the west from Riyadh.

Public prayers were made in mosques on Fridays. Consisting of the chanting of memorized praises and penitents to Allah, the prayers were performed in unison. Kneeling and prostate on prayer rugs and with sandals removed, men filled each of the many mosques in the city. It was in Friday services that clerics preached their interpretation of Islam, and men were exhorted to practice and protect the religion.

I occasionally observed Saudi Arabian women who happened to be shopping at the time of the call to prayer. While men hurried to mosques, these women knelt on sidewalks, in dirt alleys beside shops, or in any somewhat secluded place available. Their black-draped forms curled into fetal-like balls as they offered their prayers to the god of this desert kingdom – the one of whom Mohammed had declared thirteen centuries earlier, "There is no god but Allah."

At the amplified and insistent call to prayer, all work ceased. Shops closed. Doors slammed shut and aluminum shutters crashed down. The *Mutaween* enforced the call to prayer. They banged their cane poles against counter tops in markets or waved them in warning at shoppers and merchants alike, all the while screaming shrilly in Arabic. Shop-keepers never argued with the religious police. Neither did shoppers! Especially expatriate shoppers!

If you happened to be in a market when the call to prayer sounded, your transaction ended immediately. You could return in twenty minutes for your change or your purchased item unless you made the mistake of shopping just before the midday call to prayer; shops often remained closed for several hours of rest after midday prayers. By early evening the heat had dissipated somewhat and merchants returned to their shops. One could only hope the same merchant who would remember the interrupted transaction would be the one to reopen the shop.

The religious police particularly scrutinized Arab women who were not Muslim and neither veiled nor observed daily prayers. My Lebanese friend who was Christian and had lived in Saudi Arabia for fifteen years told of being startled in her own home. The prayer call was so loud, so near, she thought the religious police must have come inside to enforce prayer. Terrified, she crept to the front room expecting an unpleasant confrontation with a *Mutawa*. It turned out to be her mynah bird screaming what he had heard five times every day. His intonation was perfect.

Mutaween, religious police officially called the "High commissary for the propagation of virtue and prevention of vice," enjoyed wide powers to enforce Islamic law. The bearded old men wearing the traditional *thobe* and *ghutra* and each carrying a cane pole went about the business of judging virtue and vice for citizens and expatriates alike. The threat of being hit with the rod was very real.

The religious police had the ability to make arrests and hold perceived offenders for extended periods without trial. In recent years, some members of the Royal Family have called for an end to arrests made by Mutaween unless a legitimate police officer is present. I doubt there is any difference in practice.

With as many as 3500 volunteers who in the 1980s received a stipend from the government, the Mutaween were present in all public places: markets, business offices, residential areas, and schools. They looked for any infraction of Islamic law such as unrelated men and women engaged in conversation or a female without appropriate male escort. Using a video camera was forbidden as well. If illegal activity were suspected, the Mutaween had authority to break into private homes. The possible use of alcohol and the mingling of unrelated persons of the opposite sex were valid justifications for forced entry.

Mutaween enforced standards of dress as well. Occasionally, American men jogged in gym clothes outside their compounds but women did not. Jogging in public never would have been considered appropriate behavior for a female, and any woman who dared dress other than very conservatively was subject to scolding.

Because arms, legs, and necks had to be completely covered, we all wore long, loose dresses outside our compounds. Inexpensive cotton dresses imported from the Philippine Islands or China and sold in the local *souqs* were popular with expatriates. Some of the dresses had a slit from the hem to mid-calf to allow ease in walking. If a gust of wind caught the skirts of the souq-dresses, as we called them, and exposed any ankle, expatriate wives experienced a shrill scolding in Arabic from passing Saudi women or the raised cane pole of the Mutaween.

Saudi Arabian women were not only required to veil, every strand of hair had to be tucked inside their black coverings. Expatriate women did not veil, though the uncovered blond hair of foreign women was an offense to some of the Saudi religious police. Women were chastised in Arabic and, on occasion, experienced a raised cane in warning. Some expatriate women, sensing the need for protection or in deference to the culture in which we lived, began wearing head scarves when outside their compounds.

In the past, many Saudi men had returned to the Kingdom with blond wives. Now, we were told, it was against the law to bring a foreign wife home without the permission of the Saudi Arabian government. And yet, there were frequent stories of American and European families who were approached by Saudi males in the market places patrolled by the Mutaween and offered money for their young, blond daughters.

5
COMPOUNDS OF WALLED SECLUSION

Grateful for the really big freedoms, the Bill of Rights kind, I had scarcely recognized with any sense of appreciation the ordinary, everyday freedoms common in communities all across our great land. I had worn shorts to mow our lawn, and I waved to passing neighbors. I had stood in our doorway handing out Halloween treats, while at the same time nursing my infant, a shawl covering him. I chatted across fences and solved the problems of the world with the freedom to complain of the heat, barking dogs, the school board, or the president. I dressed as I wanted, socialized without fear, worshipped freely, and critiqued our government. It was ordinary American life. And then I moved to Riyadh, Saudi Arabia. Nothing in that Islamic state resembled the American communities I had so taken for granted.

In the Kingdom, neighborhood fences were replaced by compounds of walled seclusion that isolated residents who lived within them. An eight foot block wall surrounded our compound separating us from Arabian life and the unyielding demands of Islamic law. The wall provided a tangible barrier between us and the religious police, the Mutaween, though a tall, earthen-colored minaret towered just outside our confines, its speakers amplifying the insistent call to prayer five times each day. The melodic chant reverberated inside our wall of seclusion – a reminder of the inescapable force of the religion that unequivocally ruled the desert kingdom named for the House of Sa'ud.

Outside the wall, strict codes of dress and behavior were enforced. Assembly of any kind was forbidden, as was dissent. Islamic law governed every aspect of life in Saudi Arabian communities. Mutaween patrolled, ensuring that expatriates as well as Arabians observed long-established rules – rules that defined honor according to the seventh century traditions of the Prophet Mohammed, the Messenger of Allah.

The United States Military Training Mission Compound, known as USMTM and pronounced as the acronym "you smit'em," became our desert home for two years. Consisting of about twenty acres, the compound, which bore no resemblance to military bases, provided the essentials of a small community. Dozens of families lived within its high walls – so many in fact that two full sized buses and a mini-bus were needed to transport the children of USMTM to school.

Tall, austere, steel and concrete apartment buildings with parking spaces below stood in the center of the compound. Though built for practicality rather than architectural style, the buildings were immaculately maintained. The marble foyers and stairs of each were polished to a mirrored luster. Glass walls sparkled on two sides of the spacious lobby that made up part of the ground floor of each building.

Low, flat-topped duplexes skirted the perimeter of the compound, providing additional housing. Each duplex had a small front yard that was desert landscaped. Grass was scarce and there were only a few spindly trees. There were no gardens or flowers. The sun reflected off the gravel and concrete with unrelenting heat.

Senior officers from all branches of the United States Armed Forces who served as advisors to the Royal Saudi Arabian military lived in the apartments and duplexes with their families. Additionally, a few Lebanese and Jordanian men who filled the roles of translators and facilitators to the military mission lived with their families among us. American enlisted personnel and officers who were in the country for one-year tours without their families lived in a separate facility outside our compound but were part of the USMTM community.

Our apartment was on the fourth floor of one of the two tall buildings. We had three bedrooms, two baths, a kitchen, and three separate living areas. Balconies were adjacent to bedrooms on two sides. Major appliances were provided, including a stand alone freezer, washer and dryer, and a microwave oven. Five gallon jugs of imported drinking water were delivered to us daily. Tap water was usable for laundry and bathing, but it was not considered safe for consumption.

Furnished with adequate, though hardly tasteful furniture, every apartment was identical. Furniture had been purchased in bulk and apparently at a greatly discounted cost! Overstuffed chairs and sofas were oddly-colored and ill-matched. Residents routinely negotiated swaps of avocado green, harvest gold, or purple furnishings between apartments carpeted in the same out-dated colors.

A well-established colony of black ants shared the apartment with us. How can there be ants on the fourth floor of a steel and concrete building? I wondered. Some suggested the little six-legged pests lived in the sand that had been used to form concrete and were an integral part of the buildings. In two years, we were never able to eliminate the intruders.

Riyadh, in the interior of Saudi Arabia, is hotter than Jeddah but does not have the humidity. Despite the dry climate, we had a persistent mosquito problem inside our apartment. The mosquitoes were particularly bothersome at bedtime when their continual buzzing was most noticeable. Saudi Arabia is the only place I have lived where it was necessary to wear insect repellent to bed! We did not have the services of an exterminator who may have been able to solve both our pest problems.

Each floor of the apartment buildings had a huge central foyer with a marble floor and a windowed wall on one side. Sofas were easily slid into those communal spaces. With Persian rugs laid and tables set up, we had the perfect place for the expatriate version of block parties. Rotating AWACS crews from the United States Air Force who were in the Kingdom for three month tours flying the newly acquired surveillance aircraft, visiting members of The Foreign Military Sales Office from the Pentagon, and military promotions all provided excuses to pull out the rugs, slide the sofas, and have a party. Of course, the gatherings were safe only within the walled secrecy of our compound. Any party in which unrelated members of the opposite sex mingled subjected the participants to arrest if Mutaween had access to or knowledge of the event.

Laws restricting the mixing of genders have not changed since my time in the Kingdom as evidenced by a recent news article. Twenty foreigners in Saudi Arabia were sentenced "to receive lashes and spend several months in prison for attending a party where alcohol was served and men and women danced." The twenty were among 433 foreigners, of which 240 were women. All were arrested and held to face trial.

*　　*　　*

Our arrival in Saudi Arabia was early on a Wednesday morning or Desert Friday as we called it. We were met at the airport by an Air Force Major who was our designated guide to life in the desert kingdom. He had communicated with us for months prior, giving us valuable information.

Insisting it was in my best interest to work, the major had secured an application for employment in the international school and mailed it to me. I had resisted his presumption that I would want to work outside the home. After all, my sons were still young, and I was not ready to resume my teaching career. Undeterred by my reluctance, he explained that wives without employment were bored to discontent and prone to dangerous depression in this Islamic state. There was little to fill long days of seclusion within walled compounds.

The major scheduled my job interview despite my protestations. It was on the day of our arrival in the Kingdom that he drove me to the international school for that "timely" interview. He could not have been more correct in recommending employment. I was soon extremely grateful to have something to fill the excruciatingly tedious days in the desert of Saudi Arabia.

The Saudi Arabian International School-Riyadh was, by far, the largest of many non-Islamic schools for expatriate children in the Kingdom. Three thousand students representing at least fifty nations attended SAIS-R. Though there were students and instructors from several Middle-Eastern countries including Egypt, Syria, and Pakistan, there were none from the six Arab states of the Persian Gulf: Saudi Arabia, Kuwait, Qatar, Oman, United Arab Emirates, and Bahrain. Children from these states had no exposure to expatriate children in the Kingdom or to the international school or to Western thought or education.

About half of my students were from the United States and Canada; others were from countries as diverse as Egypt, Pakistan, China, and Norway. One of my students was a delightful child with gorgeous red hair and sparkling green eyes. Freckles adorned her nose, adding to her charm. Her Muslim parents who were from Syria had enrolled her in the international school because of its academic reputation but were terrified that exposure to the multi-national school population would result in the child's marriage to a Christian. After kindergarten, the little girl attended an Islamic school for girls. I could only hope her education lasted for more than a few years.

The USMTM compound provided the necessary buses for delivering children of American military families to school. I rode one of the buses and served as a monitor in exchange for my needed transportation to work. Having African drivers who spoke little English, coupled with erratic traffic, necessitated strict bus behavior. Students were required to sit quietly, talking only to their seatmates.

Buses from expatriate compounds throughout Riyadh filled the enormous school parking lot, which became insufferably hot during the warmest school months. Heat radiated off acres of asphalt as the outside temperature soared to as high as 130 degrees Fahrenheit. Exhaust pipes from the buses added to the inferno.

On one occasion, the bus was already loaded with children when our driver pulled into a gasoline station for fueling. It seemed odd that he had not filled the tank before picking up his passengers. After starting the pump, he leaned against the bus and crossed his ankles. Incredibly, he lit a cigarette and was ready to enjoy a break. I yelled and gestured to him to put out the cigarette. He reacted with both annoyance and curiosity. It seemed the African drivers of school buses received minimal training at best. The explosive nature of gasoline near a flame had evidently not been discussed.

One of the bus drivers had several lines of deep scars on each cheek. Starting near his nose, the parallel lines extended across his cheeks all the way to his jaw line. Etched into his dark skin, the scars were lighter in color than surrounding facial skin. I motioned to his cheeks, drawing four fingers across my own, and asked what they were. "Be-be," he replied, smiling proudly, revealing rotting and missing teeth as he did. Cut into his skin while he was still a baby, the scars on the African's face were as much a distinguishing feature as any other aspect of his appearance.

Many African tribes still practice traditional scarification. All three of Nigeria's major tribes engage in this rite, as do the people in much of the Sudan, Ethiopia, and Tanzania. In most cases, scars identify one as belonging to a particular tribe. Cutting into the skin is believed by some to have healing powers; to others it is a sign of beauty. Various tribes believe that deliberate scarring will provide the recipient with strength. Scars can also represent conquests, as do scalps on a lance; each scar indicates an enemy killed.

Scarification is sometimes used as a means to transfer pain in conjunction with the circumcision of older boys or men. Making cuts elsewhere on the body or even on a different person is believed to move pain away from the immediate area being circumcised. Open, bleeding cuts are then packed with available "ointment" made of everything from wood ash to cow dung.

* * *

The government of Saudi Arabia paid the multi-thousand dollar tuition for each of our sons to attend the highly esteemed international school in Riyadh. It also paid my salary as a teacher, though because of my gender I could not cash my own paycheck. There were no banking services within our compound, necessitating my husband's availability to drive me to a Saudi bank where he made the transaction for me.

We did not keep an account in the bank. With each cashed paycheck, I left carrying a fat stack of Saudi riyals. Theft and purse snatching were never concerns in the Islamic state. Clearly, any gains from crime were not worth the punishment of having one's hand cut off!

Saving the money, however, was extremely difficult. Having so much cash on hand made the "funny money" far too easy to spend. One hundred riyals converted to about thirty dollars, adding to the ease of spending the paper riyals, which seemed more like Monopoly bills than legal tender.

Primary grade teachers in America commonly work in their classrooms on weekends and during vacations. It is otherwise difficult to be prepared for demanding school days with small children whose short attention spans require the planning of multiple activities. The necessary transportation and the requirement that outside her home a woman must always be escorted by an appropriate male made after hours work in Saudi Arabia impractical.

Defiant of the restriction against women driving, a co-worker of mine tucked her short hair inside a baseball cap, dressed in her husband's clothes, and drove from her compound to the school. Small in stature, she looked like one of the many young boys who regularly sped their vehicles through the streets of Riyadh. If caught, unescorted and driving, she would have been arrested.

Our first evening in the Kingdom, the major escorted my husband and me, though we were still travel-weary and bleary-eyed, to the compound's Mission Room for a social event to meet other residents. Small and darkened, the Mission Room was the site of weekly happy hour. TGIF, held every Wednesday evening because the work week is Saturday through Wednesday, was not unlike the weekly event in the States.

Armed and uniformed Saudi Arabian soldiers guarded the gated entry to the military mission compound. They resided in a separate building inside the compound but did not socialize in any way with USMTM residents. The guards seemed to pay scant attention to our entering and leaving through the gate.

Knowing about the Arab boycott of all things from Israel and that Saudi Arabia did not recognize its existence, we were amused to see the guards armed with Uzis. The automatic submachine guns, designed by and named for an Israeli soldier, were manufactured in the Jewish state. Surely the Saudi military guards were unaware of the origin of the weapons they so proudly held.

One female resident of the compound was known to brag that on her early morning jogs within the privacy of the block wall, Saudi guards invited her to join them in their rooms. She also hinted that Bangladeshi houseboys would be easily seduced by her charms. The woman amazingly likened herself to Potipher's Wife, the Egyptian woman of the Bible who after attempting to seduce Joseph falsely accused him of making improper advances toward her. I dismissed her sexual bravado as foolish imaginations and perhaps wishful thinking to support her obvious need for male validation.

The guards were always circumspect as I saw them, but who knows what exchanges they had with one another in Arabic while guarding a compound in which unveiled women jogged, wore bathing suits at the swimming pool, and dressed in shorts to play tennis. No doubt they judged us all immoral due to the extreme contrast between our apparel and that required of Arabian women who lived within their own walls of seclusion.

Americans are accustomed, perhaps jaded, to the over-use of sex in everything from advertising to entertainment. It is precisely our sex-saturated society along with our children's behavior and lack of respect for elders that Muslims, particularly those living in Islamic states like Saudi Arabia, claim to be most offensive about the West. Good and evil are defined largely within the context of the sexual purity of females. Standards for behavior, including that of children and proper relations between the sexes, are set by centuries-old traditions based on the life of the Prophet Mohammed.

Despite the Islamic emphasis on sexual integrity, marital fidelity, and virginity prior to marriage, Saudi males, who were allowed multiple wives, were rumored to proposition Western men – quite commonly, openly, and persistently. Expatriate males new in the country quickly learned that jogging outside their compounds brought unsolicited sexual advances. However, just as in Iran, homosexuality is not acknowledged to exist in the Kingdom. "Sodomy is punishable by death in Saudi Arabia…"

Many Americans would agree with the values of sexual integrity, discipline, and respect for one's elders but differ greatly with Islamists in defining what proper relations between the sexes constitutes in practice. Men and women wearing swim suits at the compound swimming pool would unquestionably be a point of contention.

Hidden from outside view by the high wall, our compound housed an Olympic-sized swimming pool. Expertly maintained, the sparkling pool was the center of activity in our desert community and was used year round. Aerators sprayed the water attempting to cool it, but the water always remained a balmy temperature. Colorful, opened umbrellas lined the deck on all sides of the pool providing shaded respite. The pool was popular with residents all day and well into the night when the blistering sun was not an issue.

Other expatriate compounds sent their young team swimmers to our pool for meets. The size of our pool, plus the marked lanes and diving blocks, made it ideal for swimming contests. It was from gym bags at swim meets that we experienced our only thefts during our two years in the Kingdom. Gold chains that all young people wore and removed for swimming were easy targets of pilfering by visiting swimmers.

Even the youngest girls wore gold jewelry in play. Bangles became digging tools while valuable chains adorned sand castles. Surely many gold pieces were lost in the sand that covered much of the compound's playground. I wondered if Third World laborers who maintained the grounds ever searched with a metal detector for hidden treasures left by children.

The large, well-equipped playground was usable most of the year, except during summer. The chains on the swings and frames of the climbing toys became too hot when temperatures approached 130 degrees Fahrenheit. Outdoor play was then reserved for relatively cool mornings or in evenings after the sun went down. For residents willing to get up early enough to beat the heat, there were tennis, racquetball, and basketball courts within our compound.

The air-conditioned recreation center, managed by a United States Army Sergeant, was bustling with activity. At times, special classes in martial arts were offered for children. Boy Scout and Cub Scout troops met in the recreation center, allowing young scouts to continue working on their merit badges while living in the desert kingdom. Occasionally, the recreation center sponsored exotic field trips such as overnight camping on sand dunes or a day at the annual camel races. Additionally, a myriad of arts and craft projects were available.

We had never had time or the particular interest to work with ceramics. In the Kingdom, with abundant time to spare, this activity became a favorite pastime in the comfortably cooled recreation center. We individually made lots of "treasures:" colorful gnomes, Arabian camels, candy dishes, and fanciful unicorns!

Our favorite representation of Christmas was made while we lived in Saudi Arabia, an Islamic state that allows neither the practice of Christianity nor the observance of its holidays. Working together on a family project, we made a rather impressive ceramic nativity set that we continue to treasure. All of the Biblical characters, camels, and stable animals are included in the pearl-toned set whose pieces stand as tall as ten inches. Now it is our young grandson who carefully unwraps each piece of the manger scene and arranges the display every Christmas.

Christmas trees were not available for purchase, and any holiday decorations within our apartments had to be concealed from outside view. We were fortunate to "inherit" an old, ratty, artificial tree that had been used by countless families before us, and we were happy to pass it on when it was time to leave. A few enterprising Saudi merchants briefly added a small selection of innocuous Christmas decorations to their shelves, hoping to capitalize on the thousands of expatriates in the country. The Mutaween were quick to have the forbidden items removed and destroyed.

Saudi Arabia prohibits organizations or assembling of any kind. Because of the chance that some organizations might be subversive or give opportunity to criticize Islamic law or the Royal Family, all organizations were illegal. The teachers of SAIS-R had a loosely formed professional group aligned with regional international schools and not affiliated with the NEA or any other union. The organization did not negotiate on behalf of teachers. It did little more than create an opportunity to attend regional school conventions in places like Sri Lanka and Greece. SAIS-R funded the trips, providing a great opportunity for foreign travel with a minimum of personal expense!

When the Saudi Ministry of Education learned of the professional teachers' group at SAIS-R, immediate dismantling was ordered. So serious was the crime of having an organization of any kind, all officers and some members were interrogated and subjected to the threat of arrest and deportation.

The prohibition against assembling was enforced even inside our compound. Soon after settling into the USMTM community, I was invited to an evening wives' function. Dessert was served following a rather benign fashion show in which presenters demonstrated various ways to accessorize souq dresses. Was it really possible to create a fashionable look with the long, loose garments we all wore when outside the walls of our compound? Most women agreed that the additions of jewelry and scarves did little to feminize the "bagged" look. A smile was the best accessory available to us!

With the success of that gathering, a date was set and a hostess volunteered to plan the next month's affair. Incredibly, in the interim we were notified that our attempt to schedule regular activities constituted an organization, which even within the seclusion of our compound was illegal. All future meetings were cancelled. I marveled that an insipid fashion discussion could be perceived as a threat to the security of the Islamic state in which we lived. I marveled even more that awareness of our little group had reached authorities who would care.

Mail came through the APO military system to a small post office within the compound, which offered most of the services of a normal postal facility. Postage was charged within the States, to and from New York. Between New York and Saudi Arabia, mail was delivered by military vessel without additional cost to us. Letters took about two weeks to arrive from the States, while packages shipped by boat could take up to a month. Of course there were no other delivery options such as UPS or Federal Express.

My husband's parents had two huge avocado trees on their Southern California property. Our sons had loved climbing the gorgeous trees, and we all enjoyed the yearly harvest of nearly grapefruit-sized avocadoes. Knowing how much we loved the buttery, delicious fruit, my mother-in-law shipped a box of freshly picked but far from ripe avocadoes to us in Saudi Arabia. Unfortunately, by the time the parcel made its way through the APO system, the fruit was well past useable, even for guacamole!

Out-going parcels had to have customs declarations. We soon learned not to mail gold jewelry. With the required description of contents and declared value on the customs label, our gifts never arrived at the intended addresses. Gold necklaces formed with Arabic letters or Egyptian hieroglyphics ended up with unknown persons whose names likely didn't match those on the jewelry.

There was virtually no American-style clothing available in the Kingdom. Only Middle-Eastern styles or inexpensive souq-dresses were sold in local markets, though women's boutiques in the newer downtown buildings sold elaborate designer gowns. We began selecting all of our clothing, needed frequently for my rapidly growing sons, from a J.C. Penney's catalog. Soon birthday and Christmas gifts came from mail orders as well. This means of shopping was reminiscent of my childhood in the 1940s and 1950s when my birth family ordered from the beloved Sears and Roebuck catalog. My sons were indifferent to the catalog experience, and I admit it lacked the thrill of anticipation that my siblings and I had experienced years earlier, though I am still a sucker for catalog shopping!

Everyone was briefed, prior to moving to Saudi Arabia, that two items were absolute necessities. Both were to be purchased in the States and included in household shipments into the Kingdom: a short-wave radio that would provide our only access to outside news and a Sony Beta-Max video recorder for taped movies. The short wave radio picked up the British Broadcasting Corporation, and during our first weeks in the Kingdom we looked forward to nightly updates. But the radio's reception was unreliable and often too riddled with static to make the scant news worth the effort of listening. We quickly adjusted to the absence of sound bites and commentaries and soon gave little thought to what might be happening in other parts of the world.

Our compound's small video theater had an equally small collection of titles to choose from. Large gatherings in the theatre were rare; tapes were more likely borrowed and watched within apartments. Many of the selections were, no doubt, pirated copies made by the relatively new Sony technology. The shared tapes provided the only filmed entertainment available in the Islamic state. There were no movie theaters or video stores, and mail orders were strictly monitored. Residents of the compound were much more concerned about the Mutaween who censored filmed entertainment than about guidelines for copying videos.

Visiting chaplains occasionally led clandestine Christian worship services in the video theatre. Entering the Kingdom on "Morale Officer" visas, not as chaplains, they were part of

AWACS crews. Who would have guessed that the much debated Congressional approval of surveillance aircraft for Saudi Arabia would become a means of bringing forbidden chaplains into the country and providing formal Christian worship in that Islamic state?

The "Morale Officers," whether Catholic or Protestant, visited the various U.S. military compounds where they presented devotionals, prayer, and Holy Communion to any compound resident wishing to attend. During our two-year tenure, we had three visiting chaplains, each for one service.

Young men of slight build and dark skin from the Philippine Islands staffed the only restaurant available to us within our compound. Dubbed The Mission Inn, the restaurant was open for three meals everyday. Menus were not necessary after a few visits; each night of the week had its special meal and the choices did not vary during our two years there. Monday night, for example, always featured barbequed chicken dinners.

Persuasive residents occasionally sponsored the preparation of an unusual meal. The German-born wife of a United States Army Major was able to have a one time meal of schnitzel and red cabbage served. A soldier from the South supervised the preparation of ham, cooked greens, and grits. Both not-on-the-menu meals were well attended by compound residents happy to try different fare.

Filipino waiters doted on our sons. Treats were delivered to our table, though they had not been ordered. It wasn't long before our younger son and his friends learned to stop by the Mission Inn for free ice cream sundaes.

Because we had no medical facilities within our compound, we were allowed to use the doctor, dentist, and orthodontist at the Army Corps of Engineers Compound, which was also located in Riyadh but several miles from the USMTM Compound. Basic medical and dental care were available at the "Corps" to anyone in the military community, but orthodontia was limited to patients who had begun their treatment in the States and needed only adjustments to their braces while living in the Kingdom.

After being in Saudi Arabia for about a year and at a time my husband was away from Riyadh, I found my first breast lump. Terrified by the possibility of cancer, I did not want to wait for his return to have the lump checked, and so I secured transportation from a friend who was part of the United States Military Training Mission, though he did not live within our compound. As a female, I no longer had the independence and freedom of driving myself to a needed appointment. All transportation had to be provided by an appropriate male.

The sole doctor in the medical facility had been contracted by the Army Corps of Engineers. He determined the lump to be a harmless cyst, which he aspirated. Over the next several months, however, the cyst kept filling in the same spot until the doctor had emptied it four times.

"You need a mammogram," he instructed. "But that screening isn't available here." How strange, I thought. A country of immense wealth in the1980s did not yet have mammography. Royal hospitals had been built and were staffed by multi-national doctors and nurses, but care specifically for the health needs of women was not available. Arrangements were made for me to get the necessary screening – not in the Kingdom but in the United States. Imagine flying from Saudi Arabia to America for the purpose of a mammogram!

More than two decades later, breast cancer is still a taboo subject in much of the Middle East according to former First Lady Laura Bush who in October 2007 toured countries in that part of the world, including the cities of Riyadh and Jeddah in Saudi Arabia. Her trip was designed to emphasize the importance of early detection and treatment and to encourage women to fight this terrible disease. Arab women who find a lump in their breasts are unlikely to get an early diagnosis because any discussion of the breast is considered inappropriate, making examinations improbable, and because females need male permission to seek medical care. Further, men commonly divorce their wives who are diagnosed. The death rate from breast cancer in Arab countries, even among young women, is high.

The only barber and hair stylist available to us were also on the Army Corps of Engineers Compound. Appointments for hair care could be made with a phone call, but transportation to them was always a problem. On one occasion, while my husband was out of the country for an extended period, I desperately needed a haircut. My choices were to try to cut my own hair, have a friend with limited skills try her luck or find transportation to the "Corps Compound" where there was one stylist in a small shop. My friend offered to be my chauffeur for an appointment with the stylist, just as he had for my doctor's appointment.

Deciding that no Mutawa could possibly know that he was not my husband, I sat in the forbidden front seat as we drove through the streets of Riyadh. The law forbade any woman from sitting in the front seat if the driver were not her husband. We knew we faced certain arrest and I ninety lashes for punishment if we were stopped for any reason and a Mutawa asked for identifications. One can never underestimate how important a haircut is to a woman or what risks she will take to get one! Of course, rebellion against what was perceived as a ridiculous restriction influenced my decision to sit in the front seat.

Recent news reports from Saudi Arabia describing the arrest of a Saudi woman who rode in an automobile driven by a male to whom she was not related, the arrests and jail sentences for unrelated expatriates of both sexes who engaged in conversation in a coffee shop, and an elderly widow who was arrested and sentenced to be caned for mingling with an unrelated male who delivered food to her have demonstrated how foolish and dangerous my cavalier attitude was.

I cannot say if Saudis found ways to circumvent the rules that kept genders apart; I can only speculate that some may have had secret lives that put them at great personal risk. I do know that many Americans, as well as expatriates from other countries, engaged in prohibited behavior. Rumors of extra-marital affairs within compounds were common. The small secluded communities both facilitated the affairs and made keeping them secret impossible. More than a few reputations were tarnished and military careers stalled as a result of constant rumors of sexual intrigue.

There were numerous multi-national nurses working in Saudi Arabian hospitals and in medical facilities in remote areas of the Kingdom. The women had no difficulty meeting and dating expatriate men who were in the country for a year or two. Knowing that such relationships put the participants at risk for arrest and possible imprisonment didn't seem to deter the dating that took place. Sadly, the marriages of several of our friends, including that of my friend who provided my needed transportation, ended after their tours in Saudi Arabia. The nurses, primarily from England and Australia, became the new wives.

*   *   *

The Muslim calendar measures years from 622 A.D., the year the Prophet Mohammed fled Mecca and sought refuge in Medina, which is also in Arabia. With 622 being year number one, we arrived in the Kingdom in 1360. My younger son, a third grader at the time, found great amusement in saying, according to the Muslim calendar, "It isn't even 1492 yet. Columbus hasn't discovered America!"

Desert weekends were Thursday and Friday. The work week was Saturday through Wednesday, and for two years the different calendar continued to confuse me. If I had a school meeting or parent conference scheduled for Wednesday, for example, my mind would translate that to the middle of the week when, in fact, it was the last day. More than a few times I showed up for meetings on the wrong day.

As a teacher, I served as grade level liaison from the kindergarten to an administrative council for the international school. In one meeting, the primary school principal was stressing his absolute expectation that staff members perform recess and all other scheduled duties. Apparently, some on the multi-national staff were shirking playground duties or showing up late for them. The principal warned that any failure to perform assigned duties would be documented in the negligent teacher's personnel file.

As professionals, some of us were offended. Instead of a blanket reprimand, shouldn't he deal individually with the shirkers? As liaisons to our particular grade levels, we felt it should not be incumbent on us to pass on the principal's reprimand. Further, most of us would never consider risking the liability of not being on duty, should an accident occur during our assigned watch. My fear of having a lost or injured child in a Third World country was more than enough to convince me to be ever vigilant. Reliable medical care was limited; one shuddered at the thought of receiving emergency care in a Saudi Arabian hospital. Wealthy Saudis, after all, come to America to receive critical medical care in our hospitals.

After some heated discussion, the ringing of the principal's phone interrupted our meeting. He answered, turned ashen, and replied to the caller, "Yes, Sir. I will be there immediately." Returning to the table, the principal announced our meeting adjourned. He had forgotten an important appointment with the superintendent, who was waiting for him.

In an unusual quip for me, I patted his arm and said, "That's OK, Sir. We won't document this in your personnel file." The ice was broken, and though at first shocked at my impertinence, even he laughed with embarrassment.

Despite that encounter, he appointed me to several text book selection and curriculum development committees. I left after two years with a glowing letter of recommendation. Years later I learned that he had become Head Master in a school in Beijing, China.

Though the work week was different, school breaks basically followed the American calendar. We had a two week winter vacation at Christmas and a Spring break that was not timed for Easter. We were likely to work on Easter Sunday, just as we did all other Sundays.

Schools were closed during the insufferably hot summers, and families who could afford to do so, spent the hottest months outside the Kingdom. For those of us who did not leave, the compound's small library was a godsend during the long months when there was little to do.

In America, summer breaks pass quickly with swimming lessons, sporting events, Vacation Bible School, summer camps, outdoor concerts, trips to Disneyland, and Fourth of July fire works.

Saudi Arabia, ruled by Islamic law, was void of normal recreational choices and summer pastimes. There were no public swimming pools, water parks, theatres, libraries, gyms, bowling alleys, skating rinks, sports arenas, ball parks, or camp grounds. There were no Little League baseball games, soccer, or tennis matches. There were no shopping malls, museums, art galleries, craft shops, video arcades, or amusement parks. There were very few restaurants and, certainly no clubs or bars. Fast food restaurants such as MacDonald's or Taco Bell did not exist in the Kingdom. There were no ice cream shops, quick stops, hot dog stands or cold drink venders, and no one picnicked in parks.

There was, in fact, no social interaction at all outside the Saudi home or, in our case, outside our compound of walled seclusion. After two weeks of summer we longed for school to resume. The boredom was suffocating.

6

SA'EED

"Houseboy, Ma'am. Make clean, Ma'am."

We had barely acquainted ourselves with our apartment, our first morning there, when the doorbell rang. My sons were still deciding which bedrooms to claim as their own. We were swapping the bulky, over-sized and oddly-colored furniture between the small living room and the larger dining room. And hoping to find their point of entry, we were tracing the path of the intruding black ants as they crawled across the kitchen counter.

Small in stature and dark skinned, the young man at the door stood barely taller than my sons. His head was bowed in submission. Even as he spoke he looked down, avoiding eye contact with us. His slightly-built frame was noticeably shaking. His demeanor was of total servitude.

Sa'eed, our Bangladeshi houseboy, had come to introduce himself. Wearing the green jumpsuit of a foreign laborer, he was in the Kingdom on a two year work contract. Scarcely beyond his teens, Sa'eed, as well as other Bangladeshi young men, kept the apartments and the compound spotless. Additionally, they regularly washed the Chevrolets that were provided to compound residents and parked on a concrete slab below the first floor of apartments.

Sa'eed was painfully shy. Without attempting conversation, he went about his daily household tasks in the two apartments to which he was assigned. When asked his name, he replied in a voice barely audible, "Mohammed." All the houseboys used the same title, the name of the Messenger of Allah. We surmised this designation indicated that not only was he a Muslim but that he was also a servant. It was only when we pressed him for the name his family called him that we learned "Sa'eed."

I began insisting Sa'eed pause for tea, toast, and fruit before beginning his tasks. I showed him how to use the toaster and the electric tea pot. He was puzzled by both. One day as he was eating, I opened a can with our very basic electric can opener. The look on his face was one of astonishment. With his head cocked to the side, his mouth dropped open, his brow furrowed, and his dark eyes stared at the strange device that made a whirring sound and could cut the top off a can! Seeing his unmistakable expression of disbelief, I struggled to stifle my own amusement. He would have been humiliated, had I laughed.

When we left Saudi Arabia after our two years there, I gave the electric can opener to Sa'eed. I couldn't tell whether he was pleased or bemused to receive the strange contraption. Even if he had no use for it, I hoped he could sell or trade it for something more beneficial to him.

The annual per-capita income in Bangladesh, one of the poorest countries in the world, was no more than one hundred dollars. No doubt Sa'eed regularly sent money home to support his family, though he lived in squalid conditions in Saudi Arabia. I never saw the shelter provided for the boys from Bangladesh but heard it described as being no better than the worst of slums. Men lived in crowded barracks without privacy or air-conditioning and were always fearful of theft and attack. I imagined it to be similar to inner-city flop-houses.

Rumors of abuse of the houseboys were common. Third World Nationals arrived in the Kingdom already in debt to recruiters who had paid for visas and travel. Though laborers were hired to work for a specific wage, contracted companies could use any excuse, such as shortage of funds, to withhold pay or change the terms of contracts, which were written in Arabic – a language the laborer was not likely to know how to read. The young men from Bangladesh had no legal recourse. Neither did they have the liberty of quitting their jobs to seek others. As foreign laborers, they were obligated to their "sponsor" who provided housing and medical care. None would have had enough money to purchase a travel ticket to his home country even if his passport, which was usually held by the sponsor, were returned to him.

"You must not be kind to them," the wife of one of the Arab facilitators often scolded me. "They will not respect you unless they fear you. They will become lazy. They will steal from you." The houseboys' fear, even of the Americans they served in our compound, was obvious. Their pride was obvious as well.

Sa'eed's services were provided as part of our housing, but we paid him extra. Additionally, when I shopped for groceries I often got a supply for him – items that did not need refrigeration. To protect his pride, I left the bag of food meant for him next to the front door. Nothing was said by either of us after the initial bag, but I thought I could discern a quicker, livelier step on days a shopping sack bulging with bread, tea, juice, canned meats, and fruit waited by the door.

Food purchased in local markets was incredibly expensive. Fresh milk was priced at five dollars for two liters and was available in only a few small shops, which in size somewhat resembled American mini-marts. The demand for fresh milk was obviously limited; markets did not stock it in quantity, necessitating my husband to make four or five dairy-runs each week.

Other foods, though abundant, were still costly. Produce was imported from Lebanon, Syria, and Jordan. Despite the availability of plentiful amounts, a head of iceberg lettuce was priced at five dollars and needed to be rinsed in a chlorine solution before being consumed. Chicken, sheep, and goats were grown locally, but beef was imported. On special occasions I purchased fresh beef from Argentina. However, each pound of the imported ground beef was a ridiculous eight dollars, making even meatloaf an extravagant meal. Clearly the price made regular use prohibitive. In sharp contrast, bread was locally baked and priced at twenty-five cents a loaf.

Some products were strictly forbidden in the country, including alcohol and pork. Islam prohibits the use of both. Other products were banned as a result of a boycott, an economic jihad against Israel. The Arab League Boycott, which was initiated after the establishment of Israel in 1948, banned companies who do business with the Jewish state or, we were told, have a preponderance of stock holders who are Jewish.

Coca-Cola and the Ford Motor Companies were on the list of banned corporations during the years we lived in the Kingdom. My husband was provided a Chevrolet to drive, complete with an eight-track sound system and several Don Williams tapes. The favorite canned drink in Saudi Arabia was Pepsi Cola; *Bebsi*, as the Saudis pronounced it.

Mergers and acquisitions of companies made the boycott rather difficult to enforce. Minute-Maid orange juice, for example, was sold in local markets throughout Riyadh, though fine print on the label indicated Minute-Maid was a division of Coca-Cola, a banned company.

The boycott at one time listed more than 8,500 companies. After the 1993 Oslo Accords between Israel and Palestine and the 1994 Peace Treaty between Israel and Jordan, the number of boycotted companies decreased to about two-hundred. Coca-Cola and Ford were removed from the list, but Pepsi-Cola was added to it.

More than a decade later and despite promises to the contrary, Saudi Arabia continued the economic jihad against Israel. As a condition to joining the World Trade Organization, the Kingdom agreed in 2005 to cease its boycott of Israel. However, only months later "the Saudi ambassador admitted that his country still enforced the boycott in violation of promises made earlier to the Bush Administration." Fortunately, for most of our food I could shop at the American government commissary, which was a small, one-room market provided only to expatriates with diplomatic passports. Supplies in the commissary were limited to basic products; there was one brand of any item and only one size; take it or leave it. The commissary primarily stocked canned and boxed goods, though there was a small section of frozen meats and vegetables. The only fresh produce was that with a longer shelf life, like potatoes.

Milk was sold in the commissary, but it was boxed, European shelf milk. Stored at room temperature and packaged in small, individual servings similar to juice packs, the milk was convenient for school lunches. We never acquired a taste for the packaged milk that reminded us of evaporated milk. Chilling did not improve the flavor. It was easy to rationalize that five dollars for two liters of fresh milk from a local market was offset by the low cost of premium gasoline at thirty cents a gallon. We ignored the fact that each of our sons could easily drink more than a liter of milk every day.

The Saudi Arabian government paid to have American products in the commissary delivered by air transport, and the extra expense was not passed on to us. This was but one of many benefits that caused the $200,000 yearly estimated cost to have our family in the country.

Our civilian friends had to shop in local markets for all of their groceries. The difference that caused the most envy from them was not the much lower price we paid; it was that we could buy pork products. The commissary supplies were not subject to Mutaween or customs inspection, and the prohibition against pork was bypassed. Friends from the Bell Canada Compound often hinted, "What I wouldn't give for a B.L.T."

As patrons of the commissary, we signed an agreement that the pork we purchased would be used by our family (guests included, of course) and that we would not sell any of it.

Forbidden by the Prophet Mohammed, the meat from swine was rationed and a record kept of the amount we purchased each month. The store had a single register for check-out where a file box, about the size of a child's shoe box, contained five by seven cards, one for each authorized customer. The clerk listed all of our pork purchases by hand.

Oddly, the sense of restricted availability made the cuts of pork far more appealing than they would have otherwise been. We regularly ate pork roasts, chops, and hams. Clearly we used more of the "other white meat" than we ever had before living in the Islamic state in which it was prohibited, but we still did not come close to using our allotted amount.

* * *

Though Sa'eed normally came to our apartment in the afternoon, one weekend day he came unexpectedly in the morning. Having secured the afternoon off, he was eager to finish his tasks early. I was in my bedroom dressing and had only my underwear on, unaware that my sons had let our houseboy into the apartment. Sa'eed burst around the corner past my open door and we saw each other. I gasped in surprise. Sa'eed gasped in horror at having seen his house madam in her underwear – a clear violation of Islamic law and his servant status! Instantly ashen and with terror gripping his face, he turned and rushed to the kitchen.

After getting properly clothed, I went to the room to which he had fled. Sa'eed was shaking in fear. He would not look up from the sink where he had busied himself. "Sorry, Ma'am, sorry, sorry," he kept repeating. "Pardon, please, pardon, please, please."

In the Kingdom, the faces of Muslim women are covered, as are their entire bodies. One would never see a Muslim woman in a bathing suit, not to mention a bra and underpants! Poor Sa'eed was horrified at what could be his fate after seeing me. He certainly must have wondered if I would seek to have him punished. Would he be imprisoned, beaten, deported, or even executed? What in America would have been a mere embarrassment, to Sa'eed was life threatening. As a foreign laborer in the Islamic state, he had no standing and few legal rights in the country he served.

I told him as best I could that it was not his fault. I should have had my door closed. He would not look up nor could he stop shaking. Along with his pleading for forgiveness, he tried to explain his reason for coming at the unexpected time.

"Uncle come. Go airport. Come morning, make clean, Ma'am." I felt doubly sad for him. Not only had the unfortunate encounter terrified him, his otherwise joyous reunion with his uncle who was arriving to work in the Kingdom was marred. It was a long time before he was comfortable enough to again have tea and toast in our apartment or to raise his dark eyes when I spoke to him.

My sons, twenty-five years later, still remember the look of sheer terror on his face. Speaking recently of the incident, one son commented, "You know, Mom, Sa'eed thought he was a dead man!"

Sa'eed, submissive as he was, had difficulty taking instruction from me, a female, when it came to his cleaning duties. He, after all, was the houseboy not I. He had been given houseboy training! He undoubtedly thought I knew nothing of cleaning. In his experience, Americans had servants to do household chores. The proud Bangladeshi young man was obviously uncomfortable when I asked him to do a task differently.

The houseboys were provided cheap red cloths similar to those used in commercial car washes for all of their cleaning duties. From my balcony early one morning, I observed a group of the young men squatting around a water faucet in the yard. They were rinsing the red cleaning cloths in the pooled water on the ground, making them ready for continued use. From that time on, much to his annoyance, I insisted Sa'eed use the cloths I provided and laundered myself.

Sa'eed did not understand my insistence that he use separate cleaning materials in the kitchen than in the bathrooms. I color coded sponges and directed him to use the blue ones only in the bathrooms. He looked at me with a mixture of curiosity, bewilderment, and annoyance at my insistence on separate materials. Clearly he would have preferred his red cloths for all household duties, whether cleaning the kitchen, the bathroom, or dusting.

Our houseboy dusted every day and even wiped down the railings of our two balconies. Saudi Arabia is a desert with scant vegetation and very little rainfall. While dust was always a pervasive problem, there were times when it came in a tsunami of dirt. The desert dust storm, the *shamal,* could be seen many miles away as it approached the city.

Beginning as a strong northwestern wind moving across Syria and Iraq, the shamal became a wall of dirt that totally obliterated the horizon and sky above. Midday disappeared into darkness as the storm blew in with horrible velocity. Windows and doors, though closed and locked, could not entirely block the raging dirt. When I asked my older son for his most vivid memories of having lived in Saudi Arabia, he described the sight of houseboys scooping up the thick layer of dirt left on the marble floors of apartment lobbies after a shamal.

No one would choose to stay outdoors with a shamal approaching. Even when the storm was still miles away, outside air became too polluted to safely breathe. How the Bedouin of the desert in their tents woven with goat hair survived the onslaught of blowing dirt, one can only wonder. Fortunately, the gritty dust storm normally occurred only once or twice a year.

Besides continually dusting, Sa'eed also ensured that we had plenty of the imported water for drinking. He carried heavy five gallon jugs to our fourth floor apartment each day, with at least one extra jug in reserve at all times. We used tap water for bathing and laundry, though had we desired to use the drinking water for other purposes, Sa'eed would have kept us well-supplied.

My husband, thanks to the relatively new Sony technology, obtained a copy of Michael Jackson's music video "Thriller." Released in December 1983, the fourteen minute video was more a short film than music video. The record breaking horror-film-spoof featured choreographed zombies performing with

Jackson who transforms into both a zombie and a werewolf during the film.

I invited our young houseboy who had never seen a music video in his life nor had he heard of Michael Jackson to watch it with us. Sa'eed looked puzzled. Why was I asking him to sit down instead of doing his chores? He sat cautiously, fearing he might have misunderstood my insistence.

The music started and Michael Jackson jumped onto the screen. Sa'eed screamed. Wide-eyed, he continued to scream and flinch as the zombies and werewolf performed to the upbeat music, except when the fear was overwhelming. Afraid to watch, Sa'eed covered his eyes by burying his face in his hands. He then tugged at the front of his jumpsuit, trying to pull it up over his eyes. Still irresistibly intrigued by the video, his dark eyes peeked over his collar's edge. After the initial viewing, the young houseboy was eager to watch the film over and over with my sons, but he still jumped every time Michael Jackson did.

Though Sa'eed's English was limited, I was able to communicate with him with a few words and lots of gestures. He told me his father was a retired policeman in Bangladesh. He said his parents and entire family, including his brothers and their wives, lived together in a one-room house. There was no electricity or running water. Sa'eed pointed to our electrical outlets and water faucets. He shook his head, "No."

His mother and sisters carried water up from the river. I wondered if his task of carrying water to us, one relegated to women in Bangladesh, was demeaning to him. With motions he demonstrated how his mother did laundry in the river. I had observed the houseboys washing their cleaning cloths in pooled water beneath a faucet. In Saudi Arabia that was the closest substitute for a river, I thought.

I remembered seeing news coverage of the annual monsoons in Bangladesh. Each year rivers swell from seasonal rainfall, and resultant floods drown hundreds, even thousands of unprotected people. After the water subsides, the people of Bangladesh are left homeless and diseased from dangerously polluted rivers.

I had read that the literacy rate for women in Bangladesh was no more than twenty-five percent and that the mortality rate of infants was extraordinarily high. I asked about his mother.

"Mother very old, very old, Ma'am. Teeth, no. Hair, no." He bent over to show me how she was stooped.

"How old is your mother?" I asked, thinking perhaps she was in her 80s or even 90.

"Forty, Ma'am. Mother forty."

Certain that he had English confused, I replied, "No, Sa'eed, not forty. I am forty."

"Oh, no Ma'am. Forty old, very old."

At my insistence that I was forty, Sa'eed lifted his head slightly and hesitantly asked a most unexpected but amusing question.

"You have sister, Ma'am?"

Later, I read that life expectancy for Bangladeshi women is forty. Sa'eed did not have English confused. At that age, his mother was, indeed, very, very old.

I had made a habit of answering the phone by saying, "Hello, this is Mary." One day while out, I called my home phone, hoping to talk to my husband. After several rings, the phone receiver was picked up and I heard a male voice, highly accented, say, "Hello, this is Ma-rey." Sa'eed had learned even more English!

Winter in Riyadh, Saudi Arabia, comes with a dramatic temperature drop. It may get down to seventy degrees with an occasional dip into the sixties. We never wore a jacket and rarely a sweater. The Bangladeshi houseboys, however, dressed in jackets, ear muffs, neck scarves, and gloves when the temperature cooled. They huddled, shivered, and rubbed their hands together in the cold.

Every year pictures were taken of students and staff in the Saudi Arabian International School, just as in schools in the States. When I received mine, I dumped the entire packet of unwanted photographs into our apartment garbage chute that extended from the fourth floor to a large dumpster below.

You can imagine my surprise when days later several Bangladeshi houseboys came up to me, smiling broadly, as they proudly opened their wallets. My school photos filled all the little plastic covers in each wallet. In a culture that hides the female face, there was mine staring out of all those wallets, four or five times in each. And it was not even a photograph I thought worth keeping!

What did they tell their comrades back in the houseboy quarters where they were housed? Or their families upon return to Bangladesh? Was I known as the American woman who was seen in her underwear? Further, what had they done with the larger prints that were in the packet? Had I become a pin-up poster girl in the Bangladesh barrack? My sons only laughed at that suggestion!

Having my packet of school photographs removed from the trash dumpster was my first awareness that houseboys regularly sorted through compound refuse looking for useable items. Though possessing full-time employment in one of the richest countries in the world, the men from Bangladesh shared none of the wealth enjoyed by their Muslim brothers in the country that is the birthplace of Islam and the keeper of its holiest site, Mecca.

* * *

Sa'eed's work in the Kingdom gave him his best and perhaps only opportunity to make his pilgrimage to Mecca, the birthplace of the Prophet Mohammed and site of Islam's holiest shrine. We gave him extra money and hoped he was able to make the trip, though we never heard from him if, in fact, he had.

Hajj, the annual pilgrimage to Mecca, is one of the five tenets of Islam. It is meant to commemorate the trials and sacrifices of Abraham and Hagar and their son, Ishmael, who lived over four thousand years ago. Muslims believe it was in Mecca that Abraham was willing to offer Ishmael in sacrifice. The Hajj is also a time to give thanks for the final revelation of the Koran given to the Prophet Mohammed.

During the Hajj, Saudi Arabia becomes the focal point of the entire Muslim world. Historian Robert Lacey in *The*

Kingdom explains the importance of the pilgrimage to Muslims in general and to Saudis in particular:

> For the pilgrims the hajj is an opportunity to take a new name. It washes them of all their sins. One prayer said in the Grand Mosque at pilgrimage time is worth 100,000 said elsewhere. For the Saudis the festival is a reminder that their forefathers were the very first Muslims, that Muhammad was one of them, and that God, having revealed some of His truth through the Jewish prophets, and more of it through Jesus, chose an Arabian as the vehicle for His ultimate revelation.

Performed during the twelfth month of the Islamic calendar, the Hajj is observed annually by over two million Muslim pilgrims. Adult Muslims who are physically and financially able must make every effort sometime in their lives to make their Hajj.

Pilgrims from all over the world passed through the Hajj Terminal in Jeddah on their way to Mecca. Open only during the pilgrimage season and built exclusively to accommodate *Hajjis,* the incredible tensile structure resembled a gigantic white Bedouin tent. It was the perfect representation of traditional life in the desert land in which Mohammed had lived and taught his new religion, Islam.

Non-Muslims were prohibited from entering Mecca or even traveling on the immaculate road toward the city. Airplane flights overhead were forbidden as well. Driving on the road between Taif and Jeddah, we passed the restricted exit to Mecca It was the closest to the most revered Islamic site we would ever be. From that limited view, we could see the multi-lane super highway that was extremely well cared for; it was always freshly surfaced and painted. That highway was far better maintained than any other we ever saw in the Kingdom. The ornate signs pointing the way to Islam's holiest city were also kept in perfect condition; their gilded letters showed no indication of wear or tarnish. The Grand Mosque in Mecca was unquestionably equally adorned and maintained.

As a Christian I would never be allowed to see first hand the *Ka'aba*, the Islamic shrine of worship and focal point of the Grand Mosque. The Ka'aba is described as an enormous, fifty feet tall cube that is draped in rich black and gold hangings. So well cared for and revered is the Ka'aba, the ornate coverings are renewed every year.

The black cornerstone of the Ka'aba is believed by Muslims to have been cast down by God to Adam and Eve after they were expelled from the Garden of Eden. Now encased in silver, the cornerstone represents God's reconciliation with mankind and was given, according to Islam, to affirm that God was no longer displeased with Earth's first couple. Islam teaches that the resultant cube shaped Ka'aba was built by Abraham and his son Ishmael.

In Arabian days before Islam, the Ka'aba was used for the placement of various tribal and family idols during trading fairs. Tribal warfare and plunder were common. It was hoped that idols placed at the Ka'aba would provide both safety to traders and a profitable market for their goods. Additionally, infanticide, the sacrificing of children to appease idols, was common practice.

When the Prophet Mohammed conquered Mecca in the seventh century A.D., he destroyed hundreds of idols placed around the Ka'aba, including a specific one for each day of the year. As he destroyed the idols, he recited from the Koran a verse stating, "Truth has arrived and falsehood has perished for falsehood is by its nature bound to perish." He then ordered the destruction of all pictures in the Ka'aba.

Mohammed's establishment of Islam did not remove the Ka'aba as the shrine of worship even though it had been used for plural gods and the placement of idols. Polytheism was replaced by Allah, and worship at the Ka'aba continued. It is toward the Ka'aba that all Muslims must pray five times daily.

The flourishing slave trade in Mecca also continued after the establishment of Islam, and the descendants of Mohammed benefited financially from it. Pilgrims, primarily from Africa who were making the religious journey of their lifetime, sold their children into bondage. The sale of their offspring became a way for pilgrims to finance their trips home.

In the country's earlier days, Arabians, who lived in squalor, followed the Hajjis, gleaning items from discarded trash just as the Bangladeshi houseboys did with our garbage. Since the impact of oil wealth, Saudis have become the ones to leave trash, and now pilgrims from other countries sort through refuse left by wealthy Saudis.

The annual Hajj, with millions of pilgrims from primarily Third-World countries, always brought an influx of disease to the Kingdom. A Pakistani co-worker of mine contracted cholera during her Hajj, as did one of her children. For months after the Islamic pilgrimage, illness was prevalent in the international school and among expatriates; we had strange coughs, intestinal infections, viruses, and rashes. We faced the constant threat of parasites.

* * *

Eed al Adha, one of two principal holidays in Saudi Arabia, marks the end of the Hajj pilgrimage. On that day Hajjis offer animal sacrifices in Mecca and a feast of celebration is held. The meat from animals, which can include camels, sheep, cows, goat, and even buffalo, is divided into thirds: one part is to be given to the poor, a second to relatives, and a third part is kept by the pilgrim performing the sacrifice.

Animals used for sacrifice must be of minimum age, which varies from six months for a sheep to five years for a camel, though either gender is acceptable. The animals must be in good health and without obvious blemish or defect. While it is most desirable that each pilgrim perform the slaying of the sacrificial animal himself, he can, if needed, hire someone else to kill the animal for him. He should, at the very least, witness the slaughter.

According to the Koran, the Eed al Adha animal sacrifice is beneficial only as an act of obedience. "Neither their meat nor their blood ever reaches God, but heedfulness on your part does reach Him." The sacrifice is not considered an atonement or sin offering, unlike the animal sacrifices made during Biblical Judaism or the blood atonement of Jesus Christ in Christianity.

The ancient Jewish animal sacrifice *was* a sin offering, as prescribed in the book of Leviticus. "And he shall bring his trespass offering to the Lord, a ram without blemish from the flock, with your valuation, as a trespass offering, to the priest. So the priest shall make atonement for him before the Lord, and he shall be forgiven for any one of these things that he may have done in which he trespasses."

Sheep to be presented as sin offerings in the Jewish temple in Jerusalem were raised in the Judean hillsides of the nearby humble shepherds' settlement, Bethlehem – birthplace to both David who became King of Israel and of Jesus who was known as the King of Kings. Only sheep without blemish could be presented in sacrifice, a foreshadowing of the perfect "Lamb of God who takes away the sins of the world."

Muslims, on the other hand, have a revered Prophet whom they believe received God's final revelation to mankind, but they do not have a Savior. They make pilgrimages to Mecca and offer animals in sacrifice, not for atonement, but as acts of obedience in remembrance of Abraham's willingness to sacrifice his son Ishmael.

*　　*　　*

In the Kingdom, dogs were considered as unclean and revolting as were pigs. Packs of emaciated wild dogs roamed the desert. Rarely, a dog might be kept as a work animal but never a pet, and it would certainly never be allowed inside the home of a Saudi Arabian. It was not unusual for anti-Semitic writings to equate Jews with dogs, pigs, and monkeys. The symbolism attached to a dog in that Arab state, which refused to recognize Israel's right to exist, was profound.

Accordingly, dogs could not be brought into the Kingdom by expatriates. We had to leave our cocker spaniel, Dusty, behind with friends. I walked him just days before our departure and stopped for a Snickers, my personal comfort food. He and I sat together on a park bench and shared the candy bar, though I knew he shouldn't, and I wept that we would be leaving him behind.

Despite my certainty he would grieve for us, our friends Dave and Krissy reported Dusty never missed a meal after we left him! And while we were gone he became sire to a beautiful litter of registered puppies. When we returned after two years, it was as though we had never left him, except that his manners were ever so much better!

Cats were never kept as pets either, but we adopted a feral kitten while in Saudi Arabia, and we loved her. Sa'eed tolerated her and fed her in our absence, but he was puzzled by her presence in our apartment. It was unlikely he would have ever had an animal as a pet. Of course, when it was time to return to the States we wanted to bring Princess Leah home with us. We secured the necessary paperwork from the only veterinarian in Riyadh.

Princess Leah had lived entirely in our fourth floor apartment. The furthest she had ever ventured was onto the balconies adjoining the bedrooms. Mysteriously, one week before our departure for America, she somehow made her way down and out of the building and disappeared. We were heart-broken. Frantically we searched, called, and mewed, to no avail. I asked Sa'eed to have the other houseboys watch for our missing pet.

Early in the morning just two days before we were to leave the Kingdom, the little tiger-striped cat was spotted by one of the young men from Bangladesh as she darted under the restaurant's kitchen crawl space where wild cats hung out feeding on spilled garbage. The houseboy and two of his friends crawled under the building, caught her, and returned her to us.

The three of them, their green jumpsuits soiled from crawling on their bellies under the building, were beaming as they brought that dirty, tired, and hungry little cat to us. We rewarded them with one hundred riyals, which was about thirty dollars. Not much to us, it was one-third the annual per-capita income in Bangladesh. After a bath and lots of food, the poor little kitty slept for hours and was then ready for her flight to America.

On the day of our departure, we were stunned when many Bangladeshi houseboys, most of whom we did not know but had seen around the compound, came to our quarters to say good-bye and to shake our hands. The Filipino electrician for the compound and the tall Pakistani plumber also came. Much to our amazement, the men formed a line that extended out our front door. They waited respectfully for a turn to greet us. Some of the men teared in saying good-bye.

"We miss you," they said to our family. "We never forget you."

After returning to the United States we received several letters from Sa'eed imploring us to bring him to America to live with us. He offered to be our driver, cook, houseboy, and yard boy. Anything we needed, he said.

"I good work," he promised, again and again in his letters.

To him, a United States military family was wealthy beyond his imagination and could easily afford to bring immigrant servants to America. We surely had servants for our every need, he must have thought.

Ironically, we had brought our Saudi adopted cat home with us, though she was an animal considered worthless in the Islamic state. Sa'eed had wistfully said about her, "Cat lucky, go America." He hoped he could be as fortunate as Princess Leah and come to live in our country.

"America good place," he said.

7
TRADITIONAL SOUQS

The combined aroma of cardamom coffee and Middle-Eastern incense wafted toward us as we made our way down the narrow, dusty streets of traditional markets. Crowded one against another, tiny ancient shops known as souqs filled every available space along centuries-old streets. There was a souq for every product needed in the Arabian Desert, but none of the items was produced in the Kingdom. Everything was imported from Africa, China, or other Middle-Eastern countries.

The ramshackle one-room souqs were primarily constructed of plywood and aluminum, though in the oldest parts of Riyadh mud walls separated open stalls that formed individual markets. Shuttered fronts allowed for rapid closing at the first sound of the call to prayer.

Midas's palace, fabled for its splendor, could not have competed with the brilliance of Arabian gold souqs. Grouped together, an astonishing number of resplendent gold markets contrasted sharply with the seventh century atmosphere of traditional shops. Each gold souq was filled with dizzying opulence; there was more glitter and sheer abundance of gold than in dozens of jewelry stores combined in the States. Breath-taking for their incredible inventory, souqs immersed shoppers in gold jewelry on all sides and even hanging overhead. Fans, needed in the heat of the Arabian Desert, kept heavy, gleaming gold necklaces slightly swaying as if dancing to the music of Aladdin's flute.

Open in front, dazzling shops were brightly lit to welcome patrons inside. Walls covered in dark red velvet showcased hundreds of massive necklaces – the kind of adornments one would envision only in the palaces of sultans. The most striking piece of jewelry was a masterpiece comprised of rows of gold discs connected with thick links. Long and heavy, the solid gold wedding necklace, as we called it, completely covered the torso of any woman who wore it.

Mirrored ceilings gave added luster to the luminous, polished metal as it hung, filling every space from ceiling to floor against velvet backdrops. Boxes of shimmering jewelry and massive stacks of gleaming gold coins were visible beneath glass counter tops. Not only was every available space on walls covered with prized necklaces, burnished gold chains and bangles were draped unceremoniously in mass from nails and hooks in plywood dividing walls and wooden posts that supported ceilings in older shops. Glistening gold was piled in trays and in cardboard boxes on both glass and plywood counters.

The jewelry was made in Italy and was often tri-colored: yellow, white, and pink. Carat weights ranged from eighteen to twenty-four, instead of the ten to fourteen we typically see in America. Because of the greater concentration of gold, twenty-four carat pieces were as orange as brass. Expensive for their high gold content, twenty-four carat pieces of jewelry were soft and easily misshapen. Why pay for solid gold, I mused, if everyone will think it is inexpensive brass? I was happy to settle for the soft yellow of eighteen carats – less gold but more believable as the real deal.

Jewelry was sold both by carat weight and by grams. The price fluctuated depending on the value of gold on the world market but was generally about thirty dollars a gram (one hundred Saudi riyals) for eighteen carat pieces. Arabian merchants used small scales to determine the cost of one's selected piece without regard for style or craftsmanship.

If a particularly expensive piece were purchased, the merchant placed it in one of his assorted white boxes that he kept in a pile behind the counter, while a less expensive piece was placed in a small plastic bag with Arabic printed on the sides.

Gold merchants, who were always Saudis, usually wore crisp, long white thobes topped off with the traditional red and white headdresses. The stark white robes added to the brilliance of the shops; they perfectly complemented the glittering gold displayed against red velvet-covered walls.

Shops were sometimes left in the care of a merchant's young son. Though souqs were always busy and crowded, there was no apparent fear of theft. On occasion, merchants left the shopping space totally unattended to look in the back of their shops for a requested piece. A friend spoke of a time he and his wife were in a gold souq when the merchant did exactly that. A customer asked for a specific piece of jewelry; it was perhaps something previously ordered. Unconcerned by the number of shoppers filling his souq, the merchant went into the back for several minutes with no one left to tend the store.

"I wish I could have swallowed a dozen chains," our friend joked. Swift punishment made the likelihood of theft very remote. A gold chain was not worth having one's hand cut off.

Gold souqing was clearly the major weekend activity for Arabians and expatriates alike. Saudi Arabian women, in groups and always escorted by male relatives, crowded into gold markets. Thick, black coverings made it impossible to differentiate between mothers, wives, sisters, or daughters – all members of harems.

I wondered how one could satisfy the gold desires of four wives? Surely none would be willing to receive less jewelry than another wife! A woman's dowry, paid by her husband at their marriage, was likely to include gold jewelry. It became her financial security if her husband should die or divorce her.

To inspect the workmanship of desired pieces, women had to tuck glittering jewelry inside their veils for a closer look. As veils were maneuvered, one could catch of glimpse of sleeved arms covered with countless shiny gold bangles from wrist to elbow.

Saudi Arabia, always critically short of blood, paid cash to those willing to "donate." Many expatriates funded their gold purchases with the selling of their blood on a regular basis. Each trip to the blood bank financed one gram of the precious metal purchased in souqs.

American women wore glittering gold bangles, chains, and even whimsical earrings shaped like tea-pots, palm trees, or Arabian daggers! The heavy four-seasons bracelet, priced at about four hundred dollars, was a popular piece. I never saw an expatriate woman wear one of the massive torso-covering necklaces. Prized by Arab women, the necklaces, which resembled chain-maille except that they were made of solid gold, would have been considered garish by American standard.

Almost every expatriate woman, as well as many men, purchased gold chains with their names spelled in Arabic – except one of my more outspoken friends who asked rhetorically, "Why would I want anything in that squiggly writing?"

Not all English sounds have an equivalent Arabic letter, and substitutions had to be made in the spelling of names on gold chains. There is no letter in Arabic for the sound of p, for example, so Pamela was spelled "Bamela" just as Pepsi was pronounced "Bebsi" by the Saudis.

I admit to having purchased a number of necklace and bracelet sets. Of course, I purchased a necklace with my name in Arabic. It was a novel piece and I wore it for interest until the attack on America. It has remained in my jewelry box since then.

* * *

Leaving the opulent gold markets behind, we discovered exotic souqs at every turn. Silver souqs sparkled with jewelry that I actually preferred to gold. Other souqs sold inexpensive gold-plated knock-offs of more valuable jewelry. Brass souqs offered tea and coffee pots, plates, goblets, and bowls. Platters and trays of varied sizes, incense burners, and decorative Aladdin lamps were also available in brass. There were basket souqs, soap souqs, and sandal souqs. Fabric souqs displayed countless bolts of colorful cottons, silks, taffetas, and brocades.

"Antique pots from Syria. Hundreds years old." Merchants insisted on their age and origin, but I thought the pots and pitchers in the copper souqs looked remarkably the same as those sold in Jerome, Arizona. We were not persuaded of their age but purchased some of the pots anyway – just in case.

Bunches of yellow, perfectly ripe bananas hung invitingly from the roofs of open-air fruit markets. Delivered daily from Lebanon, Jordan, and Syria, bananas were abundant along with oranges, figs, melons, and grapes. Enormous moist dates and raw almonds were scooped from huge baskets and sold by weight.

The pungent aroma was unmistakable as one neared the numerous spice souqs. Cinnamon, pepper, cloves, garlic, ginger, sesame seeds, and cardamom were among seasonings filling tall, tightly woven, African baskets. Available for purchase in any quantity desired, spices were scooped from their containers and weighed in balance scales to determine their cost.

Valuable spices from the Indies had motivated Christopher Columbus to sail west from Spain in hopes of reaching the Spice Islands by an all water route. Still treasured five hundred years later, spices were sold in bulk and used liberally to flavor foods in Arabian households.

As we walked further into the traditional souqs, the smell of cardamom coffee and hot tea brewing over smoky wood fires and flat bread baking in ancient ovens beckoned to us. Bread merchants pushed up the long sleeves of their flowing robes and reached bare-handed into open, wood-burning stoves to slap flat bread against the inside walls of traditional ovens, while roaring fires in the centers singed the hair on their arms.

Merchants frequently offered us coffee or tea. I accepted the first tiny cup of green cardamom coffee but tried to avoid refills of the strong brew, which was served without cream or sugar to alter its bitter taste. Hot, sweetened tea served in small clear glass mugs was far more palatable. No matter how high the temperature of the day, hot tea and coffee were always being consumed. I never saw iced tea, even on summer days when the temperature soared.

Along Chicken Street, as we called it, the aroma of cooked meat filled the air. Outdoor vendors roasted fresh, whole chickens to a bronze blush. Sides of goat were roasted on spits, shaved, and served with creamy cucumber yogurt in freshly-baked pita bread for delicious *shwarma* sandwiches. Lamb kabobs, along with pungent Middle-Eastern rice, were sold street side. We were always comfortable buying and eating food from Chicken Street and never had any digestive problem from it. The biggest decision was merely which food to choose on any given day. The offerings were all delicious.

We found an interesting music souq that sold cassette tapes priced at a dollar or two each. Named "747," the souq was well-stocked with bootlegged copies of most genres of music. Unlike legitimate studio released tapes in music stores in the West, these tapes had no cover art. Instead, they all had identical generic labels; the titles and artists' names had been typed onto strips of white paper and glued onto the spines of the plastic cases! We purchased a number of the bootlegged tapes and found that their quality was equivalent to their price.

I especially enjoyed rug souqs. Persian, Afghan, Kashmir, Russian, and Chinese rugs were piled in stacks six to eight feet tall, with dozens of stacks in any given market. Souq-boys, young Middle-Eastern men who were not Saudi Arabian, endlessly pulled out heavy rugs and spread each for display until we found one we liked. The Prophet Mohammed's cloak was said to have been green, which made a rug of that color especially desirable, we were told by one merchant.

Rugs were also sold directly from trucks parked roadside. Merchants spread their prized merchandise on the desert sand or across the brightly painted paneled sides of their trucks. We purchased a Kashmir rug, woven in the disputed region between Pakistan and India, from one such roadside dealer.

Named for the village or region of their origin, rugs were hand knotted by women and young children. Valuable rugs will have millions of knots woven so tightly that only small fingers could have managed them. Working long hours and for little pay, women and children create beautiful works of art depicting the style of their particular village to be sold in markets around the world.

Nowhere had we ever seen the immense quantity of rugs for sale as we saw in Saudi Arabia. Our budget limited us to the purchase of area rugs, but Saudi Arabian homes and even desert tents of the Bedouin are adorned with numerous large rugs that cover every inch of floor space.

Not all souqs were operated by Saudis. In a rather large rug souq managed by an Iraqi merchant, we found a Persian silk Quom and Russian wool Caucasian we loved. The Caucasian rug was truly an old world antique and had likely been used for decades in a Russian home. The Persian silk rug from the village of Quom in Iran was a work of art with its tree of life design. It was intricately woven and tied with over a million knots. Its price, incredibly, was greater than that of our first automobile purchased years earlier! We knew we would love to have both rugs, but their combined cost made it impossible to purchase them outright.

Seeing our hesitation, the merchant, who knew us only by my husband's first name, asked why we did not purchase the rugs that day. While I was thinking the answer was rather simple – we could not afford them – my husband explained that we had a family safari in Kenya planned for Spring break and shouldn't put so much money into rugs with that trip ahead!

"Oh, yes," the merchant replied. "Must have family trip. Very important. You take rugs home today. Each month come and pay a little. You enjoy rugs and enjoy family trip." The men shook hands and we left with two beautiful hand knotted rugs that adorn our home to this day.

In a month we returned to the rug souq to make our payment, only to learn that the merchant with whom we had dealt had returned to Iraq. His brother was now in charge. My husband explained that he was there to make a payment on the rugs we had purchased. The puzzled man looked through records, but he could find no paperwork of our transaction.

"I take your word for it," he replied.

We made our payment and continued to make payments until the entire amount, interest free, was paid off. The power of the promised word, the handshake, but most of all the threat of dire punishment for theft made shopping in the Kingdom unique, indeed.

*   *   *

My husband, a determined photographer, shouldered his camera on every souq excursion. Fascinating glimpses of Arabian customs surrounded us, but capturing Saudi life with a camera was not easy, and it was certainly not without risk. He was able to produce a fine collection, but in some of the photographs the buildings are tilted or heads are missing from the intended subjects – the result of "shooting from the hip" without lifting his camera.

Many older Saudis still feared the "evil eye" of the camera. Just the sight of a camera provoked occasional finger-wagging and verbal scolding in Arabic from passing Saudis. However, young men working in the souqs were likely to agree to being photographed. Proud of their positions as merchants, especially in gold souqs, the men smiled broadly for the camera. Dark-haired and mustached, they invariably took time to adjust headdresses before the shutter clicked. Though happy to pose, the men never would have granted permission for unveiled female members of their families to be photographed.

Our favorite time to go souqing was at night when the sights, sounds, and smells seemed to intensify. Moderately busy during the day, souqs became crowded and filled with noisy clatter when the temperature dropped. At night one had the feeling of having stepped back into the seventh century or accidentally onto an *Indiana Jones* movie set. The ancient, narrow streets between traditional souqs, without benefit of modern street lights, were filled with shadows, mystery, and intrigue. Extension cords and light bulbs provided necessary light – though dim – in most souqs other than gold souqs, which were always well lit.

Old men shuffled along dusty streets between shops that stayed open well after midnight and even later during *Ramadhan*, the annual month of fasting. Bustling with activity, markets provided opportunity for men to socialize. Saudi women were noticeably absent.

In traditional dress, heads wrapped in ghutras, and often wearing belted daggers, bearded men squatted in groups while talking and drinking cardamom coffee that had been brewed over open fires. Others busied themselves playing an ancient Arabian and African board game. Using small stones instead of checkers or chess pieces, men played in pairs while others stood by watching and offering suggestions for strategic moves.

Arabia has a strong oral history. Story telling and the recitation of poetry remain an immensely popular pastime for men who gather around the coffee pot to tell and retell the same offerings learned in childhood. One poem in particular is loved, memorized and recited by every Saudi male. Its verses tell of the heroic feat of Abdul Aziz ibn Sa'ud who at the beginning of the twentieth century along with his half-brother Muhammad and their cousin Abdullah bin Jaluwi assassinated the governor of Riyadh and claimed the city for the family of Sa'ud.

At night one was most likely to see men purchasing tooth brush sticks from street vendors or smoking the *hubbly-bubbly*. Though drugs were illegal in the country, the popularity and smell of the curved, gurgling Turkish water pipe suggested it may have contained more than tobacco. Men sat in shadowed corners contentedly puffing while others awaited their turns. Smoking was common among Saudi males. Coughing, hacking, and spitting without benefit of spittoons, men enjoyed their smokes, whether the hubbly-bubbly or cigarettes. We always had to watch where we stepped!

Saudi men and boys wore the national clothing: long sleeved, white robes called thobes and red and white headdresses. During the cooler months of winter, thobes were made of a heavier fabric and were brown or gray in color. If the temperature dipped significantly, a sport coat was worn over the long robe and closed-toe shoes were substituted for sandals.

The ghutra was clearly a fashion accessory and worn with great individuality. Even when piled on the wearer's head, the placement was precise. Great care was taken to get the folds and drape just right.

Old, bearded Arabian men with leathered skin wrapped their ghutras around their heads like turbans or across their faces as if to protect their skin from a battering shamal, the desert dust storm. Only their eyes were exposed, though the headdress was easily maneuvered to allow them to sip hot tea and coffee or to smoke.

Younger men folded the sides of the ghutra back to give it the vague shape of a Stetson. The *aghal*, a black rope-like circle, was originally used as a camel hobble. Now part of the headdress, it was worn on top of the ghutra. Wearing their pristine, white flowing thobes and their ghutras so carefully folded, proud young Saudis walked in groups with a swagger that begged notice.

During one of our early trips to the souqs, we were looking at a stack of ghutras with the intent of buying one as a souvenir. We hadn't noticed two young Saudi men standing behind us until one said, "Those are not very good. They are made in China. You should get one from the other table. They are made in England and are of better quality." It was then that we met Ahmed and Khalid. The two became our friends, hosts, and guides, opening the extremely closed kingdom to us. Both young men had spent time in the United States, spoke English well, and were very willing to share their culture.

Ahmed and Khalid began dropping by our compound apartment nearly every week and, on occasion, brought along other male friends who shared meals with us as well. Their friends, all of whom had studied in the United States, were always gracious, but none spoke of their families nor did we ever see photographs of their wives or children. Saudi men socialized in the evening, but women and children remained secluded in their homes.

Incredibly, the friendships of Ahmed and Khalid, so freely given, led to unexpected invitations to their homes. I was allowed to meet their mothers and sisters and to attend family celebrations and Islamic holiday observances not normally open to Westerners. Of the many American and European women I knew in the country, not one had the experiences in Saudi Arabian homes that these young men gave me.

During my two year stay in the Kingdom, I knew only one Saudi Arabian woman, other than those I met because of Ahmed and Khalid. It was unusual for an expatriate to be acquainted with even one Arabian woman. Our amazing two friends opened their doors for me to meet many more.

That Ahmed and Khalid, devout Muslims, became so at ease with me – a woman and a Christian – was truly astounding. Ahmed, in particular, became a teacher to me in the most incredible ways in a country that totally separates men from women.

Anxious to convert me to Islam and most certainly hoping to convince me that Islam is the religion that most honors women, Ahmed gave me Islamic reading material. Written in English by Muslim clerics, the material was designed to give understanding of and justification for the many rules that encumber women under Islamic law. The writers all penned the same restrictions imposed on women who were expected to accept the extreme rules in total deference to men.

I learned much from the printed material and even more from Ahmed himself. The young Saudi answered my frequent questions about Shari'a with surprising candor.

8

SHARI'A

A Saudi Arabian woman, who in 2005 allowed herself to be interviewed by a female reporter for an American news program, removed her veil in the seclusion of a restroom but insisted her identity be concealed. Expressing her desire for change in her homeland, the woman said, "I like to drive. Here, the woman cannot drive. And I like here to have a cinema...a movie." Summing up her longings, she said, "I like to be free. All people want to be free."

The young woman could speak only in secret of desiring such simple liberties. Expressing even an interest in forbidden activities could result in punishment. Further, anyone who dared demonstrate against the rules enforced by the Mutaween was subject to public caning. Living under her veil of honor, the Saudi woman could not have imagined the liberties Americans treasure. Being allowed to drive or attend a cinema were her measures of freedom in the Islamic state that permitted her neither.

Islam teaches free will, its proponents claim, but in Saudi Arabia, the birthplace of Islam, there is little choice – particularly for women – and even less likelihood of change. Khaled al-Dakheel, a professor at King Saud University in Riyadh, is a leading reformer who has declared, "The most important change that must take place here in this country is to allow for the freedom of expression, for the diversity of this society to express itself freely." But, his pleas for reform have resulted in the government banning him from writing a column in the newspaper. When asked what he said that resulted in the ban, he replied, "It was the pattern of my writing. Too much call for reform and too much questioning of official positions...this government does not like you to be so daring in questioning the policy."

As recently as 2007, King Abdullah bin Abdul Aziz was queried as to when women might be allowed to drive in the

Kingdom. A few neighboring states had already granted females that legal right. The monarch whose family is charged with the preservation of Islamic law responded, "The state's duty is to provide a conducive atmosphere…that conforms with *Shari'a*."

Shari'a is Islamic law. It is based both on the *Koran*, the book of Islam and on the *Hadith*, the collection of sayings and actions of the seventh century Prophet Mohammed and his closest associates. To a Saudi Arabian, Shari'a is not only the straight path that governs every aspect of life, it is the law of God.

There were no elections when I lived in the Kingdom. The only voting that had ever taken place was briefly in the 1960s when a few cities conducted municipal polls that were open only to men. In 2005, Prince Sultan bin Salman said, "It's not important to have elections. It's important to have stability." The unquestioned rule of Shari'a and the enforced adherence to its dictates provide a "stability" that leaves little room for individual expression or personal choice.

The Royal Family, the House of Sa'ud, rules the Kingdom. Sons and grandsons of the original king Abdul Aziz ibn Sa'ud fill all the important offices of government. However, it is the Mutaween, the religious police, who exercise great authority to enforce the code of conduct required in the Islamic state. Those (usually self-appointed) judges of appropriate dress and behavior walk about all public areas. Faces stern, their foreheads are sometimes indented as a result of banging their heads on the floors of mosques during their ardent prayers. Each arbiter of virtue and vice carries a cane pole – the corporal back-up to his verbal reprimands in Arabic.

Media in the Kingdom were rigorously censored. Movie theaters and video stores did not exist. Rumors circulated of taped Egyptian soap operas, but I never saw any. Documentaries about Saudi Arabia shown in the United States were banned. Daytime television programming, which never featured women, was limited to public service shorts demonstrating basic health and sanitation practices or coverage of the annual Hajj. The public service shorts, produced in a simple one-dimensional format, more resembled cartoons or low budget commercials than government sponsored instructional material. Giving what to Americans seemed incredibly basic information, they emphasized, for example, the necessity of washing one's hands, of refrigerating perishable food, or seeking medical care if a child had persistent fever. The coverage of the Hajj, the annual pilgrimage to Mecca, filled hours and hours of air time. With narrative in Arabic, the televised film showed tens of thousands of white-robed pilgrims circling the Ka'aba, the holiest shrine of worship in Islam.

Televised evening news was little more than a recitation of greetings King Fahd received and returned to other heads of state. Each night there would be several greetings announced, and all were worded similarly to this: "King Fahd received a message from King Hussein, congratulating him on his birthday. King Fahd responded to the King of Jordan, thanking him for his kindness and long-standing friendship." I wondered why Saudi Arabians would care to know who greeted their king on any given day, particularly since the greeting and his formal response comprised the total substance of the news report.

On the occasion of an execution, a grim announcement was part of the evening news program. Reporting the beheading that had taken place, the news reader invariably included a "warning to our guests in the Kingdom" that laws of the country were to be taken very seriously.

There was no international news, no political discourse, and certainly no debate of issues. No one raised concerns about the rule of the Royal Family or publicly questioned its authority. There were no public opinion polls rating the king's popularity or approval. Members of the House of Sa'ud were not subjected to persistent photographers or enquiring reporters; the media never discussed their personal lives. Programming such as "Hardball," "Meet the Press," "The O'Reilly Factor," or "60 Minutes" did not exist. Neither did variety shows, sit-coms, or game shows.

The United States presidential campaign of 1984 was underway, but we heard none of the debates and little about the candidates. The Olympic Games of that year were neither televised nor included in news reports. We learned the names of

America's gold medalists when letters from home reached us two weeks later. None of the news common to local broadcasts in the States was available to us, prompting us to comment that California could be quaking, sliding, or burning, and we would never know.

Local newspapers were of scant value. Absent investigative reporting, one read only what the government, the Royal Family, allowed. State controlled, the articles in print all reflected the same Arab and Islamic viewpoints. "The friend of my enemy is my enemy also," was a common theme. The United States's friendship with Israel provoked frequent anti-American copy.

All religious material, other than Islamic, was prohibited. In spite of this ban, we were able to bring our Bibles into the Kingdom as part of our household goods that were shipped through diplomatic channels. We were told that not only were Bibles prohibited, illustrations within some were considered particularly offensive in Islam. Accordingly, any representation of the Prophet Mohammed was forbidden and considered blasphemous.

Magazine subscriptions coming through the mail to expatriates were closely monitored. Printed material not deemed suitable under Islamic law was confiscated. Most of the books I read in preparation for our move to the Kingdom were prohibited. Nevertheless, copies of forbidden works, having come as part of household goods, circulated among expatriates and were added to the shelves of compound libraries.

Among the books I read before moving to the Kingdom was Marianne Alireza's *At the Drop of a Veil.* An American woman, Ms. Alireza had decades earlier married a Saudi Arabian young man whom she met while both attended the University of California, Berkeley. In marriage, she became part of a wealthy and influential Saudi family. Her husband ultimately became the Saudi Arabian Ambassador to Washington D.C.

Her book gave an enlightened, inside look at life inside a harem. It even described the awkwardness in being introduced by her husband to his second wife whom he added to the harem. Ms. Alireza painted a vivid picture of Saudi life in general and life for women within the Royal Family in particular. My earliest perceptions of the Kingdom came from her remarkable book.

Ms. Alireza came to love Arabia and its people, though she was eventually divorced from her husband and subsequently returned to the States. Her book described the anguish over her children and her difficulty in taking them out of the Kingdom.

Ms. Alireza's arrival in Saudi Arabia in the mid-1940s was before the full effect of the tremendous oil wealth for which the Kingdom is known. By the time I arrived four decades later, Jeddah with its palatial villas looked very different from the city she described. However, the rules governing women's lives had not changed at all in the intervening years.

So much had changed for women in America during the same period. There was little similarity to my mother's life as a wife and mother in 1945 and mine in the 1980s. Education, employment opportunities, standard of living, and the feminist movement had all dramatically altered life in America. Women in the Kingdom, on the other hand, lived with limited rights under the same restrictions and obligations that had governed Arabian females for centuries.

In an article written by Ed Bradley, reporter for the television news program, "60 Minutes," Dr. Saleh al-Sheikh, the minister for Islamic affairs in Saudi Arabia, is quoted as saying that a number of factors determine a Saudi woman's obligations – the most important of which is raising a family. "I believe in equal rights according to their circumstances… Women do have rights, but they are based on our view of their obligations in life."

In the male-dominated system that unyieldingly enforced Shari'a, the obligations of women were marked by servitude and submission to the needs of men, while producing their offspring. For some it was a life of luxury in palatial villas, but for many women it was a life that offered little more than an unrelenting struggle to endure the demands imposed in the name of their religion. Women bore the responsibility of preserving the requisite honor, as defined by the seventh century culture in which they lived.

I also read *Oil Sheikhs* by Linda Blandford. The author, who managed to conceal the fact that she was Jewish, had been allowed into the Kingdom in 1975 to chronicle the impact of Arabia's oil wealth. Miss Blandford's winsome personality and her apparent vulnerability due to a limp made her readily welcomed into Saudi Arabian homes. (Disabilities are common in the Kingdom – attributable to the practice of marriage to first cousins.) Women, even members of the Royal Family, invited Miss Blandford into their private quarters, shared their secrets, and gave her unprecedented access to Arabian life.

Her subsequent book was a scandalous account of life of the new rich. I was struck by the blatant contradictions between actual Arabian life, as described by the author, and the purported piety of the Islamic state.

Saudi Arabians were outraged by the book, *Oil Sheikhs*. According to historian Robert Lacey, it was not that Ms. Blandford did not tell the truth about the lives of the Saudis she described. Her depiction of the newly wealthy Arabians in Jeddah was shocking in its accuracy. But the Saudis were furious that she had made public that which was told her in private. The same gossip that may be freely spoken, explains Lacey, brings shame if written about and exposed publicly.

*   *   *

There were no Barnes and Noble Booksellers, Borders, Walden, or other book stores in the Kingdom. Few books and magazines were sold in markets. Women's magazines, as we know them, were non-existent. Any female pictured on a cover or within printed pages had been blackened out with markers. One can only wonder at the number of Mutaween, the religious police officially called the "High commissary for the propagation of virtue and prevention of vice," who spent their days obscuring female images from print, just as women were veiled, obscured, and diminished in real life.

Draped in black, Arabian women moved silently in groups and always with family male escorts. I had at first been shocked at the sight of the enshrouded women and then stirred by an unsettling sense of oppression. Gradually, the women to whom we were not allowed to speak and who could not be identified or acknowledged in any way became invisible. Invisible. It was as though they didn't exist. And since they didn't exist, they could be ignored in all public settings. Was that, after all, the intent of the Mutaween – invisible women who were irrelevant and whose presence was ignored?

While women were wrapped and draped in black layers, men wore pristine white thobes and red and white ghutras. National dress, the practice of everyone dressing exactly the same, was said to eliminate class or wealth distinctions. There were, however, subtle differences. The thobe of a wealthy male, with cleaning done by servants, could be longer. He did not need to be concerned with soiling the hem of his long white robe. New thobes were always whiter than older, dingy ones worn by less affluent men. Further, as Ahmed told us, there was a definite difference in the quality of the headdress, the ghutra. Those made in England were superior to the ones produced in China.

Very young Saudi Arabian girls wore long dresses that were often made of white lace. I bought two of the "princess" dresses for my young nieces, but even as Easter dresses they were far frillier than American girls choose to wear. In the States, the elaborate dresses were relegated to dress-up tea parties and Halloween costumes.

Childhood ended early for females in Saudi Arabia. Little girls played with their young brothers in their dirt yards; it would be the only time in their lives they were afforded that freedom. At the onset of puberty, girls were confined to the indoors where they could not be seen by unrelated males. As soon as breasts started to develop or menses began, girls had to be hidden and secluded. Pubescent girls wore the veil and the long black abaya, just as their mothers did. The sexual symbolism of the veil covering their young faces was unmistakable.

The veil was said to protect females from harassment, from annoyance, and from molesting. It allowed privacy and modesty. Females were carriers of the honor, and veiling was a primary means of protecting the required family and cultural honor. Requisite honor sometimes led to appalling consequences.

In March 2002, just six months after the terrorist attack on America, the world was horrified when news agencies reported a tragic fire in a girls' school in Jeddah, Saudi Arabia. Mutaween prevented rescuers from entering the school to save the female students. Trapped inside, the girls were judged by religious police not to be wearing appropriate Islamic dress and were, therefore, not allowed to escape the burning building. Fifteen teen-aged girls died.

One can only shudder at the definitions of virtue and vice in a country whose religious police forced children to burn to death rather than have their unveiled faces exposed. The girls, with no time to reposition their coverings before escaping the burning school, would have brought dishonor to their fathers if seen unveiled. Better they burn. Death was preferable to the loss of honor.

For many Americans, this was a first glimpse into the culture from which fifteen of the nineteen 9-11 terrorists came. Young Saudi Arabian men who learned religious fervor in madrasahs, who lived in a culture with so little regard for human life, and who believed death was preferable to the loss of honor were willing to strap explosives to their bodies or fly aircraft into buildings to prove their allegiance to Allah. Paradise had been promised as their reward for the murder of "Infidels" who did not share their religious zeal and strict interpretation of Islam. Jihad was for them a religious act, a holy war for Allah.

* * *

Shari'a is Islamic law. As I learned from Ahmed and from the reading materials he gave me, it governed every aspect of life in Saudi Arabia, and it was women who bore the brunt of the restrictions imposed in the name of religion. Ahmed insisted the laws protected and honored women. I insisted laws that kept women subservient, secluded, and totally dependent on men benefited only males and their Middle-Eastern definition of honor. It was a system that had not changed significantly since the days of tribal warfare in Arabia's past.

For centuries, disparate Bedouin tribes had plundered one another's property stealing camels, horses, and the women of harems. Considered property, just as were livestock, women were part of the booty acquired in a raid and had little choice in the direction of their lives.

Juwayriya, one of twelve wives of the Prophet Mohammed, was taken prisoner after her tribe lost a battle with the Muslims. Her father offered Mohammed a payment for her release, but after negotiations she became the Prophet's wife instead of being returned to the tent of her father. Other wives of Mohammed had been given to him as slaves, while some of his marriages were arranged by relatives or associates, as was his youngest wife.

Aisha was only six years old when her father betrothed her to his old friend. The prophet, after all, needed a wife. Khadijah, Mohammed's first wife, had died and though his wife Sawda was still alive, his friends encouraged him to marry again – to a virgin, of course. Three years later when the little girl was nine, she had what was believed to be her first menses – the accepted indication that she was old enough to bear children. Aisha took her toys with her to the home of Allah's messenger where the marriage was consummated.

Still considered property in the twentieth century, females were subject to the same rules of Shari'a that gave them little or no choice in the course of their lives. They were deemed old enough to marry as soon as their bodies were believed physically able to produce babies. Emotional maturity was not required.

Abdul Aziz ibn Sa'ud, the first king of Saudi Arabia, had many wives – estimates range from seventeen to forty – as well as many concubines and slave girls. He was rumored to have told his friends that he had "no use for women older than thirty. I divorce them automatically when they reach that age." Several of his wives, including Hussah, did remain with him to the end of his life, though hers was an "interrupted" marriage.

While visiting her father, the king noticed the beautiful little girl playing in her yard; it was the only time in her life she was allowed the freedom to run and play outdoors. Enchanted by her guileless charm, the king arranged to marry Hussah as soon as she was old enough.

Hussah gave birth to a son, who died in infancy. The king then divorced her and gave her to his brother Muhammad. In time, Abdul Aziz began to regret the loss of Hussah. After persuading his brother to divorce her, the king remarried the wife who would become one of his favorites.

Hussah produced seven more sons for Abdul Aziz. Those seven became the most trusted and powerful of his estimated forty-five sons. Known as the *Sudairi Seven*, (Hussah's father was a Sudairi) they have remained extremely close and influential in the Kingdom. King Fahd bin Abdul Aziz, who ruled Saudi Arabia for two decades during the years of its phenomenal wealth and resultant modernization, was the eldest of the Sudairi Seven, the sons of Hussah.

* * *

The Prophet Mohammed lived in Arabia in the seventh century, and Abdul Aziz, who established Saudi Arabia as an Islamic state governed by Shari'a, lived in the first half of the twentieth century. It has been years since I lived in the Kingdom. Immense oil wealth has brought modern architecture and Western exposure to the Arabian Peninsula. One would expect that over time cultural practices have changed. However, the rules that govern women remain the same; females continue to have little say in the direction of their lives.

Marriages in the Kingdom are always arranged, and many brides have little choice in marital plans. In the Bedouin tradition, fathers and brothers make all nuptial decisions for the women of their households. Daughters who refuse to marry an arranged husband are subject to punishment. Even if not punished, a daughter who refuses arranged unions too many times runs the risk of having marriage offers altogether cease. As in other polygamist cultures, each additional wife is likely to be younger than existing ones. I met girls who at thirteen and fourteen were already married and pregnant.

A news article dated January 7, 2007, told of two business partners in Saudi Arabia, both in their 70s, who arranged marriages for themselves to each other's teen-aged daughter. One of the husbands, Al-Dossary, said, "When it comes to marriage there is no stopping point."

The other husband and business partner, Al-Qahtani, when asked if he consulted his daughter, said, "I did not ask my daughter. I don't have to. I know what is beneficial for her. When I told her what I had planned she was happy. If she hadn't been, she would have told her mother."

Besides the Bedouin tradition in which a girl cannot refuse a marriage arranged by her father (or brothers), both men justified the marriages with another point. As old, successful business men, they were able to present their teen-aged brides with huge dowries and valuable gifts – something younger men could not have done.

Reported in December 2008, a Saudi Arabian court refused to grant the divorce of an eight-year old girl to a forty-eight year old man. The girl's mother petitioned the court on behalf of her daughter after the child's father, who was no longer married to the mother, arranged the marriage in exchange for a payment of several thousand dollars.

*　　*　　*

My friend with whom I taught kindergarten was from India. She defended the practice of arranged marriages, saying that adults in charge were much better at choosing suitable mates than were the young. Her fifteen year marriage to an engineer was successful because her parents had chosen well for her, she insisted.

A Pakistani co-worker, the one who contracted cholera during her Hajj, voiced the same opinion. Both women, educated and themselves teachers, could not imagine the Western practice of dating and courtship. "Love has nothing to do with it," they said. "You can learn to love."

*　　*　　*

In more modern Saudi Arabian families, the older women were likely to arrange marriages for their sons and daughters, but all arrangements were subject to the approval of the family patriarch. The preferred union for a man was marriage to his paternal cousin, the daughter of his father's brother. A maternal cousin was a second choice. The new bride, if she were lucky, might have played with her cousin as a child and might have liked him.

There was no legal dating or courtship before marriage. The arranged bride and groom were allowed a one-time meeting, lasting about twenty minutes, in the chaperoned presence of both families. That single encounter formed the basis on which the couple agreed to the marriage or not. Afterwards, the bride and groom typically did not see each other again until they were married. Ahmed told me that brides and grooms were not always given the opportunity to meet prior to marriage. In the most traditional families, such as his, a bride remained veiled and was not seen by her husband until she became his wife.

The groom had to pay a dowry proposed by the bride's father or brothers. Meant to become the bride's financial security, her father could inflate the demand and ask for anything he wanted for himself, such as a new automobile, camel, or tent. Any man could decline a proposed marriage if the requested dowry were greater than he was willing to pay.

Marriage ceremonies for Saudi Arabian couples were performed by a local judge. Grooms attended, but brides did not. Instead, a bride was spoken for by a male family representative who agreed to the union. Two additional relevant males attended to bear witness to the judge's pronouncement of a valid marriage contract.

Marriage celebrations, for those affluent enough to host them, were gender separated. The groom partied with men in a hotel room or special event room where musicians provided music for them to dance. Women celebrated in a separate room and usually had a singer or singing group for their entertainment. At an appointed time, the bride and groom met in still another room.

The couple typically moved into his mother's home where several generations of Saudi women lived together in the women's quarters known as the harem. The new bride was treated like a servant until she produced male babies. Her fertility was always a concern, as was her anxiety that her husband would take additional wives.

Secluded and separated from men socially, women and girls wore the veil anytime they were likely to be in the presence of a man other than one in their immediate families. Two brothers with their wives could live in the same house, and neither brother would ever see his sister-in-law unveiled. A woman who was married was allowed to remove her veil in the presence of her father or brothers or eat with the men of her birth family only with her husband's permission. He was entitled to be the only man who would ever see his wife's unveiled face or with whom she would share a meal or have conversation. Husbands could keep their wives, who had "equal rights according to their circumstances," totally secluded.

It was rumored that King Sa'ud, the second king of Saudi Arabia and a son of Abdul Aziz, never saw the faces of some of his wives. Though they were married to him and gave birth to his children, including approximately fifty-three sons, the wives remained veiled in his presence, reinforcing the prevailing perception of women as little more than breeders.

In 2008 I read of a Saudi Arabian woman who petitioned the court for divorce because after forty years of marriage her husband was demanding to see her face!

Wealthy Saudi women filled their days with hours of boredom, sleep, or grooming in anticipation of chaperoned shopping excursions or nightly visits from their husbands. Fortunate women may have had video recorders on which to watch taped Egyptian soap operas or clandestine American movies. However, poor women, often living in squalor, spent their days of seclusion laboring with all the responsibilities of home and family, as well as the care of animal herds. Bedouin wives were not likely to be shopping in the gold souqs and dress boutiques of Riyadh or Jeddah.

Saudi women were allowed to leave their residences for limited reasons. In very traditional homes, women visited females of another harem only once a year. Family male escorts were always required. Unmarried women were accompanied by fathers, paternal uncles, or brothers, while a married woman could leave her home in the presence of her husband or perhaps an adult son. Since the "revival" of Islamic law after Desert Storm in 1991, the male escort must not only be a family relative; some reports indicate he now must be the elder member of the family.

Travel outside the Kingdom was even more restricted. Passports were kept by men, and females had to have written permission from a father or husband to travel. "Women must be protected," Ahmed insisted. "It is not safe for a woman to be alone. Our wives and sisters understand that it is our duty to protect them."

* * *

It was a culture of honor, and women were carriers of the honor. A woman's life was not her own; it belonged to the culture as a whole. As a result, any female behavior whether real or imagined that brought shame to her family dishonored the culture as well. Her punishment, therefore, had to be severe enough to avenge not only her family's damaged honor but that of her larger culture.

"Domestic violence and marital rape are problems that are well known in Saudi Arabia, but never discussed publicly." An article published by Freedom House explains that while the Muslim family is considered the fundamental building block of the culture, it is so charged with the preservation of honor and privacy that domestic abuse cannot be discussed openly without challenging the very structure of the family. Women are unlikely to reveal abuse for fear of damaging their own reputations and their families' honor. Additionally, the risks of incurring further punishment are too great.

Though not talked about openly in the Kingdom, accounts of abuse surface occasionally from women who have left Saudi Arabia. In July 2009, a Saudi princess was granted political asylum in Great Britain. The princess feared that if she returned to the Kingdom she would be honor killed. Married to a much older man, the princess had engaged in a relationship with a British man and, as a result, was in danger of being stoned.

President Obama has declared an administration policy that would allow "foreign women who are victims of severe domestic beatings and sexual abuse to receive asylum in the United States." In order to be granted asylum, however, a woman is required to show that domestic abuse is widely tolerated in her culture and that she is, therefore, unable to find protection within her own country. One has to wonder how a battered woman still living in Saudi Arabia, Pakistan, the Sudan, or Afghanistan could possibly report abuse and meet the stated requirement for American asylum.

A rare but much publicized report came from a Saudi Arabian woman who still lived in the Islamic state. Described as a "television host" – a position that didn't exist for females when I lived in the Kingdom – the woman, who wanted a divorce and custody of her two sons, made her abuse public. Though she allowed photographs of her battered face to be taken and sympathy was expressed for her plight, it is unlikely that her experience has changed any cultural attitudes toward domestic violence. In Saudi Arabia, physical abuse of wives was accepted as the right, if not the duty of the husband.

Punishment was justified, clerics wrote, in cases of disobedient females. Reported on Internet news in 2008, a cleric from Saudi Arabia produced a video in which he instructed men in the proper way to beat their wives. Reminding them that even camels and horses should not be struck in their heads, he said women should be given the same consideration. When punishing wives, he admonished, avoid hitting their heads!

Punishment ranging from beating, lashes, or even jail was meted out for perceived offences. Girls were punished for wanting to choose whom to marry or desiring to attend school. Not being a virgin, even if a doctor offered proof to the contrary, incurred severe punishment. A dishonored husband whose bride did not bleed on their wedding night was likely to return the "scandalous" woman to her birth family. Her father or brothers were certain to enact punishment against her in order to restore their family honor.

Women were even punished for sexual acts perpetrated against them. Four male witnesses to the crime of rape were required in order for a woman not to be jailed as an adulteress. And, an assaulted woman could not even report the crime without the permission of a male family member. One can speculate that accused women prefer jail as their best hope of protection against the ultimate punishment, honor killing, at the hands of their male relatives. But even in jail, women were not protected from additional rapes and possibly murder.

The requirement to have four male witnesses was instituted by the Prophet Mohammed after his young wife Aisha was accused of adultery. She had left her tent to search for a missing necklace and had not returned when Mohammed's group folded their tents and moved on from their desert encampment. Left stranded on the desert, the child bride was rescued by a man who located the Prophet's tent and returned her to him. Mere speculation led to an accusation of Aisha's adultery with her rescuer. The prescribed punishment was death, but her life was spared when Allah intervened.

Mohammed declared that he had received a revelation from Allah confirming his favorite wife's innocence. The proof? There had not been four male witnesses to the act. Incredibly, the revelation from Allah that protected the Prophet's wife from being stoned for adultery became the means of absolving men from charges of rape.

A news item in November 2007 told of a nineteen year old Saudi Arabian woman who was brutally gang raped by seven men who then repeated their assault against her. The young woman, though criminally assaulted and violated, was sentenced to receive ninety lashes when it was determined that prior to the attack she had been riding in an automobile with an unrelated male – one to whom she had previously been engaged and from whom she sought to retrieve a photograph of herself.

The victim's attorney (I was astounded that legal representation was available to her) alerted the media, no doubt in hopes of raising awareness of the injustice of her situation.

Because she made her plight public, however, her sentence was increased to two hundred lashes and six months in jail!

King Abdullah bin Abdul Aziz pardoned the woman, though he insisted the intended punishment was just under Islamic and Saudi law, after President George W. Bush spoke against the sentence given the young woman, and the Kingdom was criticized internationally. Former Saudi Arabian kings had been infuriated when the international community criticized "just punishment" prescribed in the Kingdom. One can only wonder if the pardoned woman's brothers or father enacted the punishment denied by their king – the punishment deemed necessary to restore their family honor.

*   *   *

Arizona Senator Jon Kyl recently commented on the distorted perception of honor and the application of punishment in some cultures. After an immigrant child was gang raped, the Liberian family of the eight year old victim was reportedly shamed and, therefore, shunned the little girl. Senator Kyl said in part, "It's practically impossible for us to understand a society which has precisely the opposite idea about who should be blamed and who should feel shame and who should be helped or not helped."

*   *   *

Despite the emphasis on family honor, divorce was extremely common in Saudi Arabia. There was no social stigma against it. Easy to obtain, a man was granted the dissolution of his marriage for any reason. The husband could decide, for example, that he had married a woman whose tribe or family was inferior to his. Ending his marriage was justified. A simple process, the husband was required to declare to his wife on three occasions that he intended to divorce her.

After the third declaration there was a waiting period of three months before the divorce was final and remarriage was allowed. This gave the woman ample time to know if she was pregnant. Pregnancy did not prevent the intended divorce; it merely established the paternity of the child. In Saudi Arabia, one's whole identity was tied to the father. It was, therefore, unthinkable for a woman to be divorced and remarried so soon as not to be certain who fathered a child.

While a divorced woman had to wait three months to remarry, a widow had to wait four months and ten days. I never understood why it took longer for a widow to determine if she was pregnant, than it did for a divorced woman.

The discarded wife was allowed to keep her dowry, unless her husband's divorce showed fault against her. A charge of adultery against a woman was clearly serious fault and would result in the loss of the dowry paid at her marriage, but the wronged husband would never demean himself by admitting that his wife's actions were of any relevance to him. He would divorce her for fault but with indifference.

It was the men of her birth family who were dishonored, and they would take the punishment for her accused crime into their own hands. In traditional families, the father and brothers enacted the Islamic penalty of death for adultery against a so-charged woman. Her actions stained their reputations, not that of her husband's, and the spilling of her blood restored their family honor.

Violence extended beyond the bounds of family. It was widely rumored that abuse of female servants from Africa, Indonesia, or the Philippine Islands was common. Reported by a human rights watch in 2001, the Philippines' Ambassador to Saudi Arabia revealed to his government that many Filipino women were "forcedly subjected to poor living conditions, salary underpayment, insufficient food, inhuman working conditions and long hours of work without rest or day off."

One wonders if Saudi women, secluded, frustrated, and themselves abused, took out their unhappiness on their foreign servants. Children, witnessing the pattern of mistreatment, had little hope of forming different attitudes and behavior years later as adults in their own homes.

*   *   *

There was woefully little help for women in the judicial system of Saudi Arabia. A woman's testimony was worth, at most, only one-half that of a male's. Female testimony was limited to matters of property, and two women were required to give witness to count as one. According to Islamic teachings, two women were necessary so that if one woman erred in her testimony, the other could remind her.

Women were easily persuaded by their physical limitations, emotions, and monthly hormonal cycles, it was argued. Uneducated and their lives spent secluded in harems, women were generally not considered capable of intelligent thought. Their word, therefore, was unreliable and inadmissible in serious matters of law.

If a woman's testimony were against her husband, the court was certain to disallow it. A wife's evidence of adultery, either in her own defense or against her husband, was not legally admitted. A husband's evidence in his defense or against his wife was heard in court.

While men were merely required to speak their intent to end marriages, women were not allowed to initiate a divorce or even separate from their husbands except in extreme cases of cruel treatment or conjugal neglect. Since a woman's testimony was insufficient in legal matters, especially against her husband, there had to be two witnesses to her charge in order for the divorce to be considered. But, here is the rub. Because of the seclusion of women, it was extremely unlikely that one would ever have sufficient witnesses to a man's cruelty and certainly not to his failure at conjugal duty to be heard in court.

Besides the loss of dowry, a woman was likely to lose custody of her children if she did succeed in divorcing her husband. In practice, a divorced mother could not leave the country with her children. Custody of children was in particular jeopardy if the wife were foreign born. The nationality of children was tied to the father not to the mother. Sons and daughters of an American wife in the Kingdom were always Saudi Arabian; they were never American.

There was no limit to the number of wives a man could have during his lifetime, so long as he had no more than four at any time. The Prophet Mohammed had many concubines, mistresses, slave women, and as many as twelve wives, but he was reportedly married to no more than four at a time. His example became the standard that allowed plural marriages and set the number of allowed wives. Four was also considered the maximum one could reasonably afford, financially. However, a man could change wives at will, or as in the case of Muhammad Awad bin Laden, the father of Osama bin Laden, he could keep two or three favored wives in a somewhat permanent position and rotate the fourth wife as frequently as desired.

While men were allowed multiple wives, there was no pretense for the reason. Islamic scholars who defend the practice often point out the Middle-Eastern cultural history of polygamy or the Biblical record of Old Testament patriarchs. However, when asked, any Saudi male I knew gave an excuse that was not a spiritual, cultural, or even economic justification. It had nothing to do with what was good for women or for the family. It wasn't because of the shortage of available men, although some have suggested that during earlier days of constant tribal fighting men were killed off in great numbers leaving many unmarried women. "Because men are hot!" was the answer I heard again and again. "One woman is not enough."

* * *

Traditions are treasured in Western cultures, and enduring truths provide context for our lives, but it is innovative thought that solves problems and promotes growth, advancing our people. Students schooled in the West are encouraged to question, to argue points, to challenge conventional thought, and to debate issues. As a teacher, I was thrilled when a student discovered an aspect to the lesson or a method of solving a problem that I had not previously recognized. I wanted young minds to think outside the box, to explore ideas, and find new ways to apply what they had learned.

Not surprising, academic instruction in the Kingdom and throughout the Middle East is very different than in America, and it is limited to a few years. There were no schools in Saudi

Arabia for adolescents, whether citizen or expatriate, when I lived there. Western teen-agers who were old enough for high school attended boarding schools, primarily in Europe. Saudi young men, if their educations continued, studied out of country as well. It was a convenient way to prevent teen-aged problems such as forbidden dating and the cruising of streets in downtown Riyadh and Jeddah.

The Koran and the Hadith form the basis of Saudi Arabian education, which is primarily for males. Students memorize the Koran and are taught to recite its passages with fervor. After the Prophet Mohammed's death, his followers had questions that were not answered in the Koran, prompting converts to ask, "What would Mohammed do?" A collection of the actions and sayings of the Prophet and his closest associates was compiled to form the Hadith or traditions. Each generation has passed on the same respect for the traditions of Mohammed that have been learned and treasured. Emphasis is not placed on reasoning but, rather, on accepting without question the wisdom of the elders.

Queen Rania of Jordan is a tireless advocate for reform in education and gender equality. In a recent interview, she explained that schools in the Middle East are more likely to teach students "what to think," than "how to think." Further, she noted that millions of children in Arab countries remain without any education at all, and at least two-thirds of those who never attend school are female.

Saudi Arabian girls are schooled only with written permission of the male responsible for them. Schools are gender separated and most girls receive only a few years of education. Even though Saudi Arabia is one of the richest Muslim nations, literacy rates for women are reportedly very low – lower than in other neighboring Arab States.

The Christian Science Monitor in an article titled "Voices from behind the Veil" by Nicole Gaouette reported that even when Saudi women are educated there are few opportunities for them in the work force. "Where do girls go when they graduate? Nowhere." Other than as foreign household servants, the only legal opportunities for employment available to women in Saudi Arabia were in medicine and education.

The demand for business secretaries who were fluent in English created available, though illegal, employment for any expatriate woman who wanted it. Many Western women were hired with minimal skills in grammar, spelling, or punctuation. No matter. Their Arab bosses didn't seem to recognize or be concerned with the poor quality of work. Computers with word processors were just becoming available in some offices, though most still used electric type-writers without correction features. Business communication was, therefore, often riddled with error.

Expatriate secretaries always worked in secret with their desks hidden in small back rooms. A nearby window was necessary to provide the means of quick escape, should an unexpected religious inspection occur. Transportation to and from their offices was usually provided by their employers.

American women reacted differently to their unlawful employment. Some were intrigued by the danger, as well as the tax-free money earned. Several of my friends who had secretarial jobs spoke of lavish gifts, including Persian rugs and gold jewelry, presented to them by their Arab employers. Others, having tried employment, decided the income was not worth the risk they were being asked to take.

Reported in February 2008, two expatriates living in the Kingdom, a man and an American woman who were business colleagues, were arrested and jailed for sharing conversation and Internet access at a table in the "family section" of a coffee house while waiting for electrical power to be restored to their finance offices.

Fearful of retribution when her plight was made public, the woman "was bruised and crying when she was freed from a day in prison after she was strip-searched, threatened, and forced to sign false confessions by the Kingdom's Mutaween" – the religious police whose number now approaches ten thousand.

In Saudi Arabia, because there were no behavioral norms for relating to the opposite sex, strict separation of genders was required. There was no legal social interaction of any kind between genders. It was a crime to be alone or even to converse with any man who was not part of the woman's family. There were not only separate restrooms in public buildings, there were also separate elevators for men and women.

City buses were segregated as well. Each was fitted with a partitioned section in the rear. Expatriate women, foreign servants, and Saudi females who were poor entered though a door at the back and sat in the female section with its darkened windows, while men entered at the front and filled the main part of the bus.

The total separation of genders resulted in an awkward sexual tension whenever Saudi men and women were in the same space, such as markets. The accepted belief was that women are temptresses by nature, and that whether they intend to be seductive or not, they provoke uncontrollable desire in men. Instead of teaching appropriate behaviors for dealing with sexual attraction and establishing healthy norms for gender interaction, the Saudi Arabian solution is to "minimize the opportunities for temptation to occur, by keeping the sexes apart."

After a three-hour spectacle in July 2007, British Airways removed three Arab princesses from an aircraft that had already taxied to the runway. Related to the oil-rich emir of Qatar, the three princesses in traditional dress boarded the airliner after shopping in Milan. While male members of their entourage demanded segregated seating for the women, the princesses refused to remain in their designated seats near male passengers who were not their family members.

It was no different for women in the Kingdom. One of the justifications cited for not allowing women to vote in a proposed 2005 municipal election was that there was no acceptable place in which women could cast their ballots separately from men. The enforced separation of genders trumped any "right to vote" for women.

Although men were allowed to cast ballots in this historic election, the first of its kind, they were able to vote for only one half of the open council seats.

Long before the advent of the Internet, all exchanges were made in community offices that were run by and restricted to men. Divorced or widowed, Saudi Arabian women who had finances of their own appointed a male proxy to handle all business transactions for them. I have read that Riyadh now has a separate bank for women. Veiled females can make financial transactions without risking forbidden contact with unrelated men.

The newer shopping buildings in Riyadh all had separate, partitioned areas for women. Inside, one could browse in boutiques filled with expensive designer gowns without fear of being seen by passing males.

There were very few restaurants in the capital city, and all were gender separated. We found one with a secluded family area upstairs, away from the sight of male diners. In the several times my family ate in the "Royal Chinese Restaurant," we were the only ones utilizing the family space, while men filled the tables at ground level. The capital city of Riyadh has more restaurants now, including a Starbucks coffee shop, but all continue to enforce gender separation.

Veiling provided the ultimate means of gender separation. The sexual symbolism of the face hidden from the view of men was obvious. The veil, which represented female sensuality, became the means of concealing any hint of it. Defenders of veiling argue just the opposite, saying that it is when women are seen and judged by their appearance that they are diminished to sexual objects.

Honor in Saudi Arabia was largely defined by a woman's chastity. If a female were violated, the men of her family were seen as weak and then subjected to the scorn of other men. It was, after all, their responsibility to "protect the honor." Veiling served two contradictory purposes to that end: it produced the respect of men and at the same time provided protection from them.

The veiling of women did not originate with Islam. It was practiced in various forms and for multiple reasons long before the birth of the Prophet Mohammed. One of its more common purposes in pre-Islamic times was to differentiate between a respectable wife whose veiling indicated her sexuality belonged to a husband and women whose unveiled faces indicated they were still sexually available. Slave women typically were not veiled.

The type and extent of veiling varies within Muslim cultures. In some, a head scarf, the *hijab*, suffices. Afghan women wear the *burqa* and the *chador* is worn by Iranian women. The most restrictive veiling is practiced in Saudi Arabia and other Gulf states. In recent years, a narrow eye opening in the black *niqab* has become more widely accepted, though some Islamic clerics have called for a return to the full veil or at least one in which only a single eye is exposed. Sheikh Muhammad al-Habad has said that exposing both eyes encourages women to use eye make-up and, therefore, become seductive.

* * *

In 2009, Andre Gerin, the Communist mayor of Venissieux, France, proposed the following resolution:

> A woman wearing a burqa or a niqab is in a state of unbearable isolation, exclusion, and humiliation. Her very existence is denied. The sight of these imprisoned women is intolerable when it comes to us from Iran, Afghanistan, Saudi Arabia, or other Arab countries. It is totally unacceptable on the soil of the French Republic.

French President Sarkozy added, This "is not a religious issue but rather a question of freedom and of women's dignity."

* * *

The Koran does not specify the extent of veiling but makes clear the requirement that a woman preserve her modesty. "O Prophet, tell your wives and daughters and the believing women that they should cast their outer garments over their bodies so that they should be known and not molested."

It was accepted that men could not be expected to restrain natural sexual urges. Ahmed explained that the sight of a woman's earlobes or her ankles had the power to tempt a man beyond his control. Certainly faces, especially eyes, were considered sensual by nature and irresistible to men. "Female eyes are naturally seductive," Ahmed told me.

Additionally, Ahmed and his books insisted that women must avoid the use of perfume or the wearing of shoes that click, lest they attract the attention of men. Females were expected to speak quietly for the same reason. Nowhere in any of his books was there instruction for men in either self-discipline or personal responsibility. The onus of sexual restraint fell totally upon women.

I hated the practice of scandalizing women for sexual acts while men received a pass on responsibility, just as I had bristled at that notion as a teen-ager. In America, though sexual discrimination had made allowances for teen-aged boys, grown men were expected to have matured beyond the onslaught of adolescent hormones. No such expectation existed for men in the Kingdom.

A man's behavior toward a woman did not dishonor him unless he engaged in an adulterous affair with a married woman. Rape was still generally believed to be consensual sex and considered the fault of the woman who was deemed a temptress. Groping and other inappropriate behaviors were also accepted as provoked by women. Not only were females presumed to have invited any assault against them, it was they who would be punished for dishonoring their families.

Though offended by forced veiling and the relegation of women to the back seats of cars and buses, I had an experience that made me better understand those particular restrictions imposed on Muslim females in a culture that does not have behavioral norms for interaction between genders. My husband and I were driving in a busy part of the city one late afternoon. I was in the front passenger seat as we stopped at an intersection behind a truck loaded with Yemeni laborers. The men were soiled and tired from the day's work as they stood packed like sardines in the bed of the truck, which was the usual method of transporting Third-World laborers to and from work sites.

As we sat behind the truck waiting for the light to change, I suddenly realized the men, who had been away from any normal life for years, were staring at my unveiled face with undisguised lust. Seeing them with their eyes in glassy stares fixed on my face, their mouths open and standing as in a trance, I knew I was being visually raped. There was nothing I could do to avoid their attack except duck below the windshield. It was a nauseating, disgusting feeling of violation. My unveiled face had become blatantly sexual, unintentionally inviting the lust of men in that totally gender segregated culture.

Ahmed, had I told him, would have said, "Ah, now you understand how veiling protects our women." But my response would have been, "It is your rigid culture; the total separation of genders; the absence of behavioral norms between the sexes and the obvious sexual symbolism created by the veil that cause the need for protection."

Though all Saudi women in Riyadh were veiled, we occasionally saw women whose veils had openings that exposed just their eyes. These women, who were always older, were draped in black and were often barefoot. With only their tired and joyless eyes revealed, they sat on the sidewalks with items for sale spread around them. Their wares included brass pots, woven baskets, or Bedouin jewelry. I asked Ahmed about them.

"They are poor. They are allowed to sit in the markets. They must earn money to live," he answered. "Perhaps they are divorced or have no family to provide for them. Their veils must allow them to see. They must work to live."

Had they been divorced by their husbands who desired younger females in the harem? I wondered. Were they women who had been outcast from their families because of a perceived infraction that brought dishonor to the males? Had they lost their dowry in divorce due to an accused fault? Was their inheritance lessened or omitted because of their gender? Were they widows who had not been given a sufficient dowry at marriage? My mind filled with possibilities and more questions.

"Do Bedouin women in the desert veil?" I asked.

"Of course," Ahmed answered. "But not the eyes. Their veils do not cover their eyes. They must be able to see. How can they tend the herds of sheep and goats if they cannot see? Poor women do not cover their eyes. They must see so they can work." Ahmed continued. "Women who do not work wear the veil. Women who have family and money wear the veil. Women who live in the city wear the veil."

Of all the reasons for thick veiling that covered even the eyes, a class distinction of wealth had not occurred to me as one of them.

"Women want to wear the veil." Ahmed declared. "It is an honor to wear the veil."

PART TWO
HONOR CONFLICTED

9

PHENOMENAL WEALTH

Contradictions abounded. Hypocrisy, some called it. Many labeled it schizophrenic. How long, I wondered, could the Kingdom survive the great disparity between protecting and observing seventh century Islamic law and rapid modernization made possible by the new phenomenal wealth? Sudden riches paid for burgeoning construction projects, travel and education outside the Kingdom, and for an influx of advisors and foreign laborers. But the magnitude of the oil wealth that had brought such rapid change to this desert kingdom threatened the traditional life of the proud Arabians who practiced the strictest form of Islam. Its honor conflicted, the Kingdom of Saudi Arabia was involved in a dangerous balancing act.

King Abdul Aziz ibn Sa'ud, beginning early in the twentieth century, had united a nation whose people eked out a meager existence. They were grateful to have a bit of stale bread, a few dates, and a piece of stringy camel meat to eat. When oil was discovered in 1938, authority over the fields was given to American companies with a portion of the oil revenues returned to the Kingdom. The new wealth primarily enriched the treasuries of the Royal Family and did little for its people other than to create a welfare state.

The Kingdom's capital city, Riyadh, was described by visitors in the 1940s as a "medieval walled city, surrounded by vivid greenery, and then stark desert." As late as 1953, while Americans were responding to enticing television commercials and filling their new tract homes with innovative appliances, visitors to Riyadh remarked on the "hordes of Bedouin living on royal charity in their tents around the town that still depended on water hauled from the ground in leather buckets." "The airport was a cleared sand strip with a windsock and a few old tents where visitors were offered sweet mint tea and coffee. Every plane had to receive the king's express permission to land or to take off."

Much had changed in Riyadh since the earthen wells and cleared sand strip of an airport, but some things remained the same. I, too, arrived only by permission of the government of the Royal Family of Saudi Arabia.

* * *

Two weeks in October 1973 had changed the world. Nowhere was that change more evident than in Saudi Arabia. Phenomenal wealth had come quickly and with incomprehensible magnitude by 1980. The oil embargo, the price of oil, the increased production, and ownership of oil fields all contributed to the new fabulous wealth beginning with the reign of King Faisal bin Abdul Aziz and reaching its peak under his half-brother King Fahd bin Abdul Aziz.

Following the oil embargo of 1973, the cost of oil soared from its previous price of less than two dollars a barrel to nearly one hundred-fifty dollars in 2008! Aramco, the Arabian-American Oil Company, had from the beginning kept fifty percent of the oil profits. By 1980, however, Aramco turned over complete ownership of the fields to the Saudi Arabian government, the Royal Family of Sa'ud.

Two years later, the Kingdom was exporting "black gold" at the unprecedented rate of 10.3 million barrels a day at a price of nearly thirty dollars a barrel! Simple math reveals the astonishing wealth that poured into the country as oil was sold to industrialized nations whose economies were increasingly dependent on Saudi Arabia's greatest asset.

Most Saudis were no longer poor. Sudden riches in the Arabian Peninsula had changed the country from settlements of mud huts and Bedouin tents to populated cities filled with palatial villas and modern homes. Money was available to Saudis whenever and wherever they wanted to build. Interest-free loans, grants, and gifts to male citizens were available upon request. Perhaps this practice still defined the Kingdom as a welfare state, but it was an extraordinary one.

Riyadh had changed from a medieval-looking encampment into a city exploding with high rise buildings: banks, business offices, and hospitals staffed by multi-national doctors and nurses. The capital city was getting much needed roads, infrastructure, and a reliable telephone system. Construction companies, Western advisors, and Third World laborers flooded Saudi Arabia.

Unfortunately, as companies inundated the Kingdom, there was no apparent overall development plan. Each company did what it was contracted to do, collected millions in fees and moved on. The lack of zoning was a distinct problem. Walled villas were built alongside trash heaps of rotting garbage, near piles of wrecked automobiles, or in areas of isolated desert.

The oil revenues created opportunities for enterprising Arabians, especially those closely associated with the Royal Family. Saudi middle-men who brokered construction deals were amassing fortunes, often by exerting little more effort than making a well-placed phone call.

As rulers of an Arab nation and a family-owned government, the Royal Family controlled everything. Business was done by those able to "pull strings." Saudi Arabia was rumored to award contracts more by word-of-mouth than by bids. Construction and engineering firms competed for lucrative contracts to produce modern buildings in the Arabian desert and were happy to pay the *baksheesh*. Often no more than a bribe, the gratuity or broker's fee was the means of securing a contract. With the right baksheesh, anything was possible.

Muhammad Awad bin Laden, father of the world's most hated terrorist, had decades earlier, made his fortune in building in Saudi Arabia. Originally a poor laborer from Yemen, Muhammad had become closely associated with the Royal Family. Favored by Arabian kings, particularly King Sa'ud and later his half-brother King Faisal, important projects were awarded to his business, which became the largest construction company in the Kingdom. He is credited with work on major mosques in Saudi Arabia, as well as many commercial buildings.

During the 1980s, one third of the world's construction dollars were being spent in the Kingdom. We joked that the national bird of Saudi Arabia was the desert crane – the construction crane! They were everywhere. From our balconies we could always see numerous soaring, swinging cranes – gangly birds with enormous beaks – scooping up the desert soil and forever changing the landscape. The sound of construction droned on at all hours; the diggers worked all night so the fillers could work all day!

The massive construction projects had a horrendous effect on transportation. Traffic was slowed, snarled, and completely altered by building projects throughout the capital city. Routinely clogged and delayed by the "national birds," traffic flow was also hindered by supply trucks, cement mixers, dump trucks, and loads of Third-World laborers.

Rerouting and detours were common, but signs were rarely placed to indicate roadway changes. Deep caverns and trenches appeared where streets had been the day before. Luxury automobiles, Toyota pickups, and Mercedes work trucks driven into holes by unsuspecting motorists had to be pulled out before construction projects could be resumed.

City maps were useless. Roadways changed so continually that maps were never current. Street signs, even in Arabic, were few in number and unreliable. During our first year in the country we were regularly lost during driving excursions, especially at night. What should have been a twenty-minute drive took hours in the capital city of Riyadh. Eventually we learned to recognize a few landmark buildings and sites, unceremoniously renamed by expatriates, to help us navigate our way through the maze of unfinished and ever-changing streets. We plotted our trips using specific points of reference: "Tea pot Circle," where gigantic brass pots stood in the center of Riyadh's only round-about street, the futuristic looking water tower, and "Chop-Chop Square," the downtown public area where beheadings took place at the foot of the towering, lighted clock.

The collision between the modern and the traditional created inevitable contradictions in values. As American and European construction companies poured into the country, their senior advisors, managers, and engineers were allowed to bring families to live in Saudi Arabia. Few of those expatriate families were Muslim, though Islam was the only religion allowed in the Kingdom. While Muslim women were required to veil, there were hundreds of expatriate women in the Kingdom not subject to the same requirement. To traditional Saudis, the unveiled expatriate woman was an offense and a threat to traditional Islamic life.

With immense oil wealth at their disposal, King Fahd and Crown Prince Abdullah were authorizing the construction of modern buildings and expensive walled villas. At the same time, many Saudi Arabians who resided in remote villages or in the eastern provinces lived in squalor. Nomadic Bedouins of the desert moved their herds in search of scant grazing areas and *wadis*, desert oases with life-sustaining water.

Did the Bedouin of the desert choose to live without benefit of the new wealth? Were they traditionalists who believed a

Muslim should live as Mohammed did? With money available to any citizen, did the Bedouin ask only for new tents, more camels, or perhaps a Toyota pick-up for transporting their gangly beasts? For those living in tents or mud houses, a window refrigeration unit and a generator to power it would have been luxuries.

My husband had occasion to be in a major bank building owned by Adnan Khashoggi, who was at that time the richest man in the world. (Khashoggi's sister is the mother of Dodi Fayed, the companion who died with England's Princess Diana) After commenting appreciatively on the grandeur, the rich woods, luxurious leather chairs, and gold appointments, my husband was shown the office bathroom. It was one of those "You ain't seen nothing yet" moments. Not only did the bathroom have gold fixtures, marble floors, and crystal chandeliers, the toilet seat was heated and fur cushioned!

In stark contrast, much of the nearby market place had ancient souqs, open-air vendors, and dirt floors. Bearded men wearing belted daggers squatted around coffee pots brewing over wood fires and brushed their teeth with sticks purchased from street merchants.

Though rich in oil, the country did not have enough water from within to sustain itself. All drinking water was imported. Gray water that had been used in home plumbing was reused to irrigate the small amount of landscaped vegetation in the cities. Large desalinization plants had been constructed off the coast of the Persian Gulf, but changing the salty sea water into usable water was costly and yielded limited results.

The Kingdom purchased everything it needed from other countries. There was still virtually no agriculture in Saudi Arabia. All produce came from other Arab States such as Jordan, Lebanon, and Syria. Beef was from Argentina. Saudi Arabia was importing more sand, more palm trees, and more camels than any other place in the world. Sand, though prevalent in the Kingdom, had smooth edges and was not suitable for construction. Massive loads of jagged sand were shipped into the Kingdom from Ohio, mixed with cement and used for the burgeoning construction projects. Palm trees and camels were imported from the Sudan in Africa. Water, food, gold, baskets, spices, laborers, and advisors were all imported – and along with life-saving blood – were purchased with oil money.

Proud Saudis, who would accept no employment lower in status than that of a taxi driver, held executive positions in government and business. Behind the scenes, however, was a myriad of foreign advisors whose expertise made the recommendations that drove decisions Saudis themselves "made" and kept the country on track. Even oil, the Kingdom's most valuable asset, had been managed by outside companies until 1980.

The country's wealth made it possible for Saudi males to travel around the world for business, education, and pleasure. Young men were provided educations, often in the United States, and generous living stipends while in school. Lucrative positions were available to them as soon as they were ready to enter the work force.

While traveling outside the Kingdom, many Saudis indulged in lifestyles that were strictly prohibited under Islamic law and totally contradictory to the traditions of the Prophet Mohammed – traditions they had been taught to revere.

* * *

Prince Nayef bin Sultan Al Shaalan, said to be deeply religious, attended college in Florida where he met a young woman with whom he maintained a relationship that spanned two decades. The prince, married to the granddaughter of King Abdul Aziz, was indicted in 1999 by a Miami court for drug trafficking after his 727 aircraft was believed to have transported two tons of cocaine from Venezuela to Saudi Arabia and ultimately to Paris. The conspiracy to transport the drugs was alleged to have originated in Miami with the assistance of the female friend of the prince. She spent five years in federal prison after her conviction, but Prince Nayef, who remained in Saudi Arabia, has yet to face our justice system.

There is much speculation about why a fabulously wealthy Saudi prince would engage in such risky behavior as drug trafficking. Some have suggested that as a non-Royal married to a princess, Nayef desired to increase his personal wealth to match that of males born into the Sa'ud family. The more disturbing speculation is that some members of the Royal Family use illegally gained funds to finance terrorism groups. We may never know the motivation or even the guilt or innocence of the indicted prince who is not likely to ever return to America.

*   *   *

My friends Ahmed and Khalid had both studied in the United States, and their free educations continued in Saudi Arabia. Ahmed told me that in addition to his education, he received a housing allowance, an automobile, and a $20,000 yearly stipend from his government. In 1980's dollars, he did very well. There was no doubt he would start his working career in a management position.

One could not miss the contrast with his Muslim brothers, the Bangladeshi houseboys, whose country's annual per-capita income was, at most, a mere hundred dollars! Saudi oil wealth had not benefited them, except to provide employment that amounted to little more than slavery.

There was an estimated fifty years worth of oil still in Arabian sand. Perhaps more. But fifty years pass quickly. We often heard expatriates predict that once oil reserves were depleted, Saudi Arabia would implode. There was little to sustain the country without industry or work ethic, at least by Western standards. However, there was male honor. There was immense pride in being a Saudi Arabian. And there was Islam.

Arabia is the birthplace of the Prophet Mohammed. Islam began in Arabia. Mecca and Medina, the two holiest sites in Islam, are in the Kingdom. Saudi Arabians, therefore, take great pride in their belief that God chose to deliver His complete and final revelation to Mohammed, a man who was one of them. There is pride that God chose this part of the world to deliver the "truth" and the "straight path." Further, the Koran was given in Arabic, the language of Saudi Arabians. Little wonder that the Kingdom enforces the laws of their Prophet with an unrelenting zeal.

The proud Saudis also put great value in their independence from other empires. Arabia has a long history of being ruled by foreign governments, including the Ottoman Empire, but the kingdom known as Saudi Arabia was recognized in 1932 after all other regimes ended their claims to the Arabian Peninsula. Tremendous pride, many would have said arrogance, described the prevailing attitude for having never been colonized.

"Even America was colonized," Ahmed stated. "But not Saudi Arabia. We have never been colonized." While I considered America's history of British colonization a rich heritage from which our great nation developed, Ahmed wore the absence of colonization as a badge of honor. It was as though colonization were equivalent with slavery, which was odd since the trafficking of humans did not end in Saudi Arabia until the 1960s, and some say it has not yet ended.

Slavery had always existed in Arabia. The Royal Family owned slaves as did the Prophet Mohammed who did not condemn it in Islam. Anyone who could afford to purchase another human did so. In addition to his numerous other slaves, King Abdul Aziz ibn Sa'ud purchased an African boy, an *Akhiwiya* or "Little Brother," to become the personal slave for each of his forty-five sons. The slave boys lived with and were schooled alongside the Saudi princes. They remained companions and personal servants of the sons of Abdul Aziz for their entire lives.

Robert Lacey in his book *The Kingdom* relates an interesting and enlightening dichotomy related to slavery in Saudi Arabia and, at the same time, the segregation of races in America.

When Prince Faisal ibn Abdul Aziz visited New York in 1944, the management of the Waldorf Astoria were shocked that he brought his slave Merzouk with him. But they were still more horrified when the prince insisted that his companion should eat, as he always did, at the same table as his master – for this involved admitting Merzouk to the Wedgwood Room, and no black had ever been allowed in there before.

The slave market in Arabia had coincided with the annual Hajj, the Islamic pilgrimage to Mecca. Pilgrims from African states sold their children into slavery in order to finance their trips home. The trafficking of humans became a primary source of income for the *Shareefs*, the descendants of the Prophet Mohammed.

Legalized slavery in Saudi Arabia did not end until 1962, a century after it was abolished in the United States. Freed slaves were allowed to stay in the Kingdom and become citizens; it is unlikely they would have had the resources to leave the Kingdom, had they wanted to. The cooks, drivers, nannies, and servants in many Saudi households were former slaves.

The practice of hiring foreign laborers from poorer Muslim countries now replaced official slavery. Many said there was little difference. There were rumors of servant women from Africa, the Philippines, and Sri Lanka being beaten by their Saudi mistresses and raped by the men of the household. We heard of young foreign servant girls who were jailed after becoming pregnant by their masters.

Saudi Arabian families, particularly members of the Royal Family who spend time in the United States, bring their personal servants with them. Accusations of beatings and forced servitude have surfaced during visits to our country. Some foreign workers in Saudi households whose plights have been reported by America's media have claimed they were recruited for and promised professional jobs only to be forced into menial labor.

A UPI article on March 9, 1993, reported that a U.S. Immigration Court hearing in Houston, Texas, was being told of two women, a Filipino and a Sri Lankan, who suffered regular beatings and forced servitude. Each was paid as little as one hundred dollars a month from members of the immensely wealthy Royal Family. Both abused women claimed they had been hired for positions much different than the servitude their employers imposed on them.

Laborers, predominantly Muslims who were Third-World Nationals, were being brought into the Kingdom without their families to do the work Saudis would never do. Many laborers and servants had little hope of ever leaving. Virtually trapped in an oil-rich country, the laborers were at the mercy of their contracted companies to pay them for their work. Employers were rumored to withhold wages for any reason. Just as slaves before them, the foreign nationals who were often required to relinquish their passports to their sponsors or employers rarely had enough money to leave the Kingdom and return to their home countries.

Non-Muslim laborers were in the country but were the minority. Our compound electrician, who was not a Muslim, was a gentle man from the Philippine Islands. He had been in Saudi Arabia for seven years. He told me his wife was a teacher in Manila, but without his work in the Kingdom they could never afford the educations they wanted for their children. And there was no end in sight. He expected to remain in Saudi Arabia for many more years with, at most, a brief visit home each two years. How sad. His children would be educated but would grow up without a father's guidance and presence.

There were only about six million Saudi Arabians during my tenure in the Kingdom. One half of the citizens were women and girls who were not allowed to work. Many of the men were too old, too young, or were attending school out of the country. Furthermore, the rate of birth defects – heart disease, nervous system abnormalities, and muscular/skeletal deformities – created by the practice of marrying first cousins was said to be extraordinarily high. It was no wonder it was necessary to hire foreign laborers.

Foreign laborers followed a pattern of nationalities. Yemeni were road builders and Koreans were in construction. Filipinos were electricians and waiters and servants. Pakistanis were plumbers. Bangladeshi were houseboys. Lebanese, Jordanians, and Palestinians were translators and facilitators. Africans and Sri Lankans were drivers and house servants.

The tremendous oil wealth allowed the proud Saudis to secure foreign workers for their every need. A common joke during the 1980s was that if Saudi Arabia were ever attacked, the Royal Family would pay Koreans to fight their war. Pakistani soldiers had already been hired to guard the northern border of the Kingdom. Though the government was spending billions for armaments and military advisors, one could only wonder if the Saudis would ever be able or willing to do the hard work of defending their country with its vast oil fields and Islam's holiest places without foreign help.

Little did we realize just how soon the joke would become reality, except it would not be Koreans who were hired to defend the Islamic state. When Saddam Hussein's army attacked Kuwait in 1990 with the intent of invading Saudi Arabia, it was the American military, along with a coalition of nations, who came to the Kingdom's aid and prevented plunder of the oil fields by Iraq, itself an Arab, predominantly Muslim nation.

* * *

The names of Saudi Arabians, who do not use surnames, can be confusing to the Western world. Among the few common male names are Waleed, Salam, Faisal, Ahmed, Ali, Mohammed, Sa'ud, Khalid, and Abdullah. Only the Royal Family or those closely associated with it use *bin* to designate their lineage, identifying their father.

The Saudi Arabian Ambassador to the United States for twenty-two years was Bandar *bin* Sultan *bin* Abdul Aziz. The use of bin indicates that Bandar is a member of the Royal Family. His father is Prince Sultan, whose father was King Abdul Aziz. Bin merely means "the son of" as in *Bandar, the son of Sultan, the son of Abdul Aziz.* It is a link to the genealogical record of males in the Royal Family or of those closely associated with it.

Osama bin Laden means, *Osama, the son of Laden.* Osama's sons would never be correctly referred to as bin Ladens. They would be, for example, Abdul bin Osama, or *Abdul, the son of Osama.* If one wanted more clarity, a son of Osama's could be Abdul bin Osama bin Laden – *Abdul, the son of Osama, the son of Laden.*

Ibn is often used instead of bin; they both mean "the son of." If the given name is omitted, Ibn in the capitalized form is used before the father's name, as in Ibn Sa'ud. (The son of

Sa'ud) Bin is not generally used without the given name. King Abdul Aziz, whose father was Sa'ud, could be *Abdul Aziz bin Sa'ud, or Abdul Aziz ibn Sa'ud,* or the shortened version, *Ibn Sa'ud.* All three titles mean "the son of Sa'ud."

Saudi men can also be identified by the name of their eldest son with the use of Abu, which means "the father of." King Abdul Aziz was the son of Sa'ud, but his first son was also named Sa'ud. Therefore, Abdul Aziz might be referred to as the son of Sa'ud, using either bin or ibn, or he might use "the father of" designation: *Abdul Aziz abu Sa'ud.* The shortened version is *Abu Sa'ud.* Both mean Abdul Aziz, the father of Sa'ud. The relatively few names used by Saudi males compounds the confusion. For example, Turki bin Sa'ud would not be enough to tell you which generation of prince he is. There are many in the Royal Family named Turki and many who are named Sa'ud.

My friend Ahmed scoffed when I asked if he used bin in his name. "Of course not. Everyone knows who my father is. My friends would laugh if I did that. That is something only the Royal Family does."

Women of the Royal Family are identified by their fathers as well. Nura *bint* Abdullah means Nura, the daughter of Abdullah. Leah bint Sultan means Leah, the daughter of Sultan. Wives of the king are not referred to as queens, though a daughter is a princess.

Saudi Arabian women do not have identification cards of any kind, other than a paper that states the name of their father. In marriage, a woman does not take the name of her husband and is never designated in any way by him. She remains, throughout her life, "the daughter of."

*   *   *

The Royal Family of Saudi Arabia, the *nouveaux riche,* in the 1980s was in the precarious position of trying to balance modernizing a country while adhering to seventh century Islamic traditions upon which the nation had been formed. The disparate tribes in Arabia had been united by Abdul Aziz ibn Sa'ud as an Islamic state named for the family of Sa'ud.

A deeply religious Muslim, Abdul Aziz did not trust any nation or its leaders who denied the existence of God. Though Russia courted friendship with the newly-established kingdom and recognized it as a state before America did, Abdul Aziz did not trust the leaders of the Soviet Union. Further, he and his son Faisal, who later became king, believed Communism was aligned with Zionism. They were convinced that Russia and Israel together sought to ultimately destroy Islam. His country, therefore, aligned with America in the common goal of fighting the Soviet Union.

The Kingdom remained the best friend America had among Arab nations while others in the region, apparently not sharing Abdul Aziz's perceived Communist threat against Islam, were openly hostile to the United States. At the same time, a duplicitous Saudi Arabia used oil revenues from the West to finance the procurement of weapons from the Soviet Union by other Arab nations and, it has been charged, financed terrorism groups. The Kingdom was, nevertheless, considered moderate politically. It was certainly not moderate in its adherence to Islam.

The old king's expressed concern was that every citizen, including foreign wives being brought into the Kingdom, be Muslim. No other religion was allowed in the country he founded. Defending Islam, not modernizing the country, was the fundamental responsibility of the Royal Family. But from the beginning, the House of Sa'ud, the designated guardian of Islam and of its holiest shrines, was fraught with strife.

Abdul Aziz fathered an estimated forty-five sons and twenty daughters by wives numbered from seventeen to as many as forty. One can only imagine the depth of competition, envy, subterfuge, suspicion, and greed that surely permeated the various factions of the family as sons competed for the attention and favor of their father, the king.

Sa'ud ibn Abdul Aziz, the eldest surviving son of Abdul Aziz, became the second king to rule Saudi Arabia. As monarch, he appointed many of his own fifty-three sons to important positions in government at the expense of his brothers who believed the sons of Sa'ud were ill-prepared for the responsibilities given them. King Sa'ud exercised personal control over the Kingdom's revenues and is blamed for leading the country into massive debt. After little more than a decade, Sa'ud was deposed by religious leaders and by powerful members of the Royal Family who comprised the newly and hastily formed Council of Ministers.

Invited by Egyptian President Gamal Abdel Nasser, despite persistent rumors that Sa'ud had at one time sought to have President Nasser assassinated, the deposed king went into exile in Egypt. Sa'ud's sons were subsequently removed from positions of any significant importance, numerous institutions named for the fallen king were renamed, and succession rules were quickly altered to pass the position of monarch among brothers rather than from father to son.

Sa'ud's half-brother Faisal succeeded him, becoming the third king of Saudi Arabia. Angered by America's support for Israel during the 1973 Yom Kippur War, Faisal was first to announce an oil embargo, which has resulted in the steady rise in the price of crude.

Faisal had the closest ties of any in the Royal Family to the religious leaders whose views continue to shape the culture of Saudi Arabia. His mother was a descendant of Muhammad ibn Abd al-Wahhab, the religious reformer whose radical interpretation of Islam is still taught in Saudi Arabia. Her father had served as spiritual advisor to Faisal's father, King Abdul Aziz ibn Sa'ud.

Though Faisal was a deeply religious Muslim, he is credited with moving his country toward modernization and reform, while restoring financial stability after the ruinous reign of his half-brother Sa'ud. Foreigners in his country who were accused of crimes such as using alcohol were arrested and quietly deported. That "leniency" would change during the rule of Saudi Arabia's next king.

Faisal held a weekly *majlis*. It was an opportunity for Arabian men to meet with him in his residence to make their needs known. During one such meeting, the king was assassinated by a nephew who had studied in America. Conspiracy theorists have suggested that the nephew believed the king was responsible for the murder of a relative in the young man's branch of the Royal Family. Others postulated that the young man's time spent in America had corrupted him. The most widely accepted view was that the assassin was mentally deranged. The nephew who killed the king was beheaded in the public square in Riyadh.

King Faisal's half-brother Khalid, who became the next king, was also a reformer. Recognizing the spreading threat of Communism in the Middle East, he was able to secure the purchase of advanced fighter aircraft from the United States. President Carter approved the sale of sixty F-15s that were delivered to the Kingdom in 1982.

King Khalid also desired basic health care for his people, resulting in the building of Saudi Arabia's first hospitals. He arranged television broadcasts in the country after assuring religious leaders that all programming would be carefully censored to remain consistent with Islamic law. And, it was Khalid who decided to use foreign laborers to help build the oil-rich but still developing country. However, Khalid, unlike his half-brother Faisal, determined that foreigners in his country should be subject to the same rules and punishments as were his citizens. Instead of being arrested and quietly deported for crimes against Islamic law, expatriate offenders were sentenced to jail, public caning, and for the worst of offenses, beheading.

King Khalid's modernization was repudiated in 1979 by hundreds of dissidents who attacked and seized the Grand Mosque in Mecca. Radical Islamists accused the Royal Family of not adhering to strict Islamic law and claimed, therefore, that it was unsuitable to rule the birthplace of Islam. Mohammed was revered, as was his lifestyle. To radical Islamists who opposed modernization, living as Mohammed did was seen as the "straight path."

When I arrived in the Kingdom, King Abdul Aziz ibn Sa'ud was dead, as were three of his son-kings: Sa'ud, Faisal, and Khalid who ruled in turn after him. Crown Prince Fahd had become the fifth king of Saudi Arabia. He was eldest of the seven surviving sons of Abdul Aziz by one of his favored wives

Hussah. Known as the Sudairi Seven, the sons of Hussah have remained close and powerful.

King Fahd controlled the largest petroleum reserve in the world. His personal wealth has been estimated at as much as seventy-six billion dollars. In addition to twelve palaces in Saudi Arabia, the king owned a chateau on the French Riviera. His gleaming white marble palace in Marbella on the Costa del Sol, Spain, was modeled after the United States White House, except that it was larger than America's version. He vacationed on privately owned ocean-liner yachts and traveled on his 747 aircraft.

King Fahd was rumored to indulge in wine, women, and gambling. He was known to have three wives, but it is possible there were more. Like so many in the Royal Family, he suffered from heart disease, which took his life in 2005. Fahd's half-brother Abdullah is now the ruling monarch.

Saudi Arabia experienced incredible wealth, explosive modernization, and aggressive military development during the twenty-three years Fahd was king. The Kingdom also used its phenomenal wealth to finance the spread of madrasahs and mosques throughout other countries. Students learned the Wahhabi interpretation of Islam and memorized the Koran in Arabic, the language of Mohammed, even when they neither spoke nor understood the language.

"The Koran must always be taught in Arabic," Ahmed had told me. "It is the holy language."

*   *   *

The little boy, Muhammad Atif, was only seven years old and he was blind. The national language of his people in Pakistan was Urdu, though there are many languages and dialects spoken throughout his country. Arabic, however, was taught in the madrasah, the Islamic school the little boy attended – a school quite possibly funded by Saudi Arabia. It was difficult for the child to memorize the Koran in an unfamiliar language, but only the "holy language" was acceptable to his teacher. The child had to be punished for not learning the Koran.

Muhammad Atif was hung upside down from a ceiling fan and beaten to death. It was May 2008.

*   *   *

Saudis prefer to use the term *Salafism* instead of Wahhabi, which is a term they consider demeaning. Literally, Salafism is defined as the patriarchs, the fathers, or early generations. It is a generic term for a Sunni interpretation of Islam that considers the pious ancestors (the Salaf) from the earliest days of Islam to be exemplary models. Thus, the life and teachings of the Prophet Mohammed and his closest associates, as recorded in the Hadith and the Koran, became the basis of Islamic law.

As far back as the eighteenth century, a member of the Sa'ud family, Muhammad ibn Sa'ud, made a pact with a religious reformer named Muhammad ibn Abd al-Wahhab. Ibn Sa'ud pledged to enforce al-Wahhab's teachings of Islam throughout Arabia. In exchange, members of the Sa'ud family would act as Imams, or religious leaders of the movement. The pact was strengthened in 1744 by the marriage of the son of Muhammad, who was the son of Sa'ud, to the daughter of Muhammad, who was the son of Abd al-Wahhab.

The teachings of al-Wahhab were meant to cleanse or purify Islam from various practices accumulated over the centuries since the time of the Prophet Mohammed. Much of the religion had taken on a mystical persona known as *Sufism.* Al-Wahhab condemned all vestiges of mysticism; he forbade all memorials to the dead, most acts of pleasure, and all works of art and beauty. He called for the complete veiling of women. Life was to be united in one purpose – the worship of Allah. Al-Wahhab taught that living in an austere manner removed the distractions and temptations that would otherwise pervert or dilute Islam.

The Kingdom of Saudi Arabia with its Wahhabi practice of Islam was, in the 1980s, walking a tight rope. A demoralizing and dangerous incongruity had emerged between modernizing the birthplace of Islam and preserving the revered traditions of the Prophet.

Clerics in madrasahs and mosques in Saudi Arabia and throughout the Muslim world were teaching the precepts of Islam in the Wahhabi tradition. The more radical ones taught that anyone who strayed from the strict interpretation of the religion was considered an "Infidel" and an "enemy of Islam." Reward in Paradise was promised to young men who were willing to give their lives to protect and preserve Islam and to destroy its perceived enemies.

Bereft of education that encourages critical thought, reasoning, differing points of view, or the debate of issues, students in madrasahs were taught to accept without question the traditions of the Prophet. They learned, as Queen Rania of Jordan has said about Middle-Eastern education, "What to think not how to think."

At the same time, the kings of Arabia had forged a deepening friendship with America. The country was paying richly for the advice of Americans in developing its military and in building its cities. Saudi military pilots were receiving flight instruction in the United States. The sons of kings, as well as other third and fourth generation princes, were being educated in prestigious universities in America and England. Saudi Arabia had become the best non-Jewish friend America had among Middle-Eastern nations. It was a position once held by Iran, though Iran was Persian not Arab.

Saudi Arabian leaders had not forgotten the Islamic Revolution in Iran. The Shah, too, had modernized his country and formed alliances with the West. Iranian military pilots were trained in the United States and young Persian men were educated in our universities. But radical Islamists, led by the Ayatollah Khomeini, had overthrown that government and forced the ruling monarch into exile. Freedoms ended as a new constitution governed Iran under the strict laws of Shari'a. Iran had become an Islamic state.

The Kingdom of Saudi Arabia was *already* an Islamic state, ruled under Shari'a. Would that be enough to prevent a revolution? Saudi Arabia with its five thousand princes (now a

Royal Family estimated at 30,000) serving in every important position of government, the military, and much of business was not as vulnerable as Iran had been, we were assured. A revolution was unlikely due to both the absolute control of the House of Sa'ud and the Kingdom's strict practice of Wahhabi Islam.

The government-controlled press did little to inform us of any threat the House of Sa'ud may have faced. Newspaper articles in the Kingdom praised Islam and its Prophet or reported events that had occurred in other Arab States. Rumors about government actions or the tenuous position of the Royal Family circulated widely in the Kingdom, but the press did little either to prove or quell the rumors. Separating fact from propaganda and baseless rumor from truth clearly depended upon the point of view of the reader.

Editorials in print called for Arab unity and the continual denouncement of Israel. America was criticized for her support of the Jewish state. Though Saudi Arabia had no specific dispute of its own with Israel, the strength of Arab unity prevailed; the Kingdom refused to recognize the right of Israel to exist. Editorials railing against America because of our friendship with the Jewish state were vehement.

We did not feel threatened by the anti-American copy and dismissed it as Arab rhetoric. We knew that Western advisors were in the Kingdom at the request of the ruling family. The House of Sa'ud, since the time of Abdul Aziz, had sought a working relationship between our countries. King Fahd was particularly friendly with the West. He seemed to be successfully balancing a friendship with the United States while preserving the ever-important façade of Arab unity.

Ironically, it was not Israel who threatened Saudi Arabia. All the vociferous professions of Arab unity and Muslim brotherhood did not stop Iraq, an Arab-Muslim state, from becoming the greatest threat to its neighbors Kuwait and Saudi Arabia. And it would not be an Arab brother state that would fight the invading army and liberate Kuwait. Instead, it was the "Great Satan," the friend of Israel, the United States who would rescue both Islamic governments.

10

FROM CAMELS TO MERCEDES

Women were prohibited from driving in the Kingdom. There was no law specifically making it illegal for females to drive, but in practice none could. The enforced restriction against driving was challenged by Arabian women in a remarkable demonstration in November 1990.

The American military and a coalition of nations had begun moving forces into the Kingdom after Saddam Hussein's army invaded Kuwait in August of that year. Islamic fundamentalists, already critical of the number of Western military women who were in the country as part of Desert Shield, were incensed that foreign women in uniforms drove Army vehicles in the Kingdom, just as did men. But to many of the veiled women of Saudi Arabia, the Desert Shield soldiers provided an example that produced a glimmer of hope for long-awaited change.

A group of forty-seven Saudi Arabian women bolstered by the presence of Western females who were not only capable of serving alongside men but who could drive military vehicles as well staged a demonstration claiming their right to drive. Female members of the Royal Family, doctors, and teachers were among the brave demonstrators who seized automobile keys and drove themselves into Riyadh on the day of the protest.

Mutaween demanded immediate arrest and punishment for the rebellious women whose act of driving was deemed "non-Islamic." The demonstrators were called "sluts" by some of the religious police who were charged with the propagation of virtue and the prevention of vice. All of the women were arrested, the government confiscated their passports, and the demonstrators were fired from any public employment. The women were ultimately released into the custody of male relatives. "The previously unofficial ban on women's driving quickly became official."

Women are still prohibited from driving in the Kingdom. Religious leaders insist that to allow females the right to drive would be a violation of Shari'a, the rules and traditions established by the Prophet Mohammed who lived in the seventh century – long before automobiles were invented.

*   *   *

Inconvenienced and annoyed by the restriction against women driving, I was unlikely to have chosen to drive in Riyadh's erratic traffic, even if allowed. As a passenger, I continually gasped and pressed my braking foot as if I could control the chaos that filled city streets. It is a wonder there was not a permanent indentation in the passenger's floorboard of our Chevrolet!

We had lived in Laredo, Texas, where yield signs were of little consequence. The oldest or most damaged vehicle always claimed the right of way; anyone who valued his car was more than happy to yield. We had driven on Mexico's haphazard roads, Europe's super highways, and Alaska's blankets of ice, but nothing compared to driving in Saudi Arabia.

The legal driving age for males in the Kingdom was apparently low, as was the required level of competency. Young boys barely able to peer over steering wheels swerved their Mercedes, BMWs, and Toyota pick-ups through streets filled with unpredictable drivers. Third World Nationals, many of whom appeared to have little experience behind the wheel, drove with an apparent fatalism: "If Allah wants me to die, I die."

My husband deftly maneuvered through the maze of African, Arabian, and other Middle-Eastern drivers. As a fighter pilot, he drove with two philosophies adapted from aerial combat: never hesitate, or you will be hit, and speed equals life. I learned to either close my eyes or look down as we sped through the crowded streets. Remarkably, we were never hit or even scraped, despite the frequency of accidents in the city.

A friend of ours was not so fortunate when he parked his car curbside in downtown Riyadh. After checking to make certain it was safe to exit, he cautiously opened the door. In a split second, a speeding vehicle behind him passed another on the right just in time to sever the door from our friend's automobile!

The car was replaced. There were no auto body shops in the Kingdom; damaged vehicles were replaced not repaired. Our friend, knowing first hand the risk of exiting one's car street side, vowed not to repeat his previous error. As he slid across the seat and opened the passenger door, he could not have anticipated the small pickup truck that sped by *on the sidewalk* taking the door of our friend's brand new car with him! The driver, a Third World National, had found what must have seemed to him an opportune short cut around the maze of traffic that filled the street!

We joked that people who for generations had ridden camels were now driving Mercedes, BMWs, and Jaguars – pointing and accelerating just as they had with dromedaries. The rapid transition from camel to automobile as the primary means of transport was not without cost. The reported death rate of Saudi males from car crashes in the late 1970s was higher than the Saudi Arabian birth rate of boys. Saudi males were literally killing themselves faster than they could be replaced.

High speed car crashes were common on the long roads between cities. The highway from Riyadh to Dhahran, near the Arabian Gulf to the east, was littered with crashed luxury cars. The vehicles were so mangled that any survivors were unlikely. Wrecked heaps were never removed. Traveling the Dhahran highway months later, one would see the same auto carcasses as before, plus many new ones. As a direct result of this staggering highway slaughter, a Western firm was hired to produce street signs and roadside billboards extolling safety cautions. The translations from English to Arabic and back to English produced comical results both in wording and spelling. We saw illustrated billboards written in both languages that read:

FACE IN THE DIRECTION YOU ARE GOING
DO NOT TALK OR THINK WHILE DRIVING
THE HIGH BEAMS OF YOUR VENICLES (sic) CAUSE
MANY ACCIDENTS

The frequent crashes created a critical shortage of blood. The Saudi government paid for blood, and many expatriates were happy to sell theirs. The purchased blood of Americans and Europeans was used in royal hospitals to save lives of the injured in that oil-rich country.

The department of transportation, without much success, attempted to create safer conditions for motorists. Drivers often thwarted the highway engineers' best intentions. The Saudi Arabian International School was located in an isolated, desert area outside the city of Riyadh. Speed bumps were built into the paved road alongside the school in obvious safety concern for thousands of students who arrived each day in buses and private vehicles. We were accustomed to slowing in school zones; multi-national drivers in the Kingdom were not.

Apart from those who were delivering their charges to the school, drivers rarely slowed for the traffic calming measures. Some motorists avoided reducing their speed by swerving to the sides, kicking up clouds of desert dust as they motored past. Most drivers, however, altogether ignored the speed bumps. The sound of front suspensions bottoming as they hit the raised concrete at full speed was unmistakable.

Not long after being constructed, the speed bumps were removed from the road. It was rumored that the department of transportation, headed by a member of the Royal Family as were all government offices, decided that speed bumps were damaging to automobiles! Indeed they were! Perhaps future installations would be named "slow bumps" to make their purpose clear!

At intersections, seven or eight automobiles crowded into lanes meant for two or three. Men used their vehicles to force their way ahead of others who were in front of them. Male shoppers in markets behaved the same, just as men had in the lines of entry to the Kingdom. There was little regard for any semblance of order or respect of space. Queues were usually ignored; traffic lanes always were!

Even worse, turn lanes and signals were rarely used. Drivers who were sitting in a far right lane saw no reason not to abruptly turn left. Giving only a quick honk as a signal, motorists darted across all lanes. For us a new driving guideline emerged: Always pay attention to a honk. It meant the driver was about to do something very, very stupid.

It was not unusual for a motorist in a center lane of an intersection to stop his vehicle at an angle. That awkward positioning was the only indication of his intention to turn right or left as soon as the light changed to green.

Other drivers used their hands to indicate their intentions. Regardless of the lane they were in, drivers extended their arms, palms out, as if to say, "Wait! I'm coming through," as they darted across opposing traffic.

Impatient with red traffic lights, Saudi motorists invariably laid on their automobiles' horns to make the light change. Sure enough, the incessant honking from dozens of cars always produced a green light! After rocking with brakes and accelerators pressed at the same time, the cars lurched forward the instant the light changed.

Our Palestinian friend Waleed had an amazing driving experience in downtown Riyadh. While on his way home at sunset, he was stopped in the right lane waiting for the light to change and was undoubtedly honking his horn along with every other motorist.

Young Saudi boys were riding their bicycles on a mound of dirt left roadside by construction crews. One of the boys who was about eight years old lost control on the steep bank and slammed, along with his bicycle, into the passenger side of Waleed's automobile. Fearful for the child's welfare, Waleed picked up the stunned boy whose forehead was bleeding and rushed him to the nearest hospital.

The child had only a minor cut but was, nevertheless, hospitalized for observation. Waleed, as the perpetrator of the accident, was arrested and taken to jail. Neither the boy's father nor an uncle could be located, and the child's mother did not have authority to determine the well-being of her son or to have him released from the hospital.

News that Waleed was in jail spread with an urgent request for friends to take food to him. Reportedly, prisoners were not fed – certainly not adequately fed. Friends or relatives were needed to bring provisions to the jail.

Waleed languished in his imprisonment for a week before the father of the child returned to the city and pronounced no harm done. But the judge before whom Waleed had to appear declared the accident was at least fifty percent the fault of our Palestinian friend. Had he not been stopped at the intersection, the judge reasoned, the child could not have hit his car! A fine was assessed, which Waleed happily paid for his release.

Waleed was most certainly fortunate the child had not been killed in the accident. While beheading is the penalty for murder, Saudi Arabia enforces the practice of charging blood money in the event that one's death is the result of an accident. Money is paid by the guilty party to the surviving family of the victim.

Erratic traffic, caused in part by the rapid transition from camels to Mercedes, provided ample opportunities for the payment of blood money to bereaved families. At the same time, the government paid money for blood to save the lives of the injured in the Kingdom of Saudi Arabia.

11

FAHDA

Fahda was the first Arabian woman I met and the first I would see unveiled. She was the only Arabian woman my husband would ever meet, though we lived in the Kingdom for two years. As the wife of a Saudi Arabian Air Force Officer, Fahda had spent time in the United States during the year her husband, Ali, received flight training and again when he received advanced fighter pilot instruction in the F-15. Her husband and mine worked together in the Saudi Arabian military headquarters in Riyadh where the two men became friends. They shared interests in flying and a love for the outdoors.

Convinced that dirt bikes would be the ideal recreational vehicle in the desert sand of Saudi Arabia, my husband had shipped three off-road motorcycles and a trailer as part of our household weight allowance. Needless to say, we shipped little else! Those bikes turned out to be the only ones we ever saw in the Kingdom. Saudi Arabians, we learned, do not engage in any of the recreational activities common in America.

Ali had seen dirt bikes in the States and was intrigued by the idea of actually riding one. My husband suggested a two-family outing to the desert. Amazingly, Ali accepted the invitation for himself, his wife Fahda, and their two children. The date was set and plans made.

I was tremendously excited at the prospect of meeting a Saudi Arabian woman. I had, by this time, met Ahmed and Khalid and a number of their male friends. I had met many of the Arabian men who worked with my husband, but none had ever included his wife in their frequent visits to our apartment or when they accompanied us on outings. I did not know what to expect. Would Ali's wife remain veiled during our outing? Would we need to eat our picnic in separate family groups? Would her husband stay at her side at all times to ensure both her safety and proper decorum? After all, traditional Saudis do not allow their wives to unveil in the presence of, have conversation with, or eat with unrelated males.

Our two families drove in separate automobiles with ours following theirs. Ali knew just the place for our families to meet outside the city and away from the judgmental eyes of the Mutaween. Veiled in the customary way, Fahda was, as every Saudi woman I had even seen, draped and totally covered in black.

As soon as we exited our automobiles, Fahda, with her husband's permission, removed her veil. Ali proudly introduced her and the children to us. She was beautiful. Her black hair was shoulder-length against clear olive skin that was rarely exposed to the sun. Her dark eyes gave only a hint of shyness, or perhaps it was uncertainty.

Her two children, a girl and a younger boy, were pre-pubescent. The little girl did not yet wear the veil, but she was dressed much the same as her mother. Each of them wore a long dress to the ankles, neck, and wrists. Ali was in traditional clothing, but his young son wore jeans and a striped knit shirt.

We spread our picnic lunches and ate together, sharing our combined baskets: chicken, rice, dates, bread, fruit, potato chips, cookies, and, of course, "Bebsi Cola." Incredibly, Ali seemed completely at ease with having his wife eat in the presence of another man who was not related to her. Fahda, however, made no attempt to engage my husband in conversation. Throughout the afternoon, my husband got wonderful photos of our activities, but out of respect for Ali, Fahda was not in any of them.

Our sons each had his own dirt bike, as did my husband, affording ample opportunity for all to ride. Ali made a few practice laps across the desert, kicking up sand and small plants. Once he felt comfortable with the bike, he gave a ride to each of his children. His son rode first and then his daughter.

Dust clouds followed them as they rode, making it difficult for the apprehensive mother to watch in concern for her son's safety. It wasn't long, however, before everyone was at ease with the motorized toys, and the children were ready to ride the smallest of the bikes, a little Italjet, on their own. Ali ran alongside just as every parent does when his child first rides a bicycle without training wheels.

I rode on the back of my husband's bike, despite my long dress. Surely it was seeing my enjoyment that prompted Ali, in the most astonishing moment of the afternoon, to ask my husband to give his wife a ride, as well.

My husband explained to her that it was important to lean anytime he did so that the dirt bike would be balanced. Always staying within view, they rode in circles and figure eights and jumped over small mounds of sand. Fahda hung onto my husband's waist just as I had. Her skirt billowed and she tried to lean to the left and the right as needed. She didn't dare let go to wave. Ali beamed as he watched, while his children jumped up and down in excitement.

From all I had learned from Ahmed and from his books, this was a most incredible afternoon for a young Arabian woman and her husband. Fahda, loved and respected by her Western-educated husband, enjoyed a measure of freedom that afternoon that I would not have guessed possible inside the Islamic state.

Coming at a distance, we saw an old Bedouin and a young boy riding a donkey across the remote desert. We were many miles from Riyadh, and for as far as we could see there was no tent. The old man and the boy did not appear to be in a hurry or on any particular errand. Perhaps they rode simply for the pleasure of an afternoon on the desert.

As they approached, Ali greeted them, and the two stopped to talk with our husbands and children. Ali translated. Fahda and I kept at a distance since she was not veiled. The old Bedouin wore a long, curved dagger belted on the outside of his thobe, and his head was wrapped turban style. His gray-bearded face was wrinkled and weathered from years in the sun, but his eyes sparkled in friendliness. Rough, gnarled hands gestured every word of his animated speech.

Our sons, at the invitation of the Bedouin, sat upon the donkey while the old man guided the animal with a short rope that was looped around its neck. The young boy of the desert accepted a ride on the back of one of the dirt bikes but not until the man urged him to do so.

In that brief cultural exchange, my sons were just as thrilled to ride the Bedouin's donkey as the Arabian boy was to ride the dirt bike. My husband and I enjoyed seeing the bearded old man of the desert who wore a menacing-looking dagger but was every bit a kind, loving grandpa or perhaps father to the child. The two continued their journey on their slow moving animal, and we did not see them pass our way again.

Growing tired of riding dirt bikes, the children began exploring the desert. Sea shells were abundant across the stark landscape – evidence of ocean water having long ago covered the desert floor. The children filled their pockets with shells and chased scurrying lizards. The desert was flat for as far as one could see with only short bushes and random clumps of grass that provided grazing for an occasional camel or donkey. We had no concern that the children would get lost. One could see several miles in any direction.

While our children explored and our husbands chatted, no doubt about aircraft, Fahda and I walked in the desert. She was fairly functional in English. One had only to converse with her to know she was intelligent, though her formal education in Saudi Arabia had been limited. We talked about many things: family, culture, and life for a Muslim woman in Saudi Arabia.

Fahda told me that she had been allowed to attend school only until she was old enough to veil. After that, she spent her days with the women of the harem.

"It was important for me to learn to care for a home and children. My father said school was not necessary," she said, almost apologetically.

Fahda enjoyed walking and did not want to stop. She said she normally spent her entire day indoors. She longed for exercise. It was a lovely treat to be on the desert and to have the freedom to walk.

"I wish I could walk everyday," she sighed.

"Can't you walk in your yard?" I asked. All Saudi residences in Riyadh were walled, providing seclusion.

"Oh, no, never," was her quick response. "I live in an apartment building. Other military officers and their families share the same building."

"But isn't it walled?" I persisted. "Can't you walk within the complex, within the walls of where you live?" I told her that I lived in the USMTM compound and walked in the evenings, hidden from outside view by the high wall.

"I could never do that," Fahda said. "It would shame my husband. Other men would see me walking and they would say to him, 'What is wrong with your wife? Why does she go walking about?' No, no, I could never shame my husband. I must be content. I cannot walk."

Fahda, whose husband allowed her to ride on the back of a dirt bike holding onto my husband's waist, would bring shame to him if she walked for exercise within the walled complex they shared with other Saudi military officers, all of whom had trained in the United States. As contradictory as it sounded, I understood the distinction Ali surely would have made.

No one within his culture saw his wife ride the dirt bike. He felt no shame in front of my husband because he knew our culture allowed interaction between genders. But within his culture, what other men thought of him and what he allowed his wife to do mattered greatly. He would be scorned if his wife engaged in any activity that was unusual in their culture or that other men did not consider appropriate. He would be jeered for not being able to control his wife. His honor would be damaged.

Even walking for exercise would have been scandalous behavior. Motives would have been questioned. It was presumed that a woman would never walk for mere exercise. There would surely be another unseemly explanation for such provocative behavior. Women simply did not go "walking about." Only a fallen woman would do such a thing.

Fahda understood her role perfectly. She knew her husband must not be embarrassed or dishonored in the eyes of other Saudi Arabian men. It was her responsibility to meet the needs of her husband, the master of their home, and to do nothing that would threaten his perception of honor. Further, a man could divorce his wife for any reason. Walking for exercise and the resultant shame it would bring to him were more than reasons enough for a divorce.

She was fortunate to have married a man who was close to her own age. I asked if she had known Ali before their marriage. "He is in my family," she replied. "Our mothers arranged our marriage." I assumed Ali was Fahda's cousin, but she didn't specifically say so. Because of her time spent in the States, she may have been aware of how odd the practice of marrying one's cousin seems to Americans. It was a question I thought better not to ask.

I asked about her mother.

"She is very sad," was Fahda's response. "My father took another wife and that has caused much pain to my mother." Her voice seemed to hiss the words, "another wife." "I am angry with my father. I will not see him," she continued, her expression suddenly turning dark.

I was surprised by Fahda's deep emotional response. Clearly any man in Saudi Arabia believed he was honored by having multiple wives. To be able to support his harem meant that he was not only a man of wealth but that he was also virile. His sexual stamina, so important as a measure of manhood, was affirmed if he had many wives. I continued to query the young woman.

"Fahda," I said. "I understand that it is very common for men in Saudi Arabia to have more than one wife. Is that something most women accept as normal?"

"We hate it!" She said emphatically. "But there is nothing we can do about it."

As we walked, she continued to share her feelings. I was amazed at how open and unguarded she was. Fahda was not the least frivolous or flippant. She was as honest and vulnerable as a child.

She, more than any of the women I would later meet in the homes of Ahmed and Khalid was ready for change. However, her desire for change was emotionally conflicted. The rules imposed by her culture formed the foundation and purpose of her life. Fahda had been taught that obedience to the traditions of her elders brought honor to her family. It was her duty to protect that honor. Challenging any of the rules imposed on her was not a viable option, even though some of the restrictions she bore were not part of the Prophet's experience and could not, therefore, be part of his tradition. Others, such as veiling, pre-dated the birth of Islam.

The religion of her people was the only one she would ever be allowed to know. To challenge any rule imposed by Shari'a was to criticize Islam; it was to question the authority of the Prophet and that could be extremely dangerous – especially for a female. Speaking against Islam or its prophet was considered apostasy and could result in severe punishment. Converting to another religion was the ultimate act of apostasy, and death was the certain penalty.

Despite the extraordinary conflict, Fahda desired change but not for the freedoms Americans treasure. Voting, freedom of the press, freedom of speech, the right of assembly, and freedom of religion were all so foreign to her that she did not even consider them a possibility. The change she desired was far more basic.

Fahda wanted to have the freedom not to veil. She longed for the freedom to walk for exercise. She wanted her children, her daughter as well as her son, to attend school. She wanted her daughter not to marry at the young age she had.

Most of all, Fahda wanted to be the only wife her husband would take.

12
KHALID

Khalid and his friend Ahmed had approached us in the souqs. From them we learned which ghutra to purchase. After that encounter, both young men became frequent guests in our home, but rarely did they call to arrange a visit; they simply arrived at the compound gate and announced to the Uzi-armed guards that they were there to see us.

The two Saudi men always wore the national dress. Their stark white thobes contrasted with red and white ghutras that were folded back on the sides in a way that only young men wore them. Like other young Saudis, they walked with a casual swagger that indicated their importance and self confidence. It was quite unlike the slow shuffle of older men who frequented the souqs at night.

Insh'allah, if Allah wills, was the philosophy by which they lived. It allowed patience and flexibility in their schedules; they never seemed to be in a hurry. Except when driving their automobiles! Young Saudi males were in a very big rush once they sat behind the wheel.

School projects or studying for college exams could all be dealt with later. Their easy-going attitude indicated an assurance that "If not today, then another day would be fine." They would graduate if and when Allah willed. Neither seemed to have a burning desire to enter the work force or contribute his talents in any meaningful way. As students, they lived comfortably on money provided by their oil-rich government.

The two shared many meals with us and sometimes hinted that a before dinner cocktail would be nice. We were careful to ignore such statements. Did they assume that because we were Americans we had the forbidden drink in our apartment, or were they testing us? I have no doubt Ahmed and Khalid indulged when given an opportunity to do so, particularly when they were outside the Kingdom.

All forms of alcoholic drink were prohibited by the Prophet Mohammed. As a result, the manufacture, sale, or consumption of alcohol was illegal inside the Kingdom of Saudi Arabia. Despite the prohibition, shelves of local markets were well-stocked with all the supplies needed to make beer and wine. Rumors of bathroom brews circulated, and occasional arrests were made. Caning, jail, and deportation were always threats against anyone found to be making, drinking, or serving unlawful spirits. Punishment has evidently escalated since I lived in the Kingdom. In 2009 American media reported the beating death of a man who was accused of selling alcohol.

Once comfortably slouched in the chairs of our apartment, Khalid and Ahmed were content to spend hours in our home during their impromptu visits. My sons left to play, and sometimes my husband had other obligations for which he excused himself. The young Saudi men never seemed ill at ease when left alone in my presence. I, too, was comfortable and usually enjoyed the chance to ask them questions. Their answers were punctuated by phrases such as "Naturally not," "Of course, of course," "No way," and "Are you kidding?" They responded as Americans do by prefacing their responses with "Well, I mean …," or "You know…"

Khalid was first to invite us to his home, which was also the residence of his mother. It could have been a tract home in its similarity to others, but unlike homes in America, this dwelling was not part of house-lined streets in a zoned residential section. Often built in isolated spots in the desert surrounding Riyadh, some gated and walled homes were particularly isolated. .

Earthen colored, the relatively new home appeared to have about 2500 square feet of living area. Built without adornment, it had a marked absence of windows; residences in the Kingdom were designed to provide seclusion. The sandy dirt yard was void of vegetation to soften the exterior of the property. With its harsh landscape, the foreboding walled home was typical of "middle-class" homes in Riyadh – homes that had only recently replaced tents and mud huts.

We entered the front door and stepped into a large square room that may have been the majlis – the sitting room. It had no furniture, but the floor was covered with multiple overlapping Persian rugs in a patchwork of various colors and designs.

Leaving our shoes at the door, we sat cross-legged on the floor. We knew to be careful that the soles of our feet did not point in the direction of anyone. That would have been a sign of disrespect.

Homes were separated into male and female quarters with separate entrances from the outside. Though Khalid welcomed me into the room for men, my husband and sons would never have been allowed to enter the harem. Our friend made light conversation and we complimented him on the beautiful rugs that provided the only interior color or decoration.

Khalid briefly left and returned carrying two large platters of food. A whole boiled chicken filled one, and a generous mound of pungent rice filled the other. He placed both serving dishes on a small cloth spread on the floor in the center of the circle we had formed. The abundance of food was clearly more than the four of us, plus our host, could eat. Arab hospitality requires that no guest go away hungry, and we certainly would not.

We waited for our friend's signal to begin the meal. There was no prayer or verbal giving of thanks for the food; neither were there plates, flatware, napkins, nor drinking water. Khalid pushed his long white sleeves up, smiling broadly beneath his heavy mustache. He knew his dining custom was unusual to us, and he clearly enjoyed demonstrating how easy the process really was, at least to someone with a lifetime of practice. Reaching with his right hand into the mound of rice, he deftly squeezed a ball of the aromatic, sticky grain in his palm. With the rice tightly pressed in place, he used the same hand and with a twist of his wrist pulled off a morsel of the hot chicken so both could be eaten together. As the fingers of his right hand firmly encased the food, he ate through the opening created by his thumb encircling his forefinger. The left hand, traditionally saved for toileting, remained tucked out of sight.

We each dug in, literally. Well-seasoned, the chicken and rice were really quite good. Saudi rice, whether prepared in one's home or purchased on Chicken Street, had a mixture of Middle-Eastern spices that were unusual to us but were invariably delicious. My younger son didn't seem to mind putting his hand into the sticky and greasy foods. However, my older son who had always been rather finicky about anything on his hands or different foods mixed together had more difficulty enjoying the meal. He would have been much happier with a Big Mac or a pepperoni pizza, although neither was available in the Kingdom!

While Khalid didn't drop a single grain, we found it difficult to hold the rice and pinch pieces of chicken at the same time. We dropped less rice if we alternated between the two foods instead of eating them together as our host had shown us. My left-handed husband had great difficulty in using only his right hand, but he knew better than to use his preferred hand. He and the Americans with whom he worked had been well-briefed. Not only was it offensive to eat with one's "toileting hand," to do so would have brought an abrupt end to the meal for any Saudi.

Khalid described how much Saudi Arabians, who were originally nomads of the desert, still loved to leave the city for vacations spent in large Bedouin tents. Going on "holiday" must have resembled *1001 Tales of Arabian Nights* except that now instead of traveling on camels or Arabian horses, many families drove to their desert encampments in Mercedes, BMWs, and Rolls Royces. Portable generators were used to power refrigeration units that had become modern vacation necessities. Holiday tents were ever so much more comfortable than the ones in which Arabian families had lived for generations. But some things remained the same. Multiple layers of Persian rugs covered dirt floors. Coffee was brewed over traditional wood fires. Men enjoyed their oral recitation of poetry and story telling, while women remained veiled and secluded.

By the conclusion of the meal, the chicken was largely still intact. Bite sized morsels had been pinched off rather than anyone taking a specific portion. Though we had eaten heartedly in response to Khalid's frequent urgings, the remaining mound of rice was sufficient for several more meals.

A basin near a doorway provided the means of welcomed hand washing and its use signaled the end of the meal. After removing the remaining food, our host returned with a gleaming brass pot of hot cardamom coffee, which the adults drank from tiny bowl-shaped cups without handles.

Khalid then escorted me through the darkened hallways into the kitchen to meet his mother. The woman, who was no older than I, was unveiled. She stood with her elbows resting on the laminate countertop and her face cupped in her hands as she watched television. The average sized screen was mounted on the wall just above eye level. There was a small dinette table made of shiny steel with a Formica top. Matching chairs had vinyl seat covers. The only furniture I saw in the new home built in the 1980s was that which Americans had prized in the '50s.

I too stood as we watched television together. Khalid's mother spoke no English and I spoke no Arabic except for the basic greeting of hello – *maarhaba;* thank you – *shokran;* very good – *quais;* and the often used, *Insh'allah.* Verbal communication was difficult with the language barrier, but she was friendly and made every effort to entertain me. She made comments and gestured toward the programming we viewed. I smiled and shook my head in agreement, though I could only guess at her meaning. She seemed pleased, nevertheless, with my limited input. She offered me a "Bebsi" to drink.

The televised presentation we watched was a simple public service short about the importance of washing one's hands before preparing food. It emphasized that ordinary daily objects can be covered with germs from many people. The filmed episode showed a paper riyal being blown by wind into the street and touching rotted garbage. It was then picked up by a man who passed the germ-laden bill on to others. If hands were not washed, the film demonstrated, germs from the paper currency ultimately ended up on food to be eaten. I always marveled when viewing similar messages at the need for such basic information. But without this programming, there would have been little else to watch. The televised message clearly held the attention of Khalid's mother to its conclusion.

I wondered how frequently the woman was called upon to prepare food for the men of her family and their guests. Perhaps she had a servant, an African or Asian female who cooked the meals, but I did not see one. Her kitchen was, however, spotless. Someone had cleaned very well, or perhaps the meal Khalid served had come from Chicken Street vendors.

Pointing out the various appliances and cupboards and even the contents of some, the Saudi woman gave me a tour of her kitchen. Modern kitchens were relatively new to women in the Kingdom – women who had, until the sudden oil wealth, lived in squalor in desert encampments. Khalid's mother was obviously very proud of hers with its running water and electric appliances.

Secluded for no reason other than gender, this Arabian woman had spent most of her life within the confines of her home. There was, it seemed to me, little awareness of life's possibilities outside her walls of seclusion. Televised public service ads and coverage of the annual Hajj provided her meager exposure to life beyond the harem. I was struck by the realization that I, an expatriate in her country for a relatively brief time, had probably seen more of the Kingdom than she had. There was no doubt I had experienced more freedom from the hand of the Mutaween than she ever would, and as an American woman, I had more rights than she could imagine.

A much younger Saudi woman, the one who had spent time in America, Fahda dreamed of more. She longed for the simple freedom to walk for exercise, for her daughter to be educated, and for her husband not to take additional wives.

Khalid's mother, however, seemed to have accepted the reality that dreaming was pointless; there was, for her, nothing more. Living under the same rules of Shari'a that had governed her mother and grandmother before her, she had learned early in life that to desire more could lead to punishment. Her new kitchen was probably as good as her life would ever get; her new tract-like home was markedly better than dwellings of prior generations.

Khalid returned to the kitchen when it was time to end our visit to his home. With him there to translate, I again thanked his mother and complimented the meal as I had when first meeting her. He then escorted me back through the halls to the men's section where my family remained sitting on the floor.

My husband and sons never met or even saw Khalid's mother. Though in her own home, she was not their hostess. She prepared the meal but had no part in sharing it or in greeting guests, other than females. Even as young as my sons were, Khalid's mother would have veiled in their presence.

A gracious host, Khalid was obviously happy to entertain us. He was proud of his modern home – just as Americans were proud of our new prosperity and the appliances available to us in the years following the end of World War II. He was pleased for me to meet his mother. Perhaps he hoped I would conclude that Saudi Arabian women live well.

* * *

Khalid became an enthusiastic guide to the city of Riyadh. At times he accompanied us to incredible souqs we never would have found on our own or to meaningful historical sites.

The old, moldering Mismak Fortress was one such site that held great significance for Saudis. The ancient walled mud fortress had contained government structures and residences of the former ruling family, the Rasheed. At one time a heavily fortified garrison, Mismak had been guarded with Turkish cannons. The Ottoman Empire supported the rule of the Rasheed who in the late 1800s forcibly took control of Riyadh from the family of Sa'ud.

In 1902 Abdul Aziz ibn Sa'ud recaptured the Mismak Fortress in a daring attack that resulted in the assassination of the ruling Rasheed governor. A spearhead remained lodged in the mud wall alongside the gate, providing a tangible reminder of the life and death struggle that had taken place there. The conquest of the Mismak Fortress marked the beginning of a campaign to unite the entire Arabian Peninsula under the veil of Islam.

Despite the incredible significance of the fortress, there were no signs directing visitors to its location. Nor was there any effort to restore, preserve, or even clean the historical site. Trash and cigarette butts cluttered the landscape around its crumbling walls. The Mismak was not memorialized in any way.

Saudi Arabians, a people for whom honor is extremely important, do not create places of memorial. Former kings are buried in insignificant and poorly marked graves located in common communal cemeteries. The Islamic state does not lower its flag to half-staff even at the death of its monarch. Believed by Muslims to be inscribed with the words of God, the flag of the Kingdom can not be lowered to honor any mortal.

While mortals were not honored with memorials, their deeds, especially those done in the name of Allah, were revered. The daring feat of Abdul Aziz in capturing the Mismak Fortress had been set in verse and was memorized by Khalid and every other Saudi male. With his head filled with heroic acts and memorized Koranic passages, Khalid had no need for physical monuments.

"Our memorials are in our hearts," he told us.

*   *   *

Saudi Arabians raised and used many animals, but they did not keep dogs or cats as pets. Occasionally one had a working dog, but it never would have been allowed inside a Saudi home. Camels were used as pack animals and for racing. They were milked and sometimes eaten, though goats, sheep, and chickens were more common sources of meat. Falcons were trained for hunting expeditions in the desert. We heard of majestic Arabian horses, but I never saw any in the Kingdom.

Khalid took us to an extraordinary animal store in Riyadh. "Beautiful Creatures" was filled with huge snakes: boas, pythons, and anacondas. There were young African and Asian animals in cages throughout, but the most startling was a pair of Bengal tiger cubs. We were stunned to see the caged twins and could only guess at who might buy them and for what purpose. Only the Royal Family or wealthy oil sheikhs could support the purchase of such exotic and dangerous wild animals.

A separate section of the souq was filled with tropical birds. Larger than most American pet stores, the bird souq had hundreds of African gray parrots, macaws, and other varieties of large Amazons, mynahs, parakeets, cockatiels, and Australian cockatoos.

Fascinated by the bird souq, we returned on several occasions. My older son first purchased a cockatiel and later a beautiful white, sulfur-crested Australian cockatoo that he named "Napoleon." Picked from about twenty caged similar birds, Napoleon, who was still young and smaller than the others, seemed to be the most energetic. He had a definite regal strut.

Despite the incredible wild animal and bird souq, we could never have purchased a domesticated cat in Saudi Arabia, though numerous wild cats lived in our compound. Shortly after arriving in the Kingdom we acquired our Princess Leah, an orange-striped cat with oversized ears and a tail shortened by trauma. Our younger son brought the feral kitten, which resembled a tabby bobcat, home when her tail was still bloodied. "Can we keep her?" He pled.

Princess Leah had the run of the apartment until our older son purchased his cockatoo. When Napoleon was out of his cage, we put Princess Leah behind closed doors in the opposite part of the apartment – in the harem, we joked. In no time, Princess Leah learned to jump straight up and grasp the European-style door handle until her weight pulled the latch open. Though she was small even when fully grown, she could open any door in the apartment at will and almost as quickly as we closed it. The only way to keep her out of a particular room was to lock the door with a key. She lacked the manual dexterity to manage keys, though we were convinced she had ample curiosity to figure out what was necessary. Incredibly, her nemesis Napoleon the cockatoo could pick combination locks.

A spunky little cat though she was, Princess quickly learned to stay away from Napoleon. Hissing, his yellow crest raised, he charged across the floor in an authoritative pigeon-toed run. Princess Leah recognized she was no match for that strong beaked, noisy bird who was as large as she.

Strangely, our Saudi cat found underarm perspiration odor as enticing as catnip. How she loved anyone who came in from exercising! She was happiest, purring contentedly, with her head burrowed in a sweaty armpit. Other times in a show of deepest affection she crawled onto one's chest with as close to an embrace as her short legs would allow.

Khalid made it clear that he did not like dogs or cats and couldn't understand why we Americans would allow either in our homes. He certainly did not like our Princess Leah. Inexplicably, she was drawn to our Arabian friend and tried relentlessly to be affectionate. She headed for his chest or an armpit every time he visited. Was it Khalid's catnip of the desert that so attracted her to him?

During one of his visits, my husband asked Khalid for directions to a good electronics souq. Our friend was happy to accompany us. My husband drove, and I sat in the front passenger seat. Khalid and our sons were in the back of our Chevrolet. After a number of men gestured and laughed mockingly as we passed through traffic, I realized the embarrassing position I had put Khalid in. Saudi men never sit in the back seat of an automobile with a woman in the front! The souq was filled with gadgets fascinating to my husband and sons, but I quickly tired of electronics talk. Curious if other souqs of greater interest might be nearby, I stepped the few feet toward the souq's opened entry. Of course I was properly covered in my long, loose dress, and my male escorts were only a few feet from me. Khalid, knowing that I should not appear to be unescorted, quickly moved to the entry and stood with me.

It is common in the United States to greet persons you pass on sidewalks or to speak to other shoppers in a market. In days past, men tipped their hats to women, even to those who were strangers. But in the Kingdom, a man never spoke to a woman in passing or she to him. Men and women simply did not share conversation on any level outside their homes. In fact, the Mutaween were likely to raise the cane pole against any person who attempted conversation with an Arabian woman.

As Khalid and I stood in the entry of the souq talking with one another, young Arabian men strolled by. Speaking to him in Arabic, the young men smirked and gestured as they passed. Khalid acknowledged them with curt responses, also in Arabic. From the tone of his reply, I guessed he was being jeered or that I was.

"Are they giving you a hard time for being with me?" I asked.

"No problem, I can handle it," he responded flatly, his face flushed.

I did not make that mistake again. Honor and humiliation in Khalid's world were determined by what other Saudi Arabian men thought of him. There was no room for individuality or freedom of expression. It was much like the peer pressure Western teenagers experience in wanting to fit in – to be like everyone else – except that in this Middle Eastern culture, the expectation of conformity did not end with adolescence. Anyone who dared depart from the established rules was subject to scorn. Khalid's friendship with me had clearly conflicted with the strict rules of Shari'a, the traditions of the elders, particularly the ones that separate men from women.

In retrospect, I must have seemed a scandalous, wanton female to Arabians who never would have been in the company of or engaged in conversation with an unrelated person of the opposite sex. Only later did I realize that I was fortunate to have only been jeered. I could have been arrested and jailed!

*　*　*

Ramadhan, the annual month of fasting, is one of the five tenets of Islam. It is a time for reflection, a time to gain empathy for the poor, and a time to give thanks for the Koran. During daylight hours, Muslims who are at least the age of twelve must not eat, drink, smoke, or even chew gum. Sex is also forbidden.

The month of sacrificial fasting ends on the first day of the tenth month (*Shawwal)* with a celebration. Sometimes likened to Christmas, *Eed al Fitr* is a time for families to be together. Houses are decorated and a feast is prepared. Children receive presents, gifts are exchanged, offerings are made to the poor, and cards are sent to others. Differences between Muslims are forgiven and forgotten. On this special day, women and children are included in the early morning 'Id prayers.

Khalid invited us to his sister's home for the holiday. Friends and family would drop by, and food would be served. Men and women would, of course, celebrate in separate parts of the house.

We arrived at the walled home that was very similar to the residence of his mother. Upon entering, Khalid introduced me to his brother-in-law, who immediately escorted me through the darkened halls to the women's room. In his home, only he had the right to enter that section of the house. But even he had to be circumspect with female guests. At his brief knock, Haifa, his wife and Khalid's sister, opened the door slightly, making sure her female guests inside were not visible to him. She welcomed me warmly as if we had been friends forever.

The women inside the room, about twenty of Haifa's friends and relatives, had removed their veils and black abayas but kept them by their sides. Necklines and arms were fully covered by their long, colorful dresses. Most of the women were adorned with multiple glittering gold necklaces and bangles, though none wore the torso-covering elaborate pieces. Their makeup indicated hours of careful preparation; heavy black makeup accentuated their eyes and they wore dark red or purple lipstick. Hair styles were thick and full with large looped curls pinned in place – a style that had been popular in America a decade earlier.

We sat on Persian rugs in a room without furniture. The women formed one large circle, rather than small groups throughout the room. No one seemed to be uncomfortable. It was obvious they were accustomed to long periods of sitting on the floor without their limbs numbing. Only I needed to shift frequently to a different position.

Haifa offered trays of dates stuffed with almonds and we sipped hot, sweetened tea. The dates, probably from the Bedouin settlement of Hofuf were the largest and the most delicious I had ever eaten.

The women chatted quietly, alternating between English and Arabic. Topics of conversation were rather benign: their children, the holiday, and homes they had yet to visit. They did not discuss their husbands or sex or politics – at least not in English! No one spoke to the group as a whole. Rather, conversation was directed only toward women sitting close enough that there was no need to speak loudly. There were pleasantries, but no one appeared to be making comments merely for the sake of humor or to entertain. It was a very genteel affair during which ladies did not seek individual attention. How unlike gatherings with my friends in the States where each person is eager to contribute her opinion, argue a point, relate an occurrence from work or home, or elicit laughter from the group.

Each time Haifa's husband knocked on the door to announce the arrival of a female guest or time for one's departure, all the women in the room quickly grasped the fabric of their veils to hold in front of their faces. It was unthinkable that our hostess's husband, who was likely related to many of the guests, would catch even a glimpse of the women without their coverings.

It was a drop-by occasion – an open house in a much closed Islamic culture. Guests arrived, chatted, and then left to visit other homes. As women prepared to leave, veils were fully repositioned and black abayas again covered their party dresses. Haifa lifted the veil of each departing guest to waft her with incense. It was a sign of hospitality to send one's visitors away smelling of her home. Each veiled woman was then escorted by Haifa's husband through the halls to where her husband waited. She remained always out of sight of other men.

During the afternoon, Haifa invited me to see her bedroom, much as we might give a tour of our new home. The room was furnished with a bed and a dresser made of dark wood. A beautifully ornate silver hand mirror with matching brush and comb were displayed on top of the dresser. There were no family photographs. Walls, void of any framed artwork, were earthen colored and bare. There were no potted plants or decorative items in the room. The only color came from Persian rugs that covered the floor.

Haifa moved the sliding door to show me her closet that was filled with long, formal, and obviously expensive dresses. The elaborate garments were made of silks, brocades, and taffeta and were adorned with lace, ruffles, and sequins. The dress labels I saw were in Arabic and were, no doubt, those of designers. Sold in secluded boutiques in the newer buildings of Riyadh, they were known as "Cinderella dresses" to expatriates.

Haifa pulled out the garments one by one for me to see and admire. In my limited Arabic I complimented each, gushing as much as I could. She was delighted. Only women in the privacy of a home or her husband would ever see those dresses. I wondered what Haifa and other Arabian women wore during long, monotonous days spent in the harem. There were no jeans or tee shirts in her closet.

Haifa offered to give me several of her dresses. She held each against me as a stylist might, with her arms at full length and her head tilted as she evaluated how it would look if I wore it. I think she would have been genuinely pleased had I accepted them. Instead, I insisted they were much too beautiful for me and that only someone of her beauty should wear them.

I never considered purchasing a "Cinderella dress." I was told by friends who out of curiosity did shop in the dress boutiques that it was not unusual for an elaborate gown to be priced at thousands of dollars.

While I was being graciously entertained by Haifa, my sons and husband, along with other men and boys, were in a separate room having a meal of boiled goat and rice. The time-honored tradition of Arabian men sitting around a meal is as important for wounded kinships as the peace table is in other cultures. Eed al Fitr, the breaking of the Ramadhan fast, was meant to be a time of forgiveness and the healing of relationships.

Just as before, the men sat on the floor, careful that their soles did not point toward anyone. Each used his right hand to pull off the meat and scoop the rice. Goat was not as easily pulled as was chicken, and it was particularly difficult with only one hand.

My sons were quite content to eat only rice, but when the host noticed that my older son had no goat, he reached into the steaming meat and tore off a nice, fatty chunk. An Arab host is always careful to insure his guests are well fed, and if you are an honored guest you may be offered the prized morsels – the organs of the animal!

My son gamely accepted the meat, but the more he chewed, the more it grew in his mouth. His father recounted for me the several brave attempts my son made to swallow the goat, catching his gag reflex just in time to prevent offending their host. (This son of mine had, even as a toddler, gagged if a piece of oatmeal stuck to his finger as he fed himself.) With no napkin or way to discretely dispose of it, and using all the will power he could muster, he was finally able to swallow the stringy piece of meat. After that, both of my sons opted out of all invitations to goat dinners.

My husband, on several trips within the country, was invited to the traditional meal and as the honored guest was given the eyeballs of the animal. The back and forth exchange of, "Oh no, it is much too great an honor for me," usually did not work and he received the prized treat. His Saudi hosts derived great pleasure from seeing him accept and consume their gift. Fighter pilots, after all, must be tough, and he had undoubtedly swallowed worse on dares from his American peers.

Khalid remained an enthusiastic guide for Riyadh as he proudly opened his culture to us. Additionally, his government provided us wonderful travel opportunities, both within the Kingdom of Saudi Arabia and in neighboring countries.

13
A WORLD OF TRAVEL

Though void of normal entertainment and recreational choices, the Kingdom did offer diversions to expatriates who were willing to get out of the city and explore. We took advantage of every opportunity both within the country and in travel outside Saudi Arabia. Each adventure was unique and some were extraordinary, though throughout the Middle East there were frequent contradictions between Islamic rule and actual practice.

There are lovely beaches on two sides of the Arabian Peninsula. Jeddah, the Kingdom's city that most closely resembles a resort location, is on the coast of the Red Sea while the Persian Gulf, or Arabian Gulf as Saudis prefer to call it, is on the eastern side.

Despite the warm water and sweltering climate, there was no swimming, snorkeling, or boating. No one sunbathed on the sandy beaches. Saudi families occasionally waded in the surf, but they were always fully clothed. Men lifted their long white thobes just enough to get their dusty sandals wet. Fully veiled women stayed in the shallow water where there was no need to lift skirts, which would have risked exposing ankles. Little girls wore their long lacy dresses, even for an outing to the beach.

The Red Sea has an enormous coral reef. The warm, shallow waters and constant supply of sunshine create the perfect condition for spectacular coral. The immense reef was among the most beautiful we have ever seen, to include the Great Barrier Reef in Australia.

We wore long sleeved shirts, jeans, and tennis shoes – all necessary protection from the sharp coral – into the salty and amazingly buoyant water. Without benefit of snorkeling gear, except for swim masks, we explored the jagged reef that had grown to a height barely beneath the surface. The clear water provided a stunning view of brilliantly colored fish darting through tunnels and crevices in the intricate coral. The incredible reef extended far beyond the shoreline, much further than we could explore.

There was no one else on the beach or in the water. How odd it seemed that such natural treasures could not be enjoyed by the Saudis. Shari'a's strict rules governing attire made the sport of snorkeling unlikely among Arabians, even those who lived near the beautiful reef.

When we left the water, two Saudi men in thobes strode along the beach but made no acknowledgment of us. I wondered if they were even aware of the massive and incredible coral just beyond the beach on which they walked.

*   *   *

A casual acquaintance of mine told of a bizarre incident when she, her son, and her husband were snorkeling off the coast of Jeddah. On that particular occasion, two men were also in the water, but they were further out to a point where the reef dropped off and the water's depth was much greater. As my friend swam along the surface, one of the men began floundering in the deep water, indicating, she thought, a need for help. She responded immediately by swimming to where he was, but when she tried to assist, she was pulled under water. Struggling free of the man's grip, she surfaced only to be pushed under again and again until her husband, seeing what was happening, came to her rescue. As the expatriate family left the water, the two men remained where they had been, obviously in no danger of drowning.

*   *   *

"He who plants thorns must never expect to gather roses" is an old Arabian proverb. Desert roses, also known as sand roses, are treasures that grow in the eastern provinces of Saudi Arabia in the essentially vegetation-free sandy marsh land. Salty sea water from the Persian Gulf seeps inland and concentrates at three times the salinity of sea water in the sand of the flat desert areas known as *Sabkhas.* As the water evaporates, gypsum from the briny water is left in the sand where it crystallizes in the form of roses.

The delicately shaped but firm roses could be found close to the wet surface or as deep as three feet below. Like snowflakes, no two sand roses are the same. Varied in color and size, they range from tiny quarter-inch rosettes to clusters that can be three feet in diameter.

An Arabian legend claims that Allah blesses with good luck the person who finds a desert rose. In spite of being rumored that desert roses were a national treasure and that removal of them was prohibited, the wet Sabkhas were always full of expatriates eager to gather them. Digging with small shovels or by hand, each person hoped to find a spectacular specimen that would be the only souvenir truly grown in the Kingdom.

Saudi police cars drove slowly by the fields of diggers and occasionally stopped a car for search, as they did ours, but we never heard of arrests for removal of the desert rose. Interestingly, one can find any number of Arabian sand roses for sale on Internet web sites.

*   *   *

Soccer was popular with Saudi males. We frequently saw young men dressed in their national clothing as they played impromptu games. Holding their thobes high enough to run and kick the ball, Saudis played with the same enthusiasm and freedom as sports clothing would have afforded. The Kingdom boasted of an Olympic-qualified soccer team, though we never saw the would-be Olympians practice or compete.

Camels were also a common sight even in the capital city of Riyadh. Frequently transported in the backs of small pickups, the camels barely fit in the truck beds carrying them. Imported from the Sudan, the dromedaries were almost as numerous as the flocks of sheep and goats that were herded through the same city streets.

Outside the city, camels grazed freely, though grass was scant on the desert landscape. They munched on anything, including prickly scrub brush that was more prevalent than grass. As we cautiously approached, they spat and kicked until they saw our offered treats. We discovered that of all our picnic items, camels especially loved Oreos and potato chips.

The rope-like circle, the aghal, was originally used to control camels' kicking legs; now it was part of the national dress. Each man looped the black cord into a double circle and used it to anchor his red and white ghutra on his head.

Clearly the highlight of the year in Saudi Arabia was the annual camel races. It was a sport exotic enough to have been featured years earlier in *National Geographic Kids Magazine*. Held in February, the ten day event headlined two contests each day. An estimated twenty to thirty thousand spectators attended at least one of the races.

Camel racing had for centuries been a traditional sport of Bedouin tribes. In the past, thousands of the animals streaked across the desert in an annual competition. A slow camel could cover about three miles per hour while a particularly good one traversed four miles in the same amount of time. The dromedary, well suited for the grueling challenge, could compete for five to seven days with little food or water.

Though today's races are shorter in duration, the contests are still taken very seriously. A well-bred camel is able to gallop at a speed of twenty to twenty-five miles per hour for a short race. Breeders use artificial insemination and embryo transfer techniques to produce the finest line of dromedaries. Cared for with precise nutrition, a prized racing camel commands an impressive price. Prince Fayed, when I met him at his brother's celebration for completion of advanced flight training, had told me he raised prized white camels. I wondered if his were among the many I saw competing.

Just outside the capital city, a large circular dirt track replaced the Bedouins' open desert as the racing venue. Jockeys in colorful Arab dress perched precariously high atop camels while urging them on with shouts in Arabic. Heels and sticks further prodded the animals to a gallop. Clouds of dust filled the air as the gangly beasts ran their course to the enthusiastic cheers of Arab spectators.

There was neither a grandstand nor bleacher for seating. Saudi Arabian men stood on top of automobiles, pickup cabs, and buses to get a good view of the racing camels. Others huddled in groups as if placing bets, though gambling is prohibited in the Islamic State.

King Fahd and his entourage came to the races in huge
motor homes. A path had been paved around the outside of the
track specifically for the king's convenience. His air
conditioned motor home provided the king a continual firsthand view of the race as it kept pace with the camels and their
colorful jockeys running their course!

Saudis who chose to "camp out" at the races set up
enormous tents with portable generators to power refrigeration
units that were positioned on several sides. Both luxury
automobiles and pickup trucks were parked alongside tents.
Pots of hot tea and cardamom coffee were continually being
brewed over wood fires. Male servants, who were never Saudis,
kept the embers glowing and the beverages ready for their
employers. There were no concessions or food vendors.

Additional huge tents resembling giant parachutes were
provided for the comfort of day visitors to the races. Long
tethers anchored the billowing canopies to the ground, leaving
about five feet of opening between the grounding spikes and the
lower edges of the tents. Hundreds of men in traditional dress
crowded inside to sit on the rug-covered ground while taking
advantage of the welcomed shade. Neither women nor
expatriates entered the tented areas.

Prized camels were transported to the races in Datsun and Toyota pickups. Those trucks, along with buses and automobiles, parked five to seven deep outside the king's paved path that circled the track. Crowded together, the vehicles parked vertically, horizontally, and even diagonally to the others, creating a haphazard arrangement. Visitors who did not intend to spend hours upon hours at the races and did not want to be trapped were careful to leave their automobiles parked in the desert well beyond the jumble of vehicles.

Between events, camels stood beside the pickups that had delivered them to the race track. Stretching their long necks to reach hay and oats kept in truck beds, dromedaries provided ample shade for their attendants and jockeys who sat beneath them. It was a time of respite for contenders and care givers alike.

Once satisfied with food and ready for rest, camels folded their legs at the knees and sat, causing the men to scurry from beneath their animals. Shade was not necessary for camels; they rested peacefully in full sun with blankets spread across their backs. Attendants continued to stay nearby, keeping watch over valuable, prized racers.

There were few Saudi women present at the camel races. Occasionally a woman whose veil did not cover her eyes walked between parked automobiles. Perhaps her husband was a Bedouin camel owner or an attendant. Her duties in caring for animals necessitated the less restrictive veil. I never observed a Saudi woman watching the race as a spectator. Certainly none would have loudly cheered support for her favored contender. Women were expected to be neither seen nor heard.

My husband, our sons, and I were enjoying the colorful atmosphere of the unique sporting event when several Saudi young men approached us. They offered to use our camera to take a picture of our little family with the races as a backdrop. We were pleased when two of them offered to pose with us for an even more authentic photograph.

I was stunned when, as soon as the camera clicked the last photo, one of the men who posed with us groped me in a swift motion across my chest. As quickly as they had come, the group left, perhaps proud of having shown disrespect for an American

woman who was not veiled. The fact that my husband was present was obviously not a deterrent to the men.

After all, what was he to do? The laws in Saudi Arabia were not meant to protect expatriates, especially a woman who by virtue of being unveiled had, in their logic, invited their show of disrespect.

On another day, the United States Army Sergeant who managed the recreation center at USMTM arranged a field trip to the camel races for the young people of our compound. The youngsters stayed in a group with several adult chaperones. Two of the pre-teen girls, who happened both to be blond, caught the attention of several Saudi young men. Dating is forbidden in the Kingdom, and there is no legal exchange socially between genders after puberty. Nevertheless, the two Saudi males, ignoring the presence of adult chaperones, repeatedly tried to flirt with the American girls. They coaxed, cajoled, and begged for phone numbers.

Both flattered and embarrassed, the giggling girls sat in the back seat of the bus for their return trip to the compound. The Saudi men followed closely in their car, encouraged by the girls who kept looking back at their pursuers. On a dare, one of the girls wrote a telephone number on a scrap of paper and tossed it out the window of the bus. The eager Saudis quickly stopped and retrieved the paper.

For the next several days and sometimes late at night, our phone rang again and again. Each time I answered, a Saudi male (not always the same voice) insisted that I was beautiful and he wanted to meet me. He knew that I wanted to meet him as well. After all, I had given him my phone number. We could meet in secret, he said. Anywhere I wanted. Hanging up did not deter the callers. The phone rang repeatedly.

Bewildered, I spoke to my family about the persistent calls. My thirteen year old son understood immediately. Laughing, he told me about the Saudis at the camel races and his friends who had, as a gag, put *his* phone number on the paper they tossed to the enamored men. Each time I answered the phone, the young Saudis thought I was one of the blonds they had followed. Encouraged and persistent, they were determined to meet the American girls who by virtue of having provided a phone number must be equally interested in a clandestine and unlawful date.

I was most puzzled by the lack of reasoning by the young men. Even if the girls had put their own phone numbers on the tossed paper, why would the Saudi men not suppose a mother might be the one to answer the phone instead of the girls they sought? My voice surely did not have the lilt of a twelve year old. Further, why would they think an American mother would find such overtures toward her daughter acceptable?

To stop the nuisance calls of the would-be suitors, we had to have the compound switch board monitor all incoming phone calls.

* * *

We had always enjoyed camping and decided to spend a night on the sand dunes west of the city. It was spring time. The weather was pleasant in the late afternoon when we arrived to set up our little camp on the rolling breadth of sand. No one was within miles of us. We were well beyond city lights.

We hiked the dunes, ate our picnic, and spread our sleeping bags. Alone in the dark and silent Arabian night, we were ready to watch stars come out in the expansive sky. My sons were first to notice the unusual sight to our right. Turning, we all observed a reddish light approximately twenty degrees above the horizon that initially appeared to be the anti-collision beacon of an aircraft. The craft, moving rapidly in our general direction, advanced in a zigzag manner that had us immediately curious and uneasy.

"What aircraft can make turns like that?" I gasped, barely above a whisper, hoping my husband had a logical explanation for what we were watching. The turns were extremely abrupt and squared-off, not rounded as one would expect at that apparent speed. The combination of high speed and extremely sharp turns would have, according to my fighter pilot husband, generated G-loads far in excess of what any known operational aircraft or pilots could sustain.

Though likely a number of miles distant, the roar of its engine was loud enough to be clearly heard. Soon all we could see of the mysterious craft was a light or perhaps both a white and a red light. Whatever it was, the craft had climbed to a position nearly overhead, and we lost sight of it due to a mid-level cloud layer. The engine roar continued for another half minute or so and then faded to silence.

"What in the heck was that?" was our only stunned utterance. After several minutes of pondering, no one ventured a guess. We continued to lie on our sleeping bags, marveling at the mysterious flight we had just witnessed and feeling strangely vulnerable when the itching started. Felt first on our ankles and wrists, it spread to our arms and legs. We shook out our sleeping bags and wiped our skin with wet cloths. The itching intensified until it was unbearable. We moved to the inside of our automobile, hoping that would bring relief. The torment worsened until we knew there was nothing to do but abandon our Arabian night on the sand dunes and return home.

Bathing and applying every anti-itch ointment we had did not stop the intense discomfort. There was no sleep for any of us that night. The next day we made a trip to the doctor on the Corps of Engineers Compound, but even he could not discern the source of our misery, though the irritation was obvious. "This part of the world is full of parasites," he said. Whatever the cause, the itching lasted for two weeks and then vanished as abruptly as it had come.

We were never again willing to camp on the sand dunes. However, a number of men, hearing of the strange flying object we had seen, made trips to the Arabian Desert at night, hoping to witness the mysterious craft. None, to my knowledge, ever did.

* * *

"Allah willing" was the philosophy that prevailed in all areas of Saudi life. Even if hours of operation were posted, businesses rarely opened their doors according to any predictable schedule. Appointments were only suggestions and had little bearing on when one would actually begin the day's business. Forecasts of the weather, wishes for good health, and all plans were conditioned by *Insh'allah*. The expression gave verbal acknowledgement that God alone controls the lives of mankind. It also provided an excuse for any change of plans.

During a weekend trip to Jeddah, we had a typical Arabian Insh'allah experience. In that port city on the coast of the Red Sea, we discovered an abundance of barely used luxury cars. Wealthy Saudi Arabians drive the latest models of expensive automobiles, making the used car market very interesting. One automobile in particular caught our attention. We were told that it belonged to a member of the Royal Family whose driver used it only to transport the prince's children to school. The car was in the lot on consignment.

The dealership was about to close for the evening. My husband, anxious to bargain for purchase of the automobile, made an appointment to meet the merchant at ten o'clock the following morning. Insh'allah, of course.

My husband excitedly drove to the used car market, arriving early for the appointment. Hours later, after mid-day prayers, the merchant finally arrived. No apology or explanation was offered. Merchants opened their businesses when Allah willed and it was impossible to predict when that might be.

*   *   *

Saudi military pilots were trained wholly in the United States. The Kingdom's military bases were, therefore, operational in function with contingents of American military advisors assigned to each base. Royal Saudi Air Force bases were in Dhahran on the Persian Gulf side, Taif on the north-western side, and Khamis Mushayt in southern Arabia near the Yemen border.

My husband traveled to the various bases regularly, both in his capacity as an advisor and to fly the F-15 with sufficient regularity to maintain flight proficiency. On occasion, my sons and I joined him on excursions to remote sites. The trips allowed us to visit with friends and to experience the uniqueness of each area.

We flew to Khamis Mushayt for a weekend. Rural and traditional, Khamis bore little resemblance to the capital city. There were no construction projects. Most roads were not paved. Houses were old. Most surprising, a few women and their daughters, their veils exposing their eyes, worked in the souqs. Old women, draped in black, sat on folded chairs watching the market activity and keeping their daughters and grand-daughters company.

The women were not reluctant to talk with us. In fact, they aggressively bargained the price of their wares. These women were obviously poor, but they possessed a freedom I never saw afforded women in Riyadh.

In one souq, a young girl who may have been in her teens was not wearing a veil. She smiled pleasantly, eager to sell us the goods of her particular souq. Fresh-faced, her youthful appeal was winsome and without hint of guile. We asked permission to photograph her and she agreed enthusiastically.

But first she needed time to make herself ready. And, she wanted a copy of the photo. I wondered why she did not fear the capture of her spirit in the camera – especially one that could quickly reproduce her likeness.

After several minutes out of sight behind the plywood counter, she stood up ready to be photographed. The fresh face was now covered with heavy, dark make-up and she wore dark lipstick. Her pose was rigid. The smile was gone. She had replaced her natural beauty and youthful feminine appeal with what, I supposed, she considered a more glamorous countenance.

The market place was comprised of open-air stands without roofs, much like one might expect in a swap meet. All of life's necessities for the Bedouin settlement were available for purchase. There were baskets of eggs, dates, and round flat bread. Live goats and sheep were tied to posts, bleating their opposition to being restrained. Caged chickens were for sale. Squawking and flapping, their legs were bound together for the purchaser's trip home. Or if wanted, one could have his fresh chicken killed and dressed on the spot. Feathers flew in the breeze and settled like snow over the entire market.

I was instantly reminded of my mother's chicken business on our farm in Arizona and how she, too, could wring the necks of chickens and remove their feathers while her customers waited.

There were all the usual souqs with spices, fruit, soaps, and baskets. We found a Moses basket and one for a snake charmer; both were probably from Africa. Large enough to hold an infant or a large snake, the baskets were popular with expatriates. We used ours to store cassette tapes, the many we had purchased at the *747* souq of boot-legged music.

Silver Bedouin jewelry was prevalent. Worn by women of the desert, the crudely formed jewelry had come from Yemen. I purchased a thick, heavy bracelet and a rather strange tube with an attached rod fitted inside an empty chamber. The Saudi woman who sold it to me put the rod to her eye-lashes in a motion as if putting on mascara. I could only guess what Bedouin mascara was made of and how one would fill the tube with the black, gooey substance.

We picnicked in the rugged hills outside Khamis Mushayt. Massive protruding boulders surrounded by tufts of grass shaped the slopes. A young boy who could not have been older than eight was alone on the boulders tending a flock of sheep. He watched for predators and brought back straying lambs with a roughly formed shepherd's crook. I did not see either a sling-shot or dagger belted on the outside of his thobe. His shepherd's crook may have been the only weapon he had for defense of himself and his sheep, should a wild animal threaten them.

I thought of David, shepherd boy of the Bible and author of the beloved Twenty-third Psalm, who as a child tended his father's sheep and though an unlikely choice as the youngest of Jesse's sons was anointed to become king of Israel.

Exploring the rugged hills, we came across mysterious caves. In one we found a human skull, long ago abandoned and apparently unclaimed. Bleached white with age, the skull had what appeared to be a single, large caliber bullet hole through it.

Tribal warfare was common in Arabia's past, and the region has a history of honor killings. Still, I wondered why the remains had not long ago been buried. Perhaps the cave was the scene of the killing and the murdered victim was never found. It is also possible that we had stumbled upon what was meant to be a burial cave. My husband photographed the skull and cave and we left, wondering what intrigue so long ago had ended the life of that person.

We had been asked to visit Khamis Mushayt specifically to consider moving there. My husband had been offered the command of the American Air Force contingency of advisors who served in the remote station. The existing American commander was nearing the end of his tour.

After visiting Khamis Mushayt, charming though it was, we decided it was far too remote with even fewer ways to alleviate boredom than in larger cities. The available international school was incredibly small and lacked the opportunities we wanted for our sons. Khamis Mushayt was a great place to visit, but the capital city of Riyadh provided as much cultural adjustment as I was willing to make.

*   *   *

We made several car trips, driving the approximately 275 miles from Riyadh to Dhahran on the eastern coast of Arabia. As in any trip between Riyadh and other cities, there were no places to stop for food, beverages, or even bathrooms. There was an occasional gasoline station, but none had toilets. The attendant pointed toward a sand dune or a bush – in one direction for the men and another for the women.

About three hours inland from Dhahran was the Bedouin village of Hofuf. Located in one of the world's largest oases, Hofuf is the third oldest continually inhabited city in the world. Despite its remoteness, Hofuf is considered the date capital of the world, and its weekly camel market attracts buyers from around the globe. One can, in addition to purchasing camels, secure a ride on the beast of burden known as "the ship of the desert," drink its milk, or buy raw camel meat.

The legendary Arab Friday market is what brought us to Hofuf. Expatriates who had previously visited the ancient city insisted it was well worth the trip. We were not disappointed. Dramatically different from the souqs in Riyadh and even those in Khamis Mushayt, the Hofuf market was what we envisioned trading fairs in Mecca during the days of Mohammed would have been like. The only features missing from those of earlier days were the placement of idols on the Ka'aba and the flourishing slave trade.

The covered women's market had an abundance of crafts. There was plenty of gold jewelry from which to choose and even more of the crudely hammered silver Bedouin jewelry from Yemen. Colorful African baskets woven in differing styles and sizes were neatly stacked. Copper pots in various stages of tarnish were displayed. Brass coffee pots with long pouring spouts, the traditional pot of Saudi Arabia, shone with polished brilliance. Every imaginable kind of spice was available in bulk and could be scooped from tall baskets, weighed and sold by the gram: cardamom to flavor coffee, sesame seeds, and any spice desired to cover the taste of spoiled meat. Leather camel bags and saddles hung ready for purchase. Sheaths for Arabian daggers, which so many men wore, were plentiful. Hofuf is known for its locally woven fabrics and camel wool rugs.

A huge outdoor market with dozens of stalls shaded by thatched roofs bordered the covered women's market. We were intrigued by roughly constructed Bedouin baby cradles.

The beds were made of what appeared to be the central shafts of palm fronds, trimmed and woven while still pliable. Absent mattresses, I wondered what was used for padding across the hard, round rungs. Perhaps camel leather, sheep wool, or woven rugs provided the softness needed for babies of the desert who would be rocked to sleep in those cradles.

The crowded market was noisy, not only from the clamoring of hundreds of Arab shoppers who were bargaining for the best price but also from the bleating of animals and the squawking of chickens. Animals, particularly goats, wandered freely between stalls. Along with sheep, they could be purchased and herded to their new destinations. Hobbled camels stood, their tails switching as they munched hay. Noisy chickens were crowded together in wooden cages.

Fresh eggs filled baskets, as did almonds and spices. Moist dates, grown on palm trees in Hofuf, filled other baskets. Fresh fruit and vegetables were piled on counters and placed in front of the stalls. Bunches of bananas hung from thatched roofs, along with garlic, leeks, and onions.

Large chunks of raw meat and whole slaughtered chickens were tied to ropes and suspended from roofs of the stalls without benefit of refrigeration. Permeated with the odor of a barnyard, the area was swarming with flies. No one seemed to mind the pests that covered the raw meat and the faces of children.

If after visiting the markets one had an appetite for local food, there was plenty available. Lamb kabobs, falafel, hummus, and tabouleh were ready for the serving, along with plenty of hot sweetened tea.

With our Bedouin baby cradle propping open the back of the car, we left the Friday market and drove through the residential section of the settlement. Rows of old mud brick structures similar to tenements were set back from the dirt road. None could have had plumbing, heating, or cooling, although an occasional residence had a window refrigeration unit powered by a generator. The residences opened onto dirt yards without grass, trees, or fences. There were no flowers. The only color was that of dirt.

Barefoot children whose clothing was soiled and dismal played outdoors, poking about the dirt with sticks or chasing animals that roamed freely. Several women stood in the doorways of their ancient mud huts. Leaning wearily against door frames, they stared out onto a barren, communal yard where children played.

I was immediately gripped by the haunting, desperate eyes of these women who were draped in black and wearing the veil of the poor. Their exposed eyes were neither seductive nor alluring. There was no hint of music or laughter or joy. All hope was gone from the eyes of women whose lives had been reduced to simple endurance. Life had given them little materially and apparently even less honor.

My husband remarked, "If this is not squalor, I don't know what is."

* * *

From Saudi Arabia we had wonderful travel opportunities outside the country. The Kingdom provided us a round trip home each year, and we could apply its value to any travel we wished. Africa, Asia, and Europe were all readily accessible from our residence in the Middle East.

Booking travel through local agents was frustrating and never simple. However, it was at times quite amusing. Itineraries, common in the United States, were not provided. Airline tickets showed the departure time but not the arrival time in the city of destination.

My husband planned to fly from Riyadh to New York. He asked the travel agent for the arrival time in the American city; it was not on his ticket. The agent seemed puzzled, and my husband repeated the request. "What time will it be in New York when I get there?"

After a long pause, the agent responded, "Don't you have a watch? When you get to New York, look at your watch and see what time it is."

* * *

A few years before our arrival in Saudi Arabia, a Saudia Airliner, the official carrier of the Kingdom, burned while sitting on the runway in Riyadh, killing all 301 passengers and crew members on board. A fire had broken out in the cargo area shortly after take-off, and the plane returned to the departing airport but only after the flight crew wasted several critical minutes with indecision.

Even after landing, the flight crew, apparently inept at handling an emergency of that magnitude, sat on the runway for another twenty-three minutes without initiating evacuation orders. The third officer reportedly thumbed through his flight manual muttering, "No problem, no problem," as fire and smoke filled the cabin. The burned hull of the airliner remained in full view at the Riyadh airport years later – a grim reminder of the tragic event and the Arab pride that surely contributed to the disaster.

The failure to act in a timely manner to a flight emergency was incomprehensible to me. I recalled from the first days of my husband's own flight training, the hours and hours of study necessary to memorize procedural steps for every conceivable emergency. He drilled endlessly until the emergency checklists were so familiar he could act instinctively. Even I as his "drill-mate" could recite any number of in-flight procedures.

Americans can only wonder at the pride that prevented the flight crew of Saudia Airlines from admitting a crisis existed and that emergency action needed to be taken. Who can forget, in contrast, the words of the American astronaut aboard Apollo Thirteen who was quoted as saying to the NASA control center in Houston, "Hey, we've got a problem here." The Arab answer, unfortunately, is more likely to be, "No problem. I can handle it."

The inability to admit a problem and take corrective action was reminiscent of the Iranian student pilots who trained in the United States. They, too, could not admit error. *"Masha'allah,"* if Allah wills was their mantra. It was better to die than to admit a problem or an error.

*　　*　　*

Could it be possible that his sense of Arab honor prevented Iraq's President Saddam Hussein from admitting he no longer had weapons of mass destruction when the entire world believed he did? Could his need to preserve honor have been more important than the crushing blows of United Nations sanctions against his country and the subsequent toppling of his regime?

*   *   *

Saudia Airlines, because it was the official air carrier of the Kingdom, did not serve alcohol or pork at any time. Other carriers who serviced Saudi Arabia provided both the forbidden drink and meat as soon as they were no longer over Saudi airspace. Travelers joked at how quickly the service changed and bottles came out once outside the boundaries of the Islamic state.

One of the first places we and other expatriates looked for in terminals outside the Kingdom was McDonald's. The fast food restaurant was not available in Saudi Arabia, and for that reason we dreamed of Big Macs. The air terminal in Singapore had a modern McDonald's that was always open. It did not matter if we arrived at five in the morning; our first stop, even before claiming baggage, was to satisfy a "Big Mac Attack." We were not alone. Expatriates from many nations, eager for a change from the chicken and goat meals that were common in the Kingdom, crowded into lines of the restaurant.

*   *   *

We flew from Riyadh to Cairo, Egypt, aboard Saudia Airlines. The flight was nearly full, and the seats seemed particularly close together. Despite not having requested a seating change, our family of four was ushered to the first class section though we had paid for coach. The extra space and better service helped to calm my apprehension at flying the national carrier.

The following morning as we stepped outside our hotel, I was utterly appalled by the poverty and squalor in downtown

Cairo. Strewn trash was knee deep along the curbs. Filth and garbage rotted in the streets. The resultant stench increased as the temperature rose.

Sidewalks were crowded with beggars: children, the lame, the old, and women. Desperate humans with all manner of deformities and amputations sat near buildings, their hands open and their eyes pleading for help. Wooden carts, filled with everything from trash to bundles of sticks and crude furniture, were being pulled by donkeys or by emaciated oxen. The animals moved slowly through the ancient streets of the country that long ago was home to Joseph and Moses of the Bible, to Cleopatra, and to countless Pharaohs. In the midst of all the squalor, there was no shortage of interesting places to tour, causing us to wish we had allotted more time in the ancient country.

We visited a papyrus factory for a demonstration of how the writing material, which dates back to 4000 B.C., is produced. Paper was made from cyperus papyrus, a plant that grew along the Nile River. Papyrus was Egypt's primary export, and there was no substitute for it until Arabs began producing pulp paper, which was easier to make but less durable. Eventually, the market for papyrus paper disappeared, as did the plants from which it had been produced.

Papyrus making was not revived until around 1969. The ancient methods had been kept a well-guarded secret; there remained no written records as to how to produce the writing material. Through diligent research and experimentation, an Egyptian scientist Dr. Hassan Ragab discovered the secret process and reintroduced the art to Egypt. Dr. Ragab started a papyrus plantation using roots of the papyrus plant that he found in the Sudan and Ethiopia. His initial plantation was located at Jacob Island at Giza, which is also known as the Pharaonic Village.

Eager for Egyptian souvenirs, we purchased papyrus drawings of King Tut and his Queen Nefertiti, the hieroglyphic alphabet, and a Kartouch of our family name. Next we visited the gold shops for necklaces with our names spelled in ancient hieroglyphics. We were photographed riding camels while pyramids formed a backdrop. At night we watched the light and sound show over the Sphinx with its crumbling nose.

Unfortunately, the Museum in Cairo that houses the King Tut exhibition was closed during our time in the city. We were to see a portion of that collection years later in Los Angeles instead of in Egypt.

While touring the ancient pyramids, my husband forged ahead photographing everything. Our guide, pretending seriousness, said to me, "I watch husband. You pay twenty dollars. I make sure he not find Egyptian girls." I laughed at his joke.

He responded in feigned concern, "Oh, Madam, men from Saudi Arabia look for Egyptian girls. Pay twenty dollars. I watch husband for you!"

In Giza, we toured the Cheops pyramid. Our guide led us through dark tunnels that were so low we had to stoop. About midway to the burial room, his lantern went out. Muttering in Arabic, he left us in the dark and hurried back to the entrance only to return with pieces of newspaper and matches instead of another lantern. We saw the rest of the pyramid and the hieroglyphics by the light of paper torches. Each lasted only a few seconds, and the poor man was continually burning his fingers and using Arabic expletives.

*   *   *

My Egyptian friend with whom I taught in the international school had been surprised when I told her I admired the work done to improve women's lives by the wife of Egyptian President Anwar Sadat. Mrs. Jehan Sadat, who had an M.A. from Cairo University and later earned a Ph.D., was known for promoting education for females. She spoke against plural marriages and honor killings. Mrs. Sadat was able to have laws changed, granting women more rights in custody and alimony after divorce. Her reforms were often called "Jehan's Laws."

"How do you know about her?" My friend asked. She was surprised that anyone in America knew or cared about the struggles women faced in her country or that our media had any interest in informing us of her country's issues. She then told me of outrage she felt when an Egyptian judge had divorced his wife for producing only female children.

"How could a judge be so ignorant?" she fumed. "He has been to college. He should know better."

* * *

Mohammed Atta, leader of the 9-11 attack on America, was from Egypt. Educated in Germany, he attended the Al Quds Mosque in Hamburg where radical Islam was taught. Atta's views were fueled by his disillusionment with his native Egypt, its squalor and nepotism, and most of all its failure to enforce Islamic law. Likely, Jehan's Laws, granting new rights and protection to Egyptian women, were seen by Mohammed Atta as proof of that failure.

Mohammed Atta flew American Airlines Flight 11 into the North Tower of the World Trade Center, and his cousin Marwan Al-Shehhi, who attended the same mosque in Germany, flew United Airlines Flight 175 into the South Tower.

* * *

From Cairo, we flew to Tunis, capital city of Tunisia and home to the North Africa American Cemetery and Memorial. Extremely well maintained, the cemetery was obviously a place of honor for the 2,841 military dead buried there. White crosses and Stars of David marked the graves, primarily of American soldiers who gave their lives in Morocco, Algeria, and in the liberation of Tunisia – countries with large Muslim populations.

Soldiers from every state except Hawaii and the District of Columbia were laid to rest beneath the expansive green meadow. In three instances, two brothers lay side by side in burial, compounding unspeakable grief for their families.

The adjacent chapel contained the national flag of the United States of America as well as Christian and Jewish flags. Beneath the three flags was the following inscription:

ALMIGHTY GOD, RECEIVE THESE THY HEROIC SERVANTS INTO THY KINGDOM

As I gazed across the field, I was struck by the amazing heroism of American soldiers. Our young men have always been willing to go where needed, to fight for freedom and to liberate people they will never know. Understanding full-well the cost of freedom, American soldiers do not choose death. They choose life. Despite the life-threatening risks inherent in their service, they are willing to press forward, to fight in the face of evil and against incredible odds.

Loving life, valuing freedom, and serving country, thousands of young Americans died in Northern Africa where their bodies remained buried in hallowed ground and bearing witness to their incredible sacrifice.

Osama bin Laden, after 9-11 said, "We love death. The United States loves life. That is the big difference between us." He was right. But the difference is not merely "big." The difference in our values is profound. While our soldiers risk death to free the oppressed *of any religion* from tyranny, his jihadists choose death as a means of enslaving those who are not under the veil of Islam.

There are countless examples of heroism and uncommon valor from the men and women who have served in Afghanistan and Iraq in defense of freedom. They, like the heroes buried in Tunis, are owed an immense debt of gratitude from a nation whose liberty they have secured.

*   *   *

A grenade landed in the humvee – powerful enough to implode the military vehicle and kill all five crewmembers aboard. Without hesitation and in an act of selfless heroism, the young soldier threw himself on top of the grenade, absorbing the full impact of the explosion in his own body. Private First Class Ross McGinnis died that day in Iraq in an act of extraordinary heroism that saved the lives of his four crew mates.

President George W. Bush awarded our nation's highest military honor posthumously to Private McGinnis. The Congressional Medal of Honor was presented in a ceremony attended by the young man's family and the four uniformed soldiers whose lives he saved.

Not a day goes by that we don't think about him, the four, gripped with emotion, declared.

* * *

Ongoing excavations in Tunis had uncovered evidence of several distinct civilizations. Not an independent state until 1956, Tunisia had been ruled by disparate groups: among them the Phoenicians, Arab Muslims, the Roman Empire, the Ottoman Empire, the Spanish, and the French. We were fascinated by the ancient baths and the intricate tiled designs formed by Roman artisans. There were remains of ancient Carthage. The eighth century Islamic mosque *Zitouna* still stands.

Older women in this Muslim culture were veiled as they shopped in the market places of Tunis. Teenagers of both sexes, however, wore Western clothing, met openly at coffee houses, publicly smoked the hubbly-bubbly and had few of the restrictions common in Saudi Arabia. A teen-aged boy, dressed in Levi jeans and Nikes, volunteered to become our guide to the city.

On an early morning walking tour with him, we encountered a small boy who was no older than four. Alone and abandoned, the child, without any covering for warmth, was curled in sleep on the sidewalk. Our young guide muttered in annoyance and directed us around the street waif. I was horrified, but the guide shrugged his shoulders and said, "The streets are full of these boys. They cause many problems."

On our return walk, after visiting the ancient ornate mosque and modern government buildings, we saw the same soiled child in tattered rags. He was still lying asleep but, having been pushed off the sidewalk, was now lying among the bushes.

I wondered about a culture that is proud of its centuries-old mosques, its archaeological digs, and burial grounds but discards helpless children and then is annoyed by their struggle to survive. The call to prayer five times each day was observed. Women were veiled. Pilgrims made the annual Hajj to Mecca. The month of Ramadhan was celebrated annually and the fasting was meant to create compassion for the poor. Mohammed was honored as Allah's messenger, but children, street waifs, starved and slept on sidewalks.

* * *

During Spring break we made our much-anticipated African safari in Kenya. Because we had been told to take unused clothing to use for barter, our suitcases were filled with jeans, tee shirts, and shoes before we flew across the Red Sea into Nairobi. The doorman at the hotel was the first to ask if we had items to trade. He and the bell-hops eagerly sorted through our stash of clothing, and in no time we had empty suitcases to fill with souvenirs.

The market in Nairobi was as traditional and aromatic as any in Saudi Arabia, but it was far more colorful with an abundance of plants and flowers. It didn't have the restrictions or sexual tension of the Kingdom. Neither did it have the sense of safety. One needed to be ever vigilant against theft in this African city.

Joining us on safari was a family from Sweden who also lived as expatriates in Saudi Arabia, though we had not met them prior to our safari. Our families spent a week touring Kenya, staying at luxury lodges such as The Mount Kenya Safari Club and The Ark as well as in more traditional lodgings of tents where we slept on cots draped in mosquito nets.

The Mount Kenya Safari Club with its vast, beautifully landscaped yards had peacocks and other exotic birds in residence. Wild animals came onto the grounds at night. We sat on the veranda sipping cold drinks and watched a parade of African animals we had never seen outside of zoos.

We were treated to traditional tribal dances and a reenactment of a Masaai hunting party. The guttural, throaty sound made by Masaai warriors was chilling. It was easy to imagine the terror opposing tribes must have felt when hearing the unmistakable advance of their enemy. Legend says the Masaai, who at one time was one of the most feared tribes in Africa, required each boy to kill a lion as a rite of manhood. The throaty sound Masaai warriors made was not unlike the bark, the throaty cough of male lions as they mark their territory each morning.

The Ark was elevated on stilts near a natural watering hole. Animals began coming to drink in the late afternoon and continued to come throughout the night. We were alerted by bells in our rooms or knocks on the door when particularly large game came to drink. We got up many times during the hours of darkness to see elephant, zebra, gazelle, giraffe, and hippos. The most dramatic sight was a middle of the night fight between two male rhinos. The carcass of the defeated animal lay at the edge of the water the following morning, providing food for the many eager, scavenging fowl.

Both the Safari Club and the Ark still had a strong British influence that resulted in the serving of afternoon tea and formal evening meals. We carefully heeded warnings not to eat fish or drink unbottled water in Kenya. Nevertheless, we each had a turn with the most violent digestive distress imaginable during our stay at the Mount Kenya Safari Club. So did the family from Sweden. Only our African guide escaped the twenty-four hours of misery we each endured.

The Kenyan government officially forbids tourism of the Masaai who form the most traditional tribe still living in Kenya. We were assured, however, that our tour guide for the right price would be more than happy to arrange an "off the record" visit to a Masaai village.

Our van stopped short of the village. Leaving us, our African guide, David, walked well outside our hearing to meet with a group of Masaai men. The tall, thin tribal leaders, each wrapped in red fabric, leaned against their poles and bartered our visit. I wondered how much David offered the Masaai and how much he kept for himself.

We were then driven to the traditional village that was filled with women and children. The Masaai men stayed at a distance and continued to lean against their poles, legs crossed, perhaps planning how to use their newly acquired cash.

The Masaai women wore red wraps that, in many cases, did not cover both breasts. Children rode on their mothers' hips with easy access to lunch or on their mothers' backs. Everyone was barefoot. Little girls were draped in cloths similar to those of their mothers, but young boys were naked.

Most women wore colorful, multi-strand beaded necklaces they had made. Their ears had been pierced and the lobes stretched into elongated shapes. Blocks of wood and sticks were used to stretch the openings in the ear lobes of the young females, even toddlers. Proudly, the women of the tribe decorated their pierced ears with long, looped strands of beads.

Red clay covered most of their exposed skin, including their bald scalps. Flies swarmed and I supposed the clay helped shield against bites. So prevalent were the flies that no one bothered to brush them away. They hung onto children's eyes, mouths, and noses, sucking moisture and surely spreading disease.

We had been given multiple vaccinations prior to moving to Saudi Arabia and quinine tablets to prevent malaria before traveling to Africa. The Masaai had no such protection. However, they had received small-pox vaccinations, as evidenced by a large circular scar on each woman's arm. The World Health Organization in eradicating this dread disease had reached even the Masaai, though the tribe continued to live in their traditional way.

The life expectancy for Masaai women is no better than that of Bangladeshi women. Sa'eed, our houseboy in the Kingdom, had said his mother was very, very old at forty. I could only guess at the ages of these African women who were weathered and wrinkled from years in the unrelenting sun. They lived the most primitive of lives without any semblance of healthcare. No doubt, they were much younger in actual years than their apparent age.

The women and children were happy to pose for pictures. Several of the women asked, with hand motions, to try on my sunglasses. We got wonderful photos of them grinning, some toothlessly, wearing my shades and holding my hands, something they all seemed to want to do.

One on each side of me, the women affectionately continued to hold my hands as they took me to tour one of their homes. A small domed structure shaped with tree branches and plastered with cow dung, the home was about the size of a small camping tent. Each dwelling was low, no more than five feet tall with one entry covered with a flap of cow hide. I dropped to my knees, pushed the cow hide aside and crawled through the opening into a dark, smoky space. Inside were more hides serving as beds on the bare ground. The remnants of a wood fire glowed in the center of the small living area while its lingering smoke escaped through a hole in the dung-plastered roof. I complimented the homes with smiles, oohs, and aahs, knowing my English would not be understood. The women were pleased and squeezed my hands appreciatively. As we crawled out of the home, other women pressed forward, insisting on their turn to hold my hands. Fortunately, no such gesture was made toward my sons, who may have been "freaked out" had the bare-breasted women tried to show them similar affection!

Constructed by the women of the tribe, the homes formed a circle with the herd of life-sustaining cows kept in the center. Cows' blood mixed with milk was still the primary diet of the Masaai. Long, dried gourds were the vessels for collecting both. Children who no longer rode on their mothers' backs each carried a gourd, the Masaai version of a baby bottle. These tribal people grow tall, but evidence of their poor diet shows in their rotted teeth and the pot bellies of their children.

Our day packs were filled with the small candies we had been told to bring. Both women and children began pointing and tugging at our packs in excited anticipation. We opened the bags to squeals of delight. Wrapped candy spilled out and everyone, including the women, rushed forward just as when a piñata is broken.

David, who had kept at a distance during our visit, returned for us when our arranged time was up. As we drove away from the village, the smiling women waved and the naked children ran after the van.

Not far from the Masaai village we stopped at a small trading post. Several women came to the windows of the van, their rotted teeth evident. With hands open, they begged for anything we could give them. We had a few containers of yogurt and some cookies but not much else. The African women eagerly took what we had to give.

Continuing our safari, we drove through the Rift Valley in the early morning of Palm Sunday. In a beautiful, picturesque area, we passed a whitewashed building that could have been a boarding school or a Christian mission. A long line of African children, dressed in incredibly colorful clothing, formed a parade across the grassy yard. They waved branches and joyfully sang as they reenacted the triumphal entry Jesus made into Jerusalem just five days before his crucifixion. The sweet voices of the children singing in their African language and the obvious joy of the event brought tears to our eyes.

I was instantly reminded of the contrast with Islamic life in Saudi Arabia. Unlike the Kenyan children, boys and girls in the Kingdom do not attend school together, they do not wear colorful clothing, and they do not sing or have public processionals of joy. Most importantly, they have little choice in the direction of their lives and no choice in the religion that will govern every aspect of their future.

Our van stopped at many trading posts across the country where vendors sold everything from wooden and soapstone carved animals to roughly formed machetes and spears. Beaded Masaai necklaces and woven baskets were always available. Most of the vendors spoke English, and some told of having learned our language in Christian mission schools. They were both pleased and amused by our efforts to bargain in Swahili.

One young female vendor insisted on showing me her Bible and proudly proclaimed that she knew how to read it. Missionaries had taught her, she said. The villages and landscape of Kenya looked remarkably the same as I remembered seeing in photographs thirty years earlier when missionaries visited my church and described their work on the African continent. I marveled that so little of the infrastructure had changed. But evidence of education, medical care, and the gratitude of the people was abundant.

As we traversed the Savanna, we were taken very close to a lion pride that had found refuge from the afternoon heat in the shade of a tree. The sleepy male, showing his teeth only in his languid yawns, was surrounded by females and cubs that paid little attention as our van moved slowly toward them. They stretched, shifted their heavy bodies, and twitched their long tails unconcerned by our approach. Our driver knew his limits and took us as close as possible without endangering anyone. We were able to stand inside the van, our heads outside the opened roof, to watch the lion pride just a few feet from us. As evening approached, we went to the Mara River. From our vantage point, we could see a lioness on the opposite bank as she lay in wait at the side of the path used by animals to reach the water's edge. There were numerous crocodiles in the muddy, green, foamy water of the river, compounding the danger to thirsty animals.

The Mara is considered the most dangerous river in Africa. While the waters appear peaceful on the surface, there is a treacherous undercurrent beneath. During the annual migration of wildebeests, hundreds of the massive herd animals die crossing the crocodile infested water.

From the river bank but across the plain, we caught a glimpse of a cheetah in a brief, explosive chase. We saw numerous elephants and giraffes and great herds of gazelle, zebra, and musk oxen.

When we returned to our hotel in Nairobi after the safari, we were met by the door-man who was proudly wearing the wing-tip dress shoes my husband had exchanged in barter. He told us his sons were thrilled to have the jeans, tennis shoes, and tee shirts we had brought.

*   *   *

During the morning of August 7, 1998, the United States Embassies in Nairobi, Kenya, and in neighboring Tanzania were attacked with truck bombs. Twelve American diplomats, about two hundred Kenyans, and eleven Tanzanians died in the attacks. Thousands were injured. Al Qaeda, the terrorist network of Osama bin Laden, was responsible for the attack that senselessly killed and injured so many.

*   *   *

In the year before moving to the Kingdom, my older son began having pain in his right knee. It was most noticeable when he participated in sports. The knee was examined, xrayed, and determined to have a small bone spur. We were told to monitor it. Gradually the pain increased until it could no longer be merely monitored.

There are hospitals in the Kingdom, Royal Hospitals that are staffed by multi-national nurses, but they were not recommended for the care of U.S. military families. My son and husband were flown aboard a United States C-141 med-evac aircraft from Saudi Arabia to the United States Army hospital in Wiesbaden, Germany. There, my son received state of the art surgery to remove the spur and confirm the absence of malignancy. I remained in Riyadh with our younger son and anxiously awaited daily phone calls from the hospital.

After a week of hospital care and in a full leg cast, my son was allowed to return to our home in the Kingdom. He was still in the cast a month later when we departed on a two week Greek Island cruise. During the many off-ship tours of ancient sites, he was frequently asked why his leg was in a cast. Growing tired of explaining his surgery, he resorted to an easier answer.

"I fell out of a tree," he began to say.

Some questioners scratched their heads. "Where in Saudi Arabia is there a tree tall enough for such an injury?" They wondered aloud.

Our cruise ship delivered us to ancient and exotic cities with histories as rich and varied as the designs on Persian rugs. Each island was unique in its attractions and flavor. Rhodes, a large city with modern shops, was known for luxurious fur coats, Roman and Greek pottery, and gold jewelry.

Patmos, the island to which the Apostle John was exiled in the first century A.D., gleamed with white-washed structures jutting out from sloping hills. We climbed to several of the ancient dwellings and wondered if we were near any that had been a place of refuge for the Apostle.

Small green trees stunted by wind, sandy soil, and sea water added a pleasant softness against stark white buildings. Shimmering clear ocean water reflected the island's beauty. The sky, without a hint of air pollution, was a spectacular blue with drifting puffs of clouds.

Mykonos was my favorite island. There were numerous shops nestled into the hillside ledges of the landscape, much as I might have imagined the terraced dwellings of Peruvian Incas five centuries earlier, except that these structures were all white-washed and perfectly maintained. Glass windows gleamed in the sun. Narrow foot paths zigzagged between small buildings with two or three steps at a time leading to higher ledges.

Patrons sat beneath colorful umbrellas at lively outdoor cafes enjoying pastries made of almonds and apricots and sipping wonderfully aromatic coffees. Bougainvillea, bursting with explosive color, fanned the sides of white walls. Greek music wafted down and between shops as tourists marveled at the abundance of furs and gold jewelry. Below, the beach sparkled with pristine sand against a turquoise ocean.

The island of Santorini offered a mule ride up the steep mountain whose cliffs rose more than a thousand feet above sea level to the ancient village of Thera. Only the most adventurous were willing to brave the long climb to the top, and I was not among them. My husband and sons brought a lovely hand-made lace table scarf back for me as a souvenir of the trip I did not make.

Common to all the beaches were topless swimmers and the practice of changing into one's swimsuit on the beach while, at most, a companion held up a towel for a modicum of privacy. Initially, my younger son did not notice the topless female swimmers, but my older son and my husband immediately did, though they pretended not to have.

Between islands, the cruise ship offered every activity we could imagine. My son who had learned to stop by the Mission Inn for free ice cream sundaes loved the ship. He said his favorite part was reclining in a chaise lounge on the pool deck and having hot consommé served to him. He is clearly a child of my womb! That would be my choice any day instead of a mule ride up a steep cliff!

As we left our cruise ship in Ephesus, cars formed a line and drivers held crudely made signs offering their tour services. We approached the first one. "Do you speak English?" we asked.

"Yes."

"Can you show us Diana of the Ephesians?"

"Yes."

"Do you know where the Grand Theater ruins are?"

"Yes."

"Will you take us to the Hadrian Gates?"

"Yes."

After agreeing on a price, we set off on our tour only to learn "yes" was one of very few English words he knew. He did take us to the sites we wanted to see, but we tagged along within hearing range of other tour groups so that we could listen to their guides explain the wonders of the ancient city.

*   *   *

We sailed through the Bosporus to Istanbul, Turkey. Known as Constantinople under the Roman Empire, the city is considered the gateway between Europe and Asia. There we visited the grand *Hagia Sophia*, a cathedral built as an Eastern Orthodox Church. It remained the largest cathedral in the world for one thousand years and is recognized as one of "the greatest surviving examples of Byzantine architecture. The temple itself was so richly and artistically decorated [that Emperor Justinian I proclaimed,] 'Solomon, I have outdone thee.'"

Led by Sultan Mehmet II, the cathedral was conquered by the Turks in 1453 and converted to an Islamic Mosque. A powerful symbol of the conquest of Constantinople, the cathedral was renamed *Ayasofya Mosque*. Because the depiction of human images is considered blasphemous in Islam, the incredible Byzantine mosaics that filled the church were plastered over.

Hagia Sophia remained a place for prayers to Allah for the next five hundred years until it was converted to a museum in 1935. Major restoration was then undertaken; carpets were removed revealing fabulous marble floors, and the plaster was painstakingly removed from mosaics. Hagia Sophia, as a museum, is a paradox of Christian art and Islamic symbols.

We toured the Sultans' palace, including the quarters for the eunuchs and the opulent living spaces of the Sultans. We saw the areas that had housed the harems. I wondered about Saudi Arabians who were proud to the point of arrogance of never having been colonized, though Arabia was once controlled by the Ottoman Empire. The veiling and seclusion of women had been practiced by the ruling Ottomans before Saudi Arabia became an Islamic state. It seemed strange to me that a people for whom independence was a profound measure of honor would keep and treasure as part of their religion and culture the very rules that had been imposed on them by a foreign government.

On the island of Crete we toured the Palace of Knossos, which was part of an on-going archaeological site. The excavation of this Minoan civilization was started in 1878 and still had many areas of active digging roped off. My younger son ran ahead in a game of tag with his brother who even though in a full leg cast and using crutches gave a pretty good chase.

Looking back as he ran, my son veered off the trail and fell into a dig site that was about twelve feet deep. A site caretaker saw his descent and rushed into the hole, fearing the worst. Carrying the boy out, the caretaker was ashen and speechless. Fortunately, my stunned son did not suffer an injury. The experience provided a good story for years to come. He told classmates that while touring an archaeological dig on the island of Crete, he had "dropped into the palace of a king."

In Athens, Rome, and Corinth we were continually offered "old coins" that enterprising street merchants insisted had been dug up with their own hands only the night before. The authenticity of the coins was guaranteed, we were assured. Strange that so many coins, thousands of years old, were discovered *every* night!

We made trips to Japan and Singapore during our time in the Kingdom. We spent one night in the Persian Gulf State of Bahrain. We very much wanted to visit Israel, the Holy Land, but travel there was impossible. Because Saudi Arabia did not recognize its existence, there were no flights from the Kingdom into the Jewish State. Further, once a passport was stamped with an Israeli visa, re-entrance into the Kingdom was denied.

We hoped to visit Israel on our final trip out of the Middle East, but the only way to do so was to fly from Riyadh to Amman, Jordan and then hope to find a reliable driver whom we could hire to transport us across the border into Israel. Though we hated not to visit Jerusalem, the holy city of Judaism and Christianity and the third holiest site in Islam, we decided that uncertainties about transportation made traveling with two sons, a cat, and a cockatoo quite impracticable.

Before moving to Saudi Arabia, we had thought that a follow-on tour in Europe would be our next choice of assignment. But after two years in the Middle East, even with all the wonderful travel opportunities afforded us, we longed to return to the United States of America.

Sa'eed had it right. "America good place," he had said.

14

AHMED

Ahmed was tall, dark skinned, and good looking. Still in his early twenties, he was young enough to have been my son, had I started producing children as early as Arabian mothers do. His black hair was thick and shiny, and he was mustached in a sign of virility as were all Saudi men. He walked with the swagger of a rock star. After all, he was male, he had money, he was educated, and he was a Saudi. His young female cousins, veiled and hidden from his view, could see how handsome he was, and they surely considered him a catch. Each one undoubtedly hoped her mother and his would arrange a marriage for them.

Ahmed dropped in on us frequently but rarely with prior arrangement. I would receive a phone call from a compound guard informing me there was a guest waiting. Visitors were never allowed to enter the compound unescorted, necessitating me to walk to the gate, a five minute trip, to authorize his presence.

The young Saudi, when comfortably settled into one of the over-stuffed and oddly-colored chairs in our apartment, never seemed to have time constraints. Relaxed and self-assured, Ahmed apparently assumed we would never be too busy for a conversation with him. He was happy to accompany us on souqing excursions and to the newer stores within modern buildings, but most of all, he loved to sit and talk.

His studies in the United States, as well as his travels abroad, had given Ahmed experience outside his native Islamic state. He told me of his jaunts around the world, including the beaches of Hawaii. "Did you wear your thobe on Waikiki?" I asked. The white Saudi robe was what he always wore in the Kingdom.

"Are you kidding?" he responded, laughing. "No way!"

As a male student, all of his education in the United States had been paid for by his government. Continuing his studies in the Kingdom, he traveled from Riyadh to the university he attended in Dhahran, near the Persian Gulf. He never spoke of impending exams or papers due. We heard nothing about his classes, other than his area of study – engineering.

Responding to my curiosity and interest in his culture, he often brought gifts representative of life in Saudi Arabia. One of his gifts, a lovely porcelain coffee pot with a long, curved spout, was trimmed in gold and hand painted in a grape motif. It became part of a permanent display in my home.

Ahmed gladly assumed the role of tutor in all things related to women's lives in the Kingdom, and I peppered him with questions. I realized that everything he told me would be from a male perspective but so were all of the established rules, the enforcement of them, and the honor associated with them. Women were subject to the devices of men in that male dominated culture. Ahmed's viewpoint was, therefore, totally relevant.

My young tutor spoke of the goodness of Islam and that it protects women. "Islam is best for women," he told me on many occasions. He explained that while veiling occurred in pre-Islamic days, it was now something women desired because the veil honored them. Women were set apart from men as special. "Muslim women want the veil," he said. "It is a sign of honor. It protects them."

Had he ever asked the women of his family if they wanted the veil, if they felt honored by it? Perhaps they would have given the standard answer taught them from their youth, the answer expected of them. In the States I had watched documentaries of polygamist groups and cults that diminished women and relegated them to carefully defined roles that served the interests of the men who controlled them. The women, when interviewed for the documentaries, invariably gave identical responses, word for word, to justify the repression they endured. Only a rare woman dared express a desire for change. Why would it be any different in Saudi Arabia?

Ahmed gave me books and pamphlets to read such as *Women and Islam*. I read the materials, all of which were written by Islamic clerics. I learned that under strict Islamic law, Shari'a, women were not only required to veil, they could not wear perfume. Their shoes dared not click as they walked. They were expected to be as quiet and as invisible as possible to avoid the notice of males, who by their very nature were filled with lust. An exposed ear lobe, an ankle, or the scent of seductive perfume had the power to arouse a man beyond his ability to control his actions, the books insisted.

I learned that it was always the responsibility of women, as carriers of the cultural honor, to prevent any untoward behavior against them. The restrictions of Shari'a kept women pure and their families were, therefore, not dishonored.

The written pages offered no suggestions for the care of women who were victims of sexual assault or domestic violence. There was no mention of their physical or emotional trauma. None of Ahmed's books, which he hoped would persuade me that Islam is best for women, mentioned rape counseling, medical care, or protection from further assault.

The books I read did not encourage violated women to report attacks to law enforcement or to seek justice. Saudi Arabian women had to have family male permission to report an assault, and four male witnesses to the crime of rape were required before charges would be filed. Shelters for battered women did not exist.

I knew that Islam allowed a man to have up to four wives at a time and that divorce was very easy for him to obtain. The four wives could change. Polygamy had for centuries been a practice in pre-Islamic Middle-Eastern cultures. But since Islam, Ahmed proclaimed, as though a tremendous benefit had been given women, "A husband is limited to just four wives, and the wives are to be treated equally."

I wondered about the contradiction of Abdul Aziz ibn Sa'ud, the founder of the Islamic state, who had favored wives. What about his numerous other wives? And what about his concubines and slave girls who never became wives?

More recently, the mother of Osama bin Laden was reportedly his father's least favorite wife, causing Osama to be ridiculed by his half-brothers as "The son of the slave woman." If wives are to be treated equally, how then can they be rotated in and out of the fourth wife position as Osama's mother was?

Ahmed explained that multiple wives were allowed for two reasons: First the Prophet Mohammed set the example, and in a surprising lack of discomfiture, Ahmed cited the second reason: "Men are hot. One woman is not enough." It was the same answer given by other Arabian men who had visited our home, but I was surprised that Ahmed, in his desire to present his culture in the most favorable light to an American woman, was so candid. He declared, however, that he and his friends were choosing not to have multiple wives.

"It is too expensive. It causes many problems. The wives are jealous. They pout and they are angry. They fight. They complain and cry. And they want many presents. So it is better to have only one wife."

"That is surely best for all in the family," I said to Ahmed, wanting to explain that Christianity teaches a man is to be the husband of only one wife. Ahmed continued before I could say more.

"My friends and I go out of the country whenever we want and enjoy many women. That is much better than having four wives."

"But, Ahmed," I exclaimed. "Does Islam permit such behavior?"

"Naturally not," he responded. "But that is why we have the prayers."

Men's sexual promiscuity could be prayed away, but women had to be veiled and kept at home to protect family honor! I was outraged!

I knew the preferred marriage for a man was to marry his cousin, the daughter of his father's brother. I asked Ahmed about this issue. After all, he had studied in an American university. Perhaps he had studied genetics.

"That is an old custom," he said, tossing his head. "My friends and I do not want to marry our cousins."

Ah ha, I thought. He gets it. But he continued to surprise me.

"Suppose you marry your cousin and when you see her, you do not like her. You will naturally want a divorce. But your mother will say, 'You cannot divorce her. She is family.' So I think it is better to marry someone who is not family."

Wow! Never had it occurred to me that one's wife was not part of his family unless she was related to him by birth as well. She was merely his possession. Finally, I was beginning to understand the honor code. Family honor. Males of the birth family were dishonored – not the husband who, after all, was not really her family.

As I read his books, I had more questions for Ahmed. I wanted to know about finance and security and safety. To each inquiry, Ahmed explained how Islam had made life better for women.

Before Islam, he explained, women did not receive any inheritance. Now they could receive as much as one-half of what a brother inherited. "Islam provides for women," he said.

Before Islam, women had no legal voice and could not testify. Now, with the kindness of Islam, in some legal matters, two women together giving the same testimony could count as one male voice. "Islam is just," Ahmed proclaimed.

Before Islam, women could not own property. Now, he said, a woman can keep her dowry in divorce, unless she is divorced by her husband for a grave offense. "Islam is fair to women."

He explained that if a woman chooses, she can become a patron of a building by donating money to it. In some cases her name would be inscribed somewhere within the building. And by giving birth to sons, a woman can achieve independence, at least from her husband's family.

Before Islam, women could not keep their children after a divorce. Custody was always given to the man. "Now, women have a chance to keep their children. It happens all the time," Ahmed beamed. "More and more women are keeping their children. It is because of Islam."

Islam outlawed the practice of female infanticide, the burying of unwanted infant daughters in the sand and leaving them to die. It also outlawed the sacrificing of children to idols. "Islam is merciful," Ahmed said.

There were inevitable questions about travel and driving prohibitions and not being allowed to leave one's house alone or to conduct business in public. "You have seen the traffic. We protect our women by driving for them. It is not safe for a woman to be alone. Islam protects women."

"What about education?" I asked. I knew that education is the means of ending poverty. It is the pathway to empowerment and independence. Education leads to a recognition of oppression and a determination to be free. "You have attended school most of your life, but your sisters and other girls are allowed to be educated for only a few years. Why is that?"

Ahmed's response to my questioning about female education was the only time he seemed to carefully choose his words. He knew I was a teacher. I could obviously converse with him on any number of subjects, but in his culture it was not necessary for women to be knowledgeable. Men were in charge, and only they needed to know about affairs of the world. Women could receive all the instruction they needed from the men with whom they lived.

After a few moments of quiet deliberation, Ahmed, who knew better than to say the oft' repeated stereotype, "Women are not capable of intelligent thought," finally responded.

"American men do not take care of their wives as we do. American women go to school because they must work. In Saudi Arabia, women do not need to work. Our women are fortunate. Why would my wife want to work? It is better to have everything at home. It is not important for women to fill their heads with matters they cannot understand. By nature they are best suited for the home and family. Men are better prepared to handle all other concerns."

"But couldn't women handle the same matters if they were allowed to learn?" I persisted. "And even without being educated, why is a woman's testimony not accepted. Can she not give witness to something she has experienced?"

Suddenly impatient with me, Ahmed abruptly concluded our discussion. "In legal matters, a man can speak better. Women do not understand the complexities of business or law."

The next time he visited, Ahmed seemed to want to be sure he emphasized equality of the sexes, which he knew was important to me. "The Koran," he said, "teaches spiritual equality for men and women."

I could not argue that point with him. I could not quote the Koran, nor could I read it in Arabic, which according to Ahmed was the only language in which it should be read. (I did not tell my friend that I had an English version of the Koran.) But I wondered how there could be spiritual equality when the male gender was clearly preferred on earth. He could have multiple wives and divorce them at will; the value of his word was at least twice that of a woman's; his inheritance was double; and his indiscretions were covered by daily prayers while women were subject to punishment in the name of honor. Even in the life to follow, in Paradise, a man was promised a host of virgins for his pleasure. In what sense was there spiritual equality?

There are women in Islam who are recognized for their significant contributions to the religion. They are considered righteous and worthy of praise. Two of the Prophet's wives, Khadijah and Aisha, and his daughter Fatimah are considered by many Islamic scholars to be exemplary role-models for women today.

Khadijah was the first convert to Islam. She is said to have been a "perfect woman" and spoken of by her husband as one of the four greatest women of the world. The first wife of the Prophet is credited with putting aside her own desires in order to work for the cause of Islam. Khadijah gave Mohammed six children, but both sons died in infancy.

Aisha was the Prophet's favorite wife, though she bore no children for her husband. Many of the revelations from Allah were received while Mohammed was in her tent. Despite being only eighteen years old at the time of her husband's death, she was said to have been emotionally mature beyond her years. Aisha is credited with supplying the information that forms approximately one-third of the Hadith.

Fatimah was the Prophet's youngest daughter by his wife Khadijah. (Shi'a Muslims believe she was his only daughter.) Married to Mohammed's cousin Ali, she gave birth to two sons, Hasan and Hussein, who became the second and third Imams of

Shi'a Islam. To Shi'a Muslims, Fatimah is likened to Mary, the mother of Jesus.

*   *   *

Ahmed hoped to convert me to Islam. He often spoke of the "rightness" of Islam and how it is the one true religion. "Islam is the fastest growing religion in the world," he told me as proof that it is the "true religion."

The Ontario Consultant on Religious Tolerance published numbers that indicate the spread of Islam worldwide and confirmed Ahmed's assertion of the religion's growth. According to the report, estimates of Muslims vary greatly from 700 billion to 1.200 billion as counted in 2002 by the Council on American-Islamic relations.

Second only to Christianity as the largest religion in the world, Islam represents 22% of the world's population. Further, Islam is growing at 2.9% each year. That is faster than the growth of the total world population, which is 2.3% annually

*   *   *

I could mention the Bible only when Ahmed openly discussed religion in a comparative way. To speak of religions other than Islam was forbidden in the Kingdom. The Bible, I told him, teaches us about a God of love and forgiveness, one who brings peace and joy and purpose to our lives. I told Ahmed that I believed the Bible had great truths that could make us better people on Earth and give us hope for an eternity with God. The God of the Bible, I told him, offers life, abundant life.

Ahmed was immediately dismissive. "The Bible is in many languages. You cannot know its meaning."

"Language doesn't matter," I responded. "Truth is the same in any language. God's Word can be read in all the languages of the world. The message is what is important, not the particular language it is written in."

"No, no. Only Arabic is the true and holy language. The Koran must always be read in Arabic."

I was beginning to understand the importance Arabic held for my friend and for all Saudis. Because the Prophet Mohammed spoke Arabic, the language *itself* was considered holy. Ahmed truly believed that had I been able to read Arabic, I would have naturally become a Muslim. The truth of the Koran, according to my friend, was intrinsic in the language spoken by the Prophet. Even in Muslim cultures that speak languages other than Arabic, the Koran is always taught in the "holy language."

I asked Ahmed about the Biblical account of Abraham's willingness to sacrifice his son. In Judaism and Christianity it was Isaac, the "Son of the Promise," who was offered by Abraham. But according to Islam, Ishmael was the offered son.

"Of course it was Ishmael," Ahmed insisted. "Abraham was told to take his son, his only son. Ishmael was born first. Isaac was never the only son. It had to be Ishmael."

The Bible teaches that Ishmael began to scoff at Sarah after the birth of her son, Isaac. Sarah, who was grieved by the taunting and did not want her son's inheritance shared with Ishmael, insisted that Abraham send the woman Hagar and her child away. Abraham did so.

Hagar and Ishmael had long been banished from Abraham's family and tribe when the call to be willing to sacrifice Isaac occurred. Isaac was, indeed, not only the Son of the Promise, he was in practice, Abraham's only son at the time. Ishmael was gone. He and his mother, having been forced away, were dwelling in the wilderness of Paran, today's Arabia. Scripture gives a footnote to Ishmael's life; it tells us that he took a wife from Egypt, the land of his mother.

Muslims believe Ishmael and Hagar found water and refuge in Mecca. There they were spared certain death from the ravages of the desert wilderness. To mark the significance of that place of deliverance, Abraham and Ishmael, according to Islam, constructed the Ka'aba. The black rock that had fallen from heaven became the cornerstone of the shrine.

Ahmed was the only Saudi Arabian with whom I ever discussed religion. To him I was clearly an "Infidel" but one whom he hoped to persuade that Islam is best for women. He believed the rules that governed his life had come from Allah, the God of Islam. I believe the freedoms I treasure are from Jehovah, the God of the Bible.

*   *   *

Ahmed and I had many conversations. He was surprisingly open about men's indiscretions. He was patient in answering my questions. He clearly respected me and wanted me to approve of Saudi Arabian culture. Knowing him as I did and having heard such candor from him, one day I challenged his country's rules for women. I asked, "Ahmed, do you see a time, perhaps in fifty years, when the rules might change – a time when your sisters will not have to veil. Could there come a day when women will be allowed to drive?"

"No, No, Never! I would fight to the death to prevent this," he said, abruptly rising to his feet, his face flushed with emotion.

Stunned, I asked, "But, Ahmed, why not? You've lived in the West. You have enjoyed freedoms. Why would you not want at least a small change for you sisters or for your daughters? What could be the harm if they drove a car?"

"In Islam we must, how you say in English, 'nip the bud.' We must not allow the beginning of anything that would harm our family. We must protect family. We must protect our honor. Islam protects our family. It protects our honor. It is our duty to preserve Islam. We must fight for Islam."

Ahmed was willing to fight to the death to protect his Islamic culture. But it was women – his sisters and mother, and someday it would be his wife and daughters – who bore the weight of the restrictions that protected his honor.

15
LEA'S PARTY

Still in her teens, Lea had recently been married. Her
brother had given consent to the union at a legal proceeding,
one that she had not attended. Her new husband took her to live
in the home of his mother where she became part of the harem,
the women of the household, which included her mother in law,
sisters of her new husband, wives of her husband's brothers,
and several female servants. She had moved from the seclusion
of her father's home to the secluded walls of her husband's
home where she spent her days in the rooms reserved for
females.

She had not known the man to whom she was married nor
had she unveiled in his presence prior to their marriage. Now
her husband could see her face and she tried very hard to please
him. She hoped he would grow to love her and that she would
soon bear sons for him. She knew it was possible that one day
he would add additional wives to the women of the harem. Lea
understood, above all, that in her role as a female she must not
bring dishonor to her husband or to the men of her birth family.

It was customary that after three months of married life, the
bride was allowed to visit her mother's home. A large
celebratory party was planned to welcome Lea back, and all of
her female friends and relatives would attend. Ahmed was very
proud to be able to present such a fine celebration for Lea, his
younger sister.

In an extraordinary gesture, Ahmed invited me to attend the
party, to meet Lea and his mother, and to enjoy the festivities. It
would be a joyous occasion, he said. He told me that his family
had purchased five goats for the meal. Surely that expense
indicated the importance of the occasion and the affluence of
his family in being able to host such a fine gathering. He called
frequently to remind me of the upcoming event, lest I forget.

Shortly after eight o'clock on the evening of the party,
Ahmed and Khalid arrived at my compound gate where I
waited. Without the slightest hesitation, I left with the two

Saudi Arabian young men who would deliver me to Lea's party. I had not thought to even ask for an address or a phone number to leave with my husband. The two young men chatted casually as we drove across town. Of course, this time I sat in the backseat!

I wore my usual long linen dress accessorized with two gold chains, a bangle, and earrings. I had searched my closet for something more festive, but nothing I had seemed appropriate. I had brought only one formal dress to Saudi Arabia and I was certain it would not do. Far too much skin would have been exposed. It hadn't occurred to me to shop for a new party gown, one of the "Cinderella dresses" from the Saudi dress boutiques in the newer buildings.

When finally we arrived at the home of his mother, Ahmed parked the car outside the walled villa. Khalid remained seated, waiting for his friend who escorted me inside the gate. I was thrilled to attend an authentic Saudi women's party and was filled with anticipation and curiosity. I never imagined the guests inside would be equally curious about me.

I was immediately greeted with squeals of excitement from dozens of young children. Boys and girls pressed forward to see the American woman whom they had obviously been told was coming to the party. Behind the children, Ahmed's mother and sister smiled welcomingly. Other female guests remained beyond our view until Ahmed left the yard. At his departure, they too crowded forward to get a glimpse of this most unlikely guest who had arrived at the invitation of Lea's brother.

I was stunned at the reception I received. Had I thought about it, I might have realized that few Arabian women and perhaps none of the children had ever met an American woman, though hundreds of us lived in the Kingdom. American and Saudi Arabian women normally had no contact with one another. Our communities were totally separate, and expatriates were told not to attempt conversations with veiled Saudi women. I was definitely something of an oddity to them. Their curiosity was obvious. I could not have been greeted with more enthusiasm.

As we entered the courtyard filled with guests, I realized how frightfully underdressed I was. The women wore designer gowns of taffeta, silks, and chiffons. I immediately wished I had purchased a Cinderella gown for the event, even if I were never to wear it again!

The women adorned their gowns with varied lengths of gold chains and massive necklaces that covered their entire torsos. Dazzling earrings peeked from their "sensuous" earlobes. Glittering gold bangles covered their sleeved arms. There was enough gold on display to stock many jewelry stores.

We moved slowly through the crowded courtyard, where the children remained, and finally into the house. I was taken through each room and introduced. There must have been two hundred guests: teen-aged girls, young mothers with infants, matrons, and great-grandmothers. The women were all seated on overlapping Persian rugs that covered the floor. Upholstered, padded boxes, providing the only semblance of furniture, were placed around the perimeters of two rooms. I had seen photos of Saudi Royalty sitting on the floor and leaning against similar boxes. I guessed those rooms were normally used by men. Perhaps one was the majlis, the reception or sitting room.

Lea and her mother took me outside once again to a narrow space between the house and the villa's wall. An old African servant who was barefoot, her head wrapped in a turban and her body draped in servant's garb, was tending five blackened pots of coffee that were brewing over separate wood fires built on the ground. She grinned toothlessly – pleased to show me how skillfully she managed the boiling pots without any protection for her hands. Of course I acknowledged in my limited Arabic and with hand motions how wonderful the coffee smelled. The woman, perhaps little more than a slave, had obvious pride in the work she performed.

The sun had set over an hour earlier, and darkness had spread across the yard. There was little light in the area of the coffee pots, though the burning wood glowed red and smoke filled the night air. I wondered if after the embers no longer glowed but were still hot, the old servant was able to maneuver in the dark around the piles of hot coals without burning her bare feet. She would surely remain busy at her task for several more hours. Hot coffee would be served all evening.

Brewed coffee was transferred from the blackened pots into traditional shiny brass ones. Lying in each long, narrow pour spout was a fibrous plant through which the coffee flowed. The combined aroma of the bitter green coffee, strong with cardamom, smoky wood fires, and incense wafting from the house filled the night air. I thought how different the exotic smells were from familiar ones of my youth in Arizona's night air: the sweet scent of orange blossoms, the slightly confused smell of oleander bushes, the musty aroma of sage brush, and the smell of wet dirt after a sudden summer shower.

With the tour of the yard complete, though I was not shown the boiling pots for the five goats, Lea, her mother, and I joined ladies in one of the crowded rooms. Guests, who were seated on the floor in their formal gowns, were animated as they chatted in Arabic. I imagined them to be saying, "Gee, she sure doesn't look like much – such a plain dress and so little gold!"

The women discussed make-up and hair styles. Their hair was coiffed and their make-up was thick and dark. They showed me their palms, which were elaborately decorated with henna. Webbed patterns, somewhat like tattoos, were drawn in purplish, brown dye. Fingernails, always trimmed short, were stained in a matching color. Outside her home, a Saudi woman had to be covered so that even her earlobes and ankles were not exposed. Her hands were the only parts of her body that could be seen. Was that why they were decorated in the most intricate designs imaginable? I asked how long the henna lasted.

"Only a few days," I was told. "And then it starts to blur." I had seen women in the gold souqs whose palms were still stained, though very little of the patterned design remained.

One of the guests explained that the hand decorations were typically done for special occasions such as holidays, weddings, and celebrations. Lea's homecoming was clearly an event worthy of the intricate artwork. Surely the palm artists and hair stylists must have come to the homes of the women. Or, perhaps women within a harem styled one another's hair and gave the henna treatments they proudly displayed. I was not aware of any beauty salons in Saudi Arabia.

A young woman, who could not have been older than fourteen, asked me if I would like to hold her infant. I remembered having been cautioned in Air Force cultural briefings that one must always follow a compliment of a child with a blessing for Allah to protect it. In the Saudi culture, it was believed that evil spirits, specifically the Evil Eye, lurked about wanting to harm a beautiful child. If the Spirit had not already noticed a vulnerable child, it surely would after hearing the infant praised. To omit the blessing would have been reckless and frightfully insensitive.

The Evil Eye had tremendous power. Given an opportunity, it was capable of inflicting disease and even death. Birth defects such as muscular-skeletal deformities, heart abnormalities, and neurological problems are common in Saudi Arabia – the result of generations of marriages within families and tribes. No doubt the genetic maladies are attributed to the Evil Eye, which was thought to be always looking to create mischief. An Arab-Bedouin proverb warns that, "The Evil Eye can bring a man to his grave and a camel to the cooking pot."

As the favored gender, a boy child was in particular danger from the Evil Eye. It was, therefore, not unusual for protective mothers to dress their sons in girls' clothing in an attempt to fool the spirit and make the baby less vulnerable. The evil spirit was not as likely to waste his time harming girls who, after all were not so valuable. In the West, we understand that female infants tend to be stronger than males at birth. In Saudi Arabia, the Evil Eye was the explanation for the higher mortality rate among males.

The young mothers beamed with pride as I cooed to their children, again and again invoking Allah's protection. "Ma'shallah." I hoped I had remembered the correct blessing in Arabic – or at least, I hoped the one I used was adequate.

Lea, the honored new bride, wore an elaborate wedding necklace. The gold coins glistened across her chest, all the way to her waist. She wore several additional chains and multiple bangles. It was obvious her dowry, her personal security, was much greater than that of the Bedouin women whose desperate eyes still haunt me – the ones I had seen as they leaned wearily against the doorframes of their mud huts in Hofuf.

"I am going to have a baby," she proudly told me. It was too early for the new life to be obvious beneath her flowing gown, though she affectionately patted the child who was growing inside her. She told me how much she hoped to have a son. In typical households the bride is servant to her mother-in-law until she produces sons. Clearly Lea believed the responsibility for the baby's gender was hers. Obviously, no one had told her that her husband's sperm determined the sex of the child she bore.

"Does your husband love you?" Lea abruptly asked me. What an odd question, I thought. I was to be asked the same question from several of the young women that evening. Marriages in the Kingdom were arranged without benefit of dating or courtship. Men divorced their wives with ease, and there was no stigma against the dissolution of marriages. Whether or not a wife was loved by her husband was normal conversation among those young women.

In a voice more hesitant and wistful than with certainty, Lea said, "My husband loves me." It was as if she were saying she had passed the test, or at least she hoped she had. Since love was not a prerequisite for marriage, one could only hope it was the result.

I remembered Ahmed's comment that when a wife is seen for the first time, her husband may not like her and will, therefore, "Naturally want a divorce." Lea's husband had given her the treasured gold wedding necklace. That was a good sign. She had become pregnant immediately. That, too, was a good sign. Now, if she was able to produce a son – and in time, many sons – surely he would, with certainty, love her.

Lea told me that her husband would be out of country on business for several months. She would remain in her mother-in-law's home, waiting for his return. Again, Ahmed's comments came to mind. "My friends and I go out of the country and enjoy many women." I wondered if Lea, as well as I, thought about this.

Without the required male escort, Lea would, no doubt, be confined to the harem during her husband's absence. Pregnancy would surely lengthen the confinement. The loose clothing of Saudi women was covered with the draped black abaya, but I could not remember ever seeing a woman in any of the markets who was obviously pregnant.

The older guests at the party did not speak English but were friendly, nonetheless. They smiled and nodded their heads when I attempted conversation or complimented their dresses and hair. Many of them were probably no older than I but were already grandmothers. As such, their maturity quelled the exuberance they might have once had.

Among the guests was a woman from Iraq. Tall, poised, and dignified, she wore a gorgeous green velvet gown. Her black hair shone against fair skin. Fluent in English, the Iraqi woman translated questions and comments throughout the evening. She told me she was a teacher in a girls' school in Riyadh and had lived in the Kingdom for twelve years. She was not familiar with the international school in which I taught nor was the curriculum similar to the one in her school. She said she gave some instruction in English. That explained why many of the girls understood my language.

The younger women knew enough English that we could communicate without translation. They were most eager to ask questions of this underdressed American woman who wore far too little gold. I was asked how many children I had. When I answered, "Two sons," the young women were shocked.

"Why only two? Don't you like children?" they asked.

Obviously, I was old enough to have had many offspring. Married as soon as she is old enough to bear children, a Saudi woman continues to give birth until her body refuses to produce more – much as my own mother had. I could have been having babies for at least twenty-five years by that time. It was unthinkable that I had only two. But at least my children were both sons. That redeemed me to some extent.

Noticing my two gold chains, they asked if I liked gold. I wore woefully less jewelry than anyone in the room. The women, no doubt, thought I either did not like gold or that my husband did not like me and, therefore, did not buy the prized pieces to add to my dowry.

The designer dresses and fabulous jewelry indicated that most of the women enjoyed significant wealth. My attire indicated no such riches. However, the young women treated me as though I had wealth of a different kind, a life of freedoms they could scarcely imagine and about which they were immensely curious. Their questions were punctuated with giggles, as though the mere mention of forbidden activities was titillating.

They asked if I drove in America. "Doesn't it scare you to drive?" they asked. I had to admit that traffic in Riyadh did scare me, even though I didn't drive in their country.

They asked if I had gone to school and for how long. When I told them that my schooling had lasted sixteen years and as a teacher I was required to continue taking classes, they were stunned. For most of the women, attending school for more than a few years was inconceivable. Unless you were going to become a medical doctor, why would you ever need to be in school for so many years? They asked.

A young girl who told me she was thirteen years old said she longed to go to school. "I want to learn," she said. "I want to be a teacher."

"Is it possible for you to go to school?" I questioned. "Is there a school for girls your age?" With saddened eyes she said, "My husband will not allow it. He says school is not necessary. He says I must be content in my home."

In Western cultures we are so private, so guarded with our secrets, our longings, and our hurts. It was amazing to me how open these women were, especially the young ones, to a total stranger whom they would never again see.

However, their questions were not all serious ones. They wanted to know about Hollywood. Did I know any film stars? Did I live near any? Those were such frequent questions, I wondered why they would think I might know film celebrities. The Saudi population at six million was so small and the population of Riyadh smaller still. Perhaps they had no idea of the enormity of the American population or the unlikelihood of one knowing a movie star.

I told them that when I was a girl I acted in school plays, but that was the closest I ever was to knowing anyone in theatre or movies. (My dear friend, Annie, however, was related to Katharine Hepburn.) They wanted to know what kinds of roles I played, even though they had never heard of any of the typical high school theatrical productions. They seemed to be awed at the thought of being in a theatrical production – even one in school.

The young women decided to dance. I remembered reading in one of Ahmed's books that women were forbidden to dance, sing, whistle, or even listen to music. I did not question the invitation to join them as they left the room in which older women sat. We moved to a room where there was a sound system. Soon loud music erupted from large speakers. I sat with others on the floor watching as young women, two or three together, danced. Swaying and spinning to the music, they primarily moved their hips. Several began asking me to dance. With them, I thought.

The Iraqi woman said, "They want you to dance *for* them. Disco, like John Travolta." Yikes! Not only was I not a dancer, I definitely could not swing to anything that resembled *Saturday Night Fever* or even *Grease*! Their urgings were so insistent, I did my best, but I am sure I was a major disappointment to them.

Much to my relief, dinner was announced putting an end to my feeble disco demonstration. I was told we would eat in several shifts and that I was to go in the first group. Accompanied by young women, I walked through the halls of the house toward an outdoor courtyard. We stopped for a quick rinse of our hands at a basin located by the door as we exited the house.

The large square courtyard was about thirty or forty feet long on each side. The ground of the entire area was covered with dozens of Persian rugs. White plastic, about a meter in width, had been unrolled around the perimeter of the square, leaving enough space to sit on the rugs outside the plastic. Each place had a bottle of water and a plate.

Food had been placed on enormous platters and then onto the plastic strips. I was directed to sit in front of one of the boiled goats. Steaming hot, the entire animal was still intact, though the hairy skin was sloughing off from the heat. I remembered Ahmed's pride that five goats were being prepared for the occasion.

Goat, when boiled, does grow in your mouth, just as my son had told me. I was immensely grateful that I was not considered enough of an honored guest to be offered the prized morsels: the goat's liver, a kidney, or an eyeball. Perhaps if I had worn a Cinderella dress and more gold ...

On either side of the goat was a platter of rice. The mounds of pungent, sticky rice were about two feet long and over a foot high. Raisins were mixed throughout, which unfortunately resembled the many flies swarming about. I tried not to constantly wave off the persistent insects; no one else seemed to be bothered by them. Normally I enjoyed Saudi rice with all its spices and Middle-Eastern flavors, but the uncertainty of whether I was pressing raisins or flies into the rice in my palm was very disconcerting.

Bananas, peaches, and grapes filled huge bowls. I ate a banana, making it last as long as possible, while reaching into the hot goat and raisin-filled rice as necessary to appear to eat as appreciatively as those who sat near me. We ate with our right hands only, without benefit of stemware or napkins.

It was a surreal moment. Women whose hair was coiffed in elaborate styles, whose torsos were covered in gold, and whose dresses were befitting of fairy tales sat on the rug-covered ground eating boiled goat with their henna decorated hands while flies, disguised as raisins, swarmed about the food!

With the meal concluded, we washed at the basin near the door. The next group of women moved into the courtyard and filled the places we had occupied, using the same plates. They too pulled meat from the ample goats and mounds of rice, which because of their abundance showed little evidence of anyone having already eaten from them. The shifts continued until every guest had opportunity to dine.

As each group finished eating and moved back indoors, hot cardamom coffee was served by several of the women. Without spilling a drop, they poured the hot liquid from pots held about twelve inches above tiny, bowl-shaped cups. Each cup held no more than two tablespoons of the bitter, green brew that had been prepared by the African servant who remained out of sight.

Groups now formed according to age. Older women sat in a separate room from the giddy teen-agers. Though I was probably the age of many of the older women, Lea directed me to a room of young wives. At forty years old I was well aware that I could have been among the grandmothers, the matrons, who by virtue of their age ruled the harems.

Gradually, guests began leaving for their homes. I saw none of the men who came to escort mothers, wives, sisters, or daughters back to their residences. About fifteen teen-aged girls remained with Lea, her mother, and me.

We moved into a small outside patio that connected to the kitchen. Again we sat on Persian rugs. There were dozens of dish towels drying as they hung across the stuccoed half-walls that formed two sides of the enclosed area.

The young girls, who still bubbled with energy, laughed, teased, and enjoyed the night air. Now it was their chance to quiz me, and they peppered me with questions. They either giggled or grimaced, depending on my answers. The very first question the girls asked and continued to ask, perhaps hoping I had misunderstood and would give a different answer was, "Is it true that in America you do not marry your cousin?"

"Yes, that is true," I answered.

"But, why not?" Their voices whined. Facial expressions revealed both bewilderment and pain at the very idea of not being able to marry their cousins. Surely marriage to relatives with whom as children they may have played was much preferred to unions with older men whom they had never known.

I decided not to attempt genetics or the likelihood of birth defects, so I just answered, "It is against the law in America."

They shook their heads, totally bemused. It was so strange to them that one would not be allowed to marry a cousin. After all, paternal cousins were the preferred marriage partners in Saudi Arabia.

"Did you want to marry your cousin?" they asked.

"Did you have lots of cousins?"

"Did you like them?"

"Were they handsome?"

As I thought back, I remembered my cousin Dave on whom I did have a crush as a child. I remembered that at one time I wished he were not my cousin.

The brief years of freedom to play in their dirt yards would have been their only time of interaction with males, other than within immediate families. Unlike me, they could not have attended school, church, or community activities where they met lots of boys and had crushes on any number of them throughout adolescence.

"Was your husband chosen for you?" they asked. I explained that I had known my husband for many years before we married. We had been friends and classmates in school before we became interested in one another and decided to marry.

"Did you like him?" They asked if my husband was kind to me. How long had I been married to the same man? Did I still like him after so many years?

"Does your husband buy gold jewelry for you?" they asked. Did I have lots of dresses? Did I have servants?

"Why do you work?"

"Don't you want to be at home?"

No one asked if my husband had more than one wife.

Questions turned to my sons. What were their names and were they handsome? Good looks were obviously important to these teen-agers, just as they are to America's youth. The girls giggled at the unusual sound of my sons' English names and even more when I said, though they were very handsome, my sons were much too young for them.

The questions continued. Did I know whom my sons would marry? Was I going to have more children? Why hadn't I already had more? Was there something wrong that I could not have babies? They asked if American women wait three months after a divorce before marrying again. When I answered there was no law requiring that, they were stunned.

"But what if you are pregnant?"

"How will you know who the father is?"

"You must always know who the father is." Both men and women in Saudi Arabia are identified by their fathers.

They asked if I had been to Hollywood. Again, with embarrassed giggling, they inquired if I had met John Travolta? I was amazed how popular the actor was with Arabian young women and how frequently I was asked about him. With movie theatres nonexistent and videos so censored, I wondered how they even knew about John Travolta. They seemed to know far more about the star than I did. They talked about how he could dance and how handsome he was. They said they liked the way he walked. I remembered the scenes of Travolta's character walking down the street with the beat of music in his head in *Saturday Night Fever.* Both Ahmed and Khalid walked with self-confidence, but their swagger didn't approach the strut of Travolta in that movie.

The girls asked questions related to themselves. Did I like their hair and their make-up? They were especially proud of the patterned designs drawn on their palms. They told me it took hours of sitting very still to have their hands so decorated.

Except for the Iraqi woman who was a teacher, not one woman with whom I conversed throughout the evening spoke of anything that I would consider of substance. There seemed to be little awareness of a larger world. None spoke of politics, of issues women faced, of presidential elections, governments in turmoil, or the Olympics. The teen-agers did not mention school events. They knew nothing of Friday night football games, cheer-leading, homecoming pep rallies, student Council elections, flirting with classmates, movie dates, or Spring proms.

It was nearly one in the morning when Ahmed returned for me. Word spread quickly that he was about to enter the women's area. Giggling with teenage giddiness, the girls who may have been his cousins grabbed damp dishtowels from the half-walls. Since their veils were not readily accessible, those lovely adolescents in their Cinderella dresses quickly wrapped their faces in rags that had been used to clean the kitchen. Veiling was clearly tied to sexual development; prepubescent girls would not have hidden their faces.

There was immediate sexual excitement beginning with the announcement that Ahmed was coming and reaching a dizzying level as he stood in the room filled with young females. The handsome Saudi obviously enjoyed entering the room of girls who were excited by his presence and hiding their faces from his view. He was the only man who had been allowed to enter the harem that evening, and he strode confidently into the patio. Ahmed reminded me of a proud young rooster strutting back into the hen house after making the sun come up!

After giving many thanks and hugs to Lea and her mother, while all the girls remained behind their damp dishtowels, I returned with Ahmed to the car where Khalid waited. They delivered me to my compound shortly before two in the morning. My husband, waiting for me and by that time growing anxious, said it was only when it began to get so late that he questioned the wisdom of sending me off with two Saudi Arabian men on this big adventure.

I didn't sleep much that night. After telling my husband every detail of the evening, my mind repeated the events again and again. I could hardly wait to put them to pen, lest I forget the incredible evening with about two hundred Saudi Arabian women who celebrated Lea's first return to her mother's home.

* * *

Six months later Lea had a baby daughter. I did not see her. Ahmed gave me the news and I sent a lacy tooth-fairy pillow I had made for her child. Hopefully, her next child would be a boy.

16
ADVISING THE ROYAL SAUDI AIR FORCE

As a military advisor to the Royal Saudi Air Force, my
husband's work was classified; I rarely heard about his day
except in a most general way. Advising the military of a
Middle-Eastern government necessitated having his Top Secret
security clearance expanded to include Sensitive
Compartmented Information. In its simplest terms, the
expanded clearance implied not that there were more secrets to
keep, but rather, the fact that he knew any of them potentially
put others in jeopardy. Instead of "What do you know?" the
question became "How do you know that?"

With Arab-Israeli tensions boiling, it was increasingly
important to forge strong relationships for the United States,
making his assignment both critical and challenging. Annual
military evaluations described his work environment as
"internationally sensitive, highly charged, and potentially
volatile."

On most days, my husband reported to the Royal Saudi Air
Force offices of the Military Headquarters, the Saudi equivalent
of our Pentagon. Work in the United States Pentagon is fast
paced, exacting, and hard charging; there is no tolerance for
ineptitude or slacking. The Saudi Arabian Air Force General
and his senior officers were no less motivated or professional.
Committed to building a strong military defense, the Saudi
Arabian top brass took seriously the advice given by their
American counterparts.

My husband had the utmost respect for General Fahd, the
Royal Saudi Air Force Commander. "He was a brilliant man
and a fine leader – as adept as a warrior pilot as he was a staff
officer." According to my husband, whose job it was to advise
the commander, the Saudi pilots agreed with his assessment.
"General Fahd was held in high esteem by the RSAF pilots for
his legendary bravery and skill as an aviator."

American advisors understood the importance of respecting Saudi cultural practices that were unusual to Westerners. There had to be recognition of Arab honor, Saudi pride, and always a deference to Allah's will. Scheduled meetings and appointments were invariably conditioned with a verbal reminder of "Insh'allah." The meeting would take place as planned, only if Allah willed it to do so. Further, there was no guarantee that briefings would begin on time. Once all participants were present, there had to be an opportunity for tea, served by a foreign-national tea-boy, as well as polite exchanges and affable conversation before work could begin. Any attempt to "get the ball rolling," or press the participants for decisions, or even start on time was met with suspicion. If you were in a hurry, you must be trying to "pull a fast one." The American work ethic of "Let's get going and get the job done," was seen as a sign of dishonesty. If you were honest, there was no need to rush. Anything could be accomplished in good time, if Allah willed.

On occasion, my husband would be called during weekends to respond to an emergency. I learned not to ask questions when his American commander summoned him; the situation, often fraught with international ramifications, was rarely made immediately public. There were times, even in social gatherings, when the commander tapped his shoulder, signaling another potential crisis. I could not predict, on such occasions, when my husband would return.

Acts of terrorism were being perpetrated throughout the Middle East, and we were well aware of the very real threat of an attack. Rumors, usually circulated by expatriate wives who claimed privileged information, warned that the American community might face imminent evacuation. Events such as a defecting pilot from Iran, threats against oil fields, the struggle for Islamic control of the government in Lebanon, the attack on the Marine barracks in Beirut, the U.S. Embassy bombings in both Beirut and Kuwait, the murder of the President of the American University of Beirut, and an attack near a U.S. airbase in Spain resulted in tightened security to our compound.

Anti-terrorism measures were enacted. Military advisors and their families altered daily travel routes. School buses were searched for bombs before being driven into the compound. Identification was required of visitors, making it more difficult for drop-in guests to get past guards. Automobiles could no longer be parked near the compound gate.

After the attack on the United States Marine barracks in Beirut in which two hundred forty-one Marines died, the threat of terrorism seemed awfully close to our home in Saudi Arabia. The perpetrator of that murderous attack, a Hezbollah terrorist, did not face justice until February 2008 when he died as a result of a car bomb – the very method he had used to murder American Marines. Hezbollah, which continues to commit despicable acts of terrorism in Lebanon and against Israel, was established as a Shi'a militia proxy group for Iran after that nation became an Islamic Republic in 1979.

Security was enhanced at the entrance to our walled compound, which had always been guarded by Saudi soldiers. Armored personnel carriers were positioned under awnings of desert camouflage mesh and large concrete barricades, designed to slow traffic to a crawl, were added just inside the compound gate for increased security. Finally, the addition of two heavy machine gun emplacements, one on each side of the gate, completed the more obvious new security features, all of which combined to make the entry to our compound look like an armed fortress.

The increased weaponry and additional guards gave us an awareness of the looming threat but did little to reassure us of their capability of stopping a concerted attack. However, the extra security did have an unexpected, pleasant consequence; it provided impetus for exciting war games played at dusk by older children of the compound. Akin to team hide and seek or capture the flag, each group of players had a base that had to be defended and held, while other team-mates searched for opposing players whom they could capture and bring back to home base.

The game was often led by a bald and muscular U.S. Army Special Forces full Colonel, who enjoyed playing just as much as did the youngsters. The mustachioed warrior became a champion to the boys, both because of his formidable physique and the fact that he joined in their games, teaching them military reconnaissance tactics.

Because of the sensitive nature of my husband's work, he could not tell me if military intelligence had determined a specific impending threat, but we knew that if evacuated we would leave the Kingdom on very short notice. He suggested a code to alert me. I had fallen in love with the graceful porcelain figurines from Spain, *Lladros*, and I had collected several of my own. It was decided that if an evacuation were likely, my husband would call and say, "Pack the Lladros."

No serious terrorist attack occurred in the Kingdom while we were there, but in 1995 the United States-operated Saudi National Guard Training Center in Riyadh was attacked with a car bomb. Five U.S. military servicemen were killed. Four Saudis were arrested and forced to make public confessions in which they claimed to have been inspired by Osama bin Laden. The four men were beheaded before United States officials could interrogate them.

In 1996 a car bomb exploded outside Khobar Towers, a U.S. military complex in Dhahran where my husband stayed when deployed to that air base. (My sons and I accompanied him on occasion and lodged in the same facility.) Believed to have been perpetrated by Islamic jihadists, the attack killed nineteen United States servicemen and injured hundreds more. For reasons known only to them, Saudi officials rejected all requests from the United States to have an FBI counter-terrorism team assist in the investigation of the Khobar Towers attack.

*   *   *

Saudi Arabians were originally desert nomads and tribal people. A large portion of the Saudi desert, the *Ar Rub al Khali*, was known to us as the "Empty Quarter," indicative of its desolate topography. Even outside the Empty Quarter, much of the desert was unyieldingly hot and dry and as stark as anything imaginable. Many Saudis continued to live the harsh Bedouin life as nomads who lived in tents. They were in constant search of grazing vegetation and water for their herds of camels, sheep, and goats. Occasional natural wells, called wadis, provided small oases and brief respites from the desert heat.

"When I visit my parents I must search for their tent," a Saudi F-15 pilot who was first generation out of the desert and whose parents were Bedouin told my husband. "My father always asks, 'My son, tell me, what is it you do?'

"I fly jet airplanes through the sky, I tell him. My father shakes his head and says, 'No, Son, tell me what you really do?'"

As desert dwellers, the parents of the military pilot had never seen an airplane fly overhead and could not imagine such a thing. Surely their son was teasing them.

* * *

The city of Riyadh held a celebratory day in which a military air show was planned. All aircraft were relatively new in the Kingdom and most civilians, even in the city, had never seen a jet fighter. Impressed by the speed and power of his somewhat recently acquired aircraft, Crown Prince Abdullah, in an impromptu decision made in the midst of the air show, requested that an F-5 make a supersonic pass so that he and his guests could hear a sonic boom. In America we reserve breaking of the sound barrier for unpopulated areas, although those of us from the Desert Southwest who are old enough can still remember the startling ba-boom! of sonic power.

As ordered by the then Crown Prince, now King Abdullah, the lead solo F-5 pilot passed at very low altitude and at supersonic speed directly over the reviewing stand. The heavy thud of the resultant sonic boom was deafening, providing not only the Crown Prince and the other dignitaries seated with him a truly impressive display of military might but most of Riyadh as well. Millions of dollars in window glass throughout the capitol city shattered, and plastered walls of new buildings cracked. The cost of repairing the massive damage was well worth the splendid display of military airpower the Crown Prince and his guests enjoyed that day!

*   *   *

Ramadhan, one of the five tenets of Islam, is the annual month of fasting. It is a time of sacrifice that is meant to create empathy for the poor, provide a time of reflection, and to express thankfulness for the book of Islam, the Koran. Observed during the ninth lunar month, the fast occurred during summer when temperatures soared to 130 degrees Fahrenheit and in early fall during our two years in the Kingdom.

Muslims were not permitted to smoke, eat, drink, or chew anything during daylight hours for a full month. To enforce the fast, all public drinking fountains were turned off, and all food and drink concessions were closed. No chickens or goats were roasting on Chicken Street. Non-Muslims were expected to refrain from eating, drinking, chewing gum, or even using breath mints in the presence of fasting Muslims.

For the wealthy, there was not a lot of sacrifice. While servants cared for children and maintained the homes, Saudis with financial means slept during daylight hours. At dusk the cannon sounded, announcing the break in the fast. Food and drink, prepared by servants, were plentiful all night. At daybreak the fast resumed, and the wealthy Saudis went back to sleep.

Laborers, however, the Yemeni road crews, the Korean builders, the Bangladeshi houseboys, the African and Filipino servants experienced a very real sacrifice during the month of fasting. Their daytime work continued in the unrelenting desert heat but without nourishment or hydration. Ramadhan, meant to increase awareness and empathy for the needy, seemed to me to inflict the greatest sacrifice on the poorest Muslims living in the Kingdom.

In cases such as pregnancy or the nursing of an infant, one's Ramadhan fasting could be postponed until a safer time. The Royal Saudi Air Force pilots were at tremendous risk flying thirty million dollar aircraft without eating or drinking for hours. RSAF pilots were encouraged by United States advisors to postpone their fasts on days in which they had scheduled flights. Their answer was always the same. "I must perform my duty to Allah. If Allah asks me to die, I die."

* * *

A young Saudi Arabian who was neither a licensed aviator nor a member of his country's military was willing to die for Allah in a jihad against America. Hani Saleh Hanjour was born in the mountainous community of Taif, Saudi Arabia, in 1972. A shy teenager of slight build, Hani announced that he wanted to drop out of school and become a flight attendant. As the most religious member of his family, he attended daily prayers in local mosques and shared a piety with religious extremists, though his family was apparently unaware of any radical affiliations.

When he was nineteen, he visited the United States for the first time and enrolled in an English course at the University of Arizona in Tucson. Though never considered a capable flight student, he studied in multiple aeronautical courses, including one in Scottsdale, Arizona.

Over the next eleven years he hop scotched between several American cities, returned to Saudi Arabia, and then briefly visited Afghanistan where he helped with a relief agency. On September 11, 2001, Hani Hanjour commandeered American Airlines Flight 77 and crashed it into the United States Pentagon.

* * *

One early morning my husband called me from the Saudi Air Force base near the community where Hani Hanjour, then only ten or eleven years old, lived.

"Guess how I'm calling you," he effused. Of course I couldn't. Phone service in the 1980s was still not reliable in the Kingdom. Long distant calls were particularly difficult. Dropped calls were common with land lines, and no one had cell phones. Bell Canada was in the country establishing the rudiments of phone service.

"Prince Bandar is giving me a ride to the base. I'm using his car phone," my husband reported. "We're in his Mercedes Benz 560 SEL."

My husband, when not in his presence, referred to the prince as "Little Bandar" so as not to be confused with Prince Bandar bin Sultan bin Abdul Aziz who was also a military pilot and served as the Saudi Arabian Ambassador to the United States for twenty-two years.

"Little Bandar" had what most of us in America did not have until more than two decades later – a car phone – and his automobile was a highly prized, prestigious vehicle. The prince lived a life of luxury of which American military pilots could only dream. He told my husband how easy it was for him to make money.

"I just made fifteen million dollars," the prince said, as he hung up his car phone. "It is easy to make money. All I have to do is make a phone call. My fee for being a go-between is millions."

Baksheesh. Companies eager to be granted lucrative contracts were happy to pay the fee or bribe to anyone in the Royal Family or anyone who had enough clout to secure the contract. Additionally, as a member of the House of Sa'ud,

"Little Bandar" would never lack wealth. Oil had secured that wealth.

*   *   *

"The Saudi ambassador is one of the most influential diplomatic positions in Washington and is arguably the most important overseas post for the oil-rich desert kingdom."

The Ambassador, Prince Bandar bin Sultan bin Abdul Aziz is the son of Sultan, one of the powerful Sudairi Seven – the most influential of Abdul Aziz's forty-five sons. His mother was a servant, not a wife of Sultan. However, under Islamic law, all sons have legitimacy regardless of birth circumstances.

Considered a close ally and friend of the American government, the Ambassador, who was educated in the West, was a calm voice in Washington throughout his term. Prince Bandar resigned as Ambassador to the United States in July 2005. He likely took a high-level appointment within the Saudi government increasing his chances of becoming the first second-generation prince to become king.

Prince Bandar's cousin Prince Turki bin Faisal bin Abdul Aziz, a 1968 graduate of Georgetown University, became the next Saudi Arabian Ambassador to the United States and served in that capacity for fifteen months until his resignation in December, 2006.

Prince Turki, the youngest of eight sons of King Faisal, was the former Director General of the General Intelligence Directorate. It was he who suggested to Osama bin Laden that he use his considerable finances to fund relief services for Afghan refugees.

Both former Ambassadors to the United States, Prince Bandar and Prince Turki, as second generation princes are seen by many in the West as moderates from whom the United States would benefit, should they continue to have an influential voice in the Kingdom. Not everyone agrees.

Following the attack on 9-11 a lawsuit for damages was filed against the former Ambassador Prince Turki bin Faisal, along with Prince Sultan bin Abdul Aziz and Prince Mohammed bin Faisal. The legal action claimed that influential members of the Royal Family had contributed financial support to Al Qaeda. The former ambassador was quick to point out the following in his defense:

> "Remember that we face the same threat: Bin Laden targeted Saudi Arabia before he targeted America...That he chose fifteen Saudis for his murderous gang, many of whom he boasted, did not even know the ultimate goal of their mission, can only be explained as an attempt to disrupt the close relationship between our two countries..."

The Ambassador may be completely accurate in his assessment that Osama bin Laden used Saudi jihadists in order to weaken the close ties between our governments. But, the question remains: Why were those young men from Saudi Arabia so vulnerable to recruitment by Al Qaeda? Fifteen of the nineteen terrorists who attacked America were from the Kingdom of Saudi Arabia.

Prince Bandar bin Sultan bin Abdul Aziz has suggested the root of his country's terrorist problem can be found within. "The editorial [he wrote] accused the Kingdom of seeking to blame its problems with terrorism on foreign influences while failing to look at the domestic causes of violence, and urged clerics to support a 'jihad against terrorist campaigns.'"

In 2004 the government of Saudi Arabia was reported to have taken action to curb the tide of Muslim young men from that Islamic state who perpetrate acts of terror. Males who had been recruited by terrorist organizations were being retrained in a residential intervention program described as resembling a luxurious half-way house. Young men, who at one time considered suicide bombings a noble sacrifice for which Allah would reward them, were being taught that Islam is a religion of peace.

Three years later, Saudi Arabia released fifteen-hundred Al Qaeda jihadists. According to the Royal Family of the Islamic state, the men had been "reformed" with the help of counseling and were no longer a threat. Ironically, instead of remaining in the Kingdom, the "reformed" terrorists, all of whom had pledged allegiance to Osama bin Laden, were transported to Iraq.

The former Saudi Minister of Education, Prince Mohammed Al Abdullah Al Faisal recently addressed the terrorism question in a phone call he placed to the Saudi Arabian television channel, *Al Arabiya*. Recognizing the grave consequences of his country's religious education of males, the prince criticized the Wahhabi interpretation of Islam being taught in the Kingdom. Admitting that it produces terrorists, the prince said:

> "Education in Saudi Arabia suffers from a big problem. One day I went to the Minister of Education, Hassan El Sheikh, and told him, 'The religious books we teach are the books of Sheikh Mohammed Bin Abdel Wahab [the founder of Wahhabism] and we should change their interpretations and understanding for the student.
>
> I am not happy with the level and results of education in the Kingdom, and I personally sent my children after their middle school to study abroad…since we realized from experience that our curriculums produced terrorists who went and blew themselves up. We have to find out how to get our students out of that path."

* * *

The Airborne Warning and Control System surveillance planes known as AWACS had been delivered to Saudi Arabia by America. Congress had debated the AWACS deal endlessly, and the Israeli government had vigorously lobbied against it. Beginning in the 1980s, United States Air Force crews rotated into the Kingdom in three month cycles to fly the surveillance planes alongside Saudi pilots.

The American crews, on temporary assignment, stayed in guest quarters provided by USMTM. They were welcomed and entertained in off-duty hours by permanently stationed military members within various American military compounds throughout Riyadh.

I met one AWACS crew in a most inadvertent way. Having just arrived in the country, the men were invited to a party held in the lobby of our apartment building. There was plenty of food, conversation, and laughter. I remember one of the crew members who was particularly entertaining. He could play the spoons better than anyone I had ever seen. To the delight of all, he made his special brand of music by tapping two spoons against his knee. Having just written that, I realize how void of normal entertainment our lives were if spoon playing was memorable!

The morning following the party, though it was Desert Sunday, the AWACS crew was tasked to take several Saudi Arabian dignitaries on a demonstration flight while assisting Saudi pilots in the newly acquired surveillance plane. The American crew obliged.

During the many hours in the air, in-flight refueling was necessary. Both the American and Saudi crews of the AWACS and the KC-135 tanker were proficient at in-flight rendezvous. The surveillance plane pulled away when fueling was complete, as its crew had done without incident hundreds of times before. On that day, however, the two multi-million dollar aircraft collided instead of achieving normal separation of airspace. Both aircraft landed safely but with significant damage, though no crew member or distinguished guest was injured.

The aerial mishap necessitated a thorough investigation facilitated by senior United States Air Force officers who were serving in the Kingdom. My husband received a call from his commander shortly after the two aircraft landed. He rushed out of our apartment to respond to the incident and the subsequent investigation.

Accidents involving primary mission aircraft are not taken lightly by the United States military. Any damage to aircraft is a very big problem, indeed. Someone is always held accountable. Never in the U.S. military is there an attitude of, "No problem." This collision in the airspace over the Kingdom not only involved two valuable military planes, it had international significance as well; American crews were flying Saudi Arabian aircraft. Blame would be assessed. The potential impact on military careers was significant.

When my husband returned hours later, the AWACS crew was with him. Shaken, nervous, and having been questioned all afternoon, the men needed to decompress, vent their fears and have a safe place to collect their thoughts. They spent the remainder of the day and much of the next several days in our apartment waiting for a judgment to be made on the accident. They surely rehashed mentally, step by step, every flight decision made. Each man was overwhelmed with incredible apprehension. They had little appetite for food or drink or conversation.

Many months later, the sentencing portion of the investigation continued. Several military careers ended as a result of the mishap over the Saudi Arabian desert.

*　*　*

I had been taught from the day my husband entered Officers' Candidate School that military wives had significant responsibilities related to the success of their husbands. There were standards of dress for various required activities, etiquette classes, protocol lessons, and recommended volunteer work. Though most wives of officers were college educated, employment was considered quite impractical; wives were thought to have sufficient duties in their supportive roles of their husbands. I had begun my teaching career prior to my husband's military induction, and I continued employment after his commission until my sons were born, making me something of an exception.

The wives of Saudi Arabian Air Force officers had no such support-role expectations. Few would have received more than a basic education, and with only two professions open to women, employment was highly unlikely. All organizations were prohibited in the Kingdom. There were no Saudi officers' wives' luncheons, teas, or volunteer assignments. There were no candy stripers in the hospitals of the Kingdom. It was obvious Saudi Arabian wives were never included in military social life. They remained secluded in the harem, as did all other Arabian women.

My husband's RSAF counterparts frequently visited us in our apartment, usually at unexpected times. None ever brought along a wife or children. The men would drop by to see my husband and then stay for hours. I offered meals and was grateful if the men had not come on an evening in which I had prepared pork. More than a few times, my husband made unplanned trips to Chicken Street when unanticipated guests arrived at meal time.

Conversations with these Arabian men were usually about work, their training experiences in America, or casual subjects, though sometimes we discussed Saudi practices. Proud of their Islamic state, the birthplace of Islam, and their oil-rich country, the men seemed eager to elicit our approval of life in the Kingdom.

We frequently entertained visiting Americans as well. Senior officers from the Pentagon's Foreign Military Sales Office or military service members on temporary assignment spent time in Riyadh. Providing the visitors a place to relax and unwind after a rushed, even volatile, day was part of my husband's role in Saudi Arabia. On one such occasion my husband told me we would have five guests for dinner two nights later.

I had long before learned to put together short notice dinner parties, even those my spouse forgot to tell me about until the last moment. Entertaining in Saudi Arabia was a completely different challenge. Because of my gender, I could not drive to shop for groceries. The Air Force Commander's wife was provided a driver, but I was not. Transportation via the weekly compound mini-bus was not an option with my work schedule.

With two days notice, I managed to prepare a buffet of chicken curry, replete with all the condiments, and a dessert. Stored in the refrigerator, the meal would be easily heated and ready to serve. The table was set, and I was confident that at the end of the school day I could pull off the dinner party without appearing frazzled.

The morning of the party I received an "Oh, by the way" notice. The five men had been deployed to Dhahran and would not be coming to dinner after all. Since I had prepared so much food, I promptly invited another family to join us that evening.

Shortly after returning from school, my phone rang. It was one of the visiting officials who apologized for the mix up. The five had returned to Riyadh early and would love to dine with us as planned. What a scramble! Now, I had too many people for the quantity of food prepared. There was no way I could say, "Sorry, you lost your chance." Clearly, my husband was expected to entertain visitors from the States.

The restrictive nature of the culture in which we lived and the stressful work environment for advisors created a tight knit community of expatriates who were always ready to help one another. I learned to confidently ask for help when it was needed. And I did so on that occasion. A neighbor who was home from his office agreed to make an emergency food run for me. Instead of the meal I had planned, we had hot steaming roast chickens and pungent rice. The evening was a success. The visitors ate, relaxed, and enjoyed conversation.

Social events were always a welcomed diversion. We were able to meet interesting Americans who were in the Kingdom in roles related to the military but were not part of USMTM. All of the major aircraft companies, such as Northrop, Pratt-Whitney, McDonald-Douglas, and Lockheed, had senior management representatives living in Saudi Arabia to facilitate the sale of their equipment.

As an advisor to the Royal Saudi Air Force, my husband recommended specific military aircraft for purchase by the Kingdom. This resulted in our being regularly invited to wonderful, elegant dinner parties. Of course we knew the representative hoped his particular equipment would be recommended to the Saudis for purchase, but during social occasions, great care was taken not to discuss the capabilities of aircraft sold by that company.

The representatives and their wives lived in walled villas with beautifully groomed yards, at least by Arabian standards. We were greeted at the gate and ushered to the door where a Filipino butler announced our arrival. With uniformed servants to offer canapés and beverages and others to prepare and serve the meal, our hostess was relaxed and gracious no matter how large the group for dinner. Having never had hired assistance with my dinner parties, I was particularly impressed by the sophistication and luxury of these evenings.

Unlike my Chicken Street dinner party, the hostesses of these elegant affairs served entrees such as stuffed beef tenderloin and standing rib roasts with Yorkshire pudding. Desserts were equally impressive. It was obvious the price of imported beef from Argentina was not prohibitive for the entertainment budgets of aircraft companies.

"I've forgotten what we are eating this evening," one hostess commented. With so many parties given in a week, she didn't keep track of any particular meal. She planned menus with her staff well in advance and then left the shopping, preparation, and serving to her many male servants.

While most of the dinner parties were elegant, indoor ones, we attended a creative, outdoor event planned in traditional Arabian style and unceremoniously called a "goat grab." The invitations instructed us to wear our Arabian clothes – my husband in his thobe, ghutra, and sandals and I in my long, loose dress, accessorized with gold baubles.

Our host couple lived in a lovely villa that had an unusually large and well shaded grass lawn. It was the only such lawn I would ever see in the Kingdom; its maintenance surely required a great deal of gray water. After a social hour, the approximately one hundred guests were seated in long, facing rows on Persian rugs spread on the grassy lawn.

Entire goats had been boiled in large pots over outdoor fires. Heads and legs still intact, the steaming hot animals were served on immense platters that were placed between the rows of seated guests. Huge mounds of Middle-Eastern rice alternated between the several goats.

Everything was eaten by hand without benefit of flatware, plates, or napkins. If guests were hesitant to dig in, one of many African servants, in the Arab tradition, pushed his right sleeve up and reached into the incredibly hot meat. Pulling off chunks of goat dripping with fat, he served guests as if to say, "Look, no problem; this is how it's done."

It was a memorable evening filled with laughter and conversation and opportunity to meet other expatriates. We shared, as we always did in such gatherings, all our accumulated Arabian stories. After such events, I always wondered, "What in the world does one do with an entire leftover boiled goat?"

* * *

The military mission in Saudi Arabia was comprised of joint forces with officers from all branches of the United States Armed Forces represented, and there was natural competition between the various services. Each officer thought his branch of service was far more important to the military mission in the

Kingdom than were the others. The competition continued in the planning of social events. Parties were frequently given, and each was meant to be more interesting or novel than any before. There were western hoedowns, Mongolian barbeques, beach parties at the swimming pool, a German Oktoberfest, and dress like Saudis parties.

The officers of the Navy and Marine Corps decided we were long overdue a "proper" military social event. With great enthusiasm, they planned a Navy Ball to be held in our compound. A formal affair, dinner was served in our only restaurant. I have forgotten the menu, but it was, no doubt, whatever the normal meal for that day of the week was. The Filipino waiters, however, had been instructed to serve the food with particular finesse. Dancing continued in the recreation center, which was amazingly transformed for the occasion by the Navy officers and their ladies. A Navy Ball sounds unlikely in the desert, but the creative talents of those who planned it produced a memorable evening.

I had brought only one formal dress to Saudi Arabia. It was a classic, strapless black evening gown, which I had worn once before in the States. It was my only choice for the formal event. Women in our compound generally wore lots of gold jewelry, but I decided to accessorize my gown with a simple silver choker.

Compliments flowed that evening much to my surprise but delight. I heard comments such as, "You sure don't look like a kindergarten teacher in that dress!" No wonder I thought it was a terrific party!

*   *   *

During the time my husband was an advisor to the Royal Saudi Air Force, the United States of America shared a number of common goals with the Kingdom of Saudi Arabia. One of the most obvious was the defeat of the Soviet Union in Afghanistan. Soviet troops had invaded that Muslim country on Christmas Eve in 1979, and the war continued. Saudi Arabian King Fahd bin Abdul Aziz had agreed to match dollar for dollar

America's funding of the freedom-fighters, the Mujahadeen in Afghanistan.

Decades earlier, Soviet weapons meant to "bloody Israel" had been stockpiled in Egypt. Now, those weapons were being brokered by Americans for use in Afghanistan against Soviet troops. But more importantly, in 1986 President Reagan authorized the delivery of Stinger-shoulder-fired missiles to the Afghan rebels. Soviet helicopters began to drop from the sky!

* * *

Shortly before our departure from Saudi Arabia, a diplomat from the United States Embassy in Moscow, Russia, visited our military compound. A dinner party was arranged and the diplomat agreed to be the evening's speaker. With my keen interest in government and politics, no doubt learned from my father, it was an event I will always remember, though I have forgotten the name of our esteemed guest.

During his fascinating presentation, the diplomat showed slides of Russian life as it was in the 1980s. We saw peasant women washing their laundry by hand in freezing rivers. We saw long lines of people who waited daily, hoping to buy bread, meat, or produce, only to be turned away because the limited supply of food was exhausted early in the day. We saw decrepit buildings, rat infested and filthy, being used by embassies. We saw bottles on store shelves, each filled to a different level, indicating no uniformity or standard for production. We learned that vodka, the curse of the nation, had reduced the effectiveness of the work force to a few hours each day.

I understood that in the socialist republic there was no incentive to work. Everyone was paid the same and productivity was, as a result, achieved at a minimal level. Workers knew that each day's quota had to be met, but there was no motivation to produce anything beyond the required amount. Income was the same whether one exerted effort or not. There was no personal benefit to be gained from working harder or producing more. Work for the common good meant, in reality, work that benefited no one.

The diplomat told us about a recent state-allowed experiment that had permitted a mere two percent of Russia's farm land to be privately farmed instead of being under the state's control. The farmers of this small area were allowed to grow and sell their produce as they wished and to keep the proceeds of their labor.

The Soviet government was shocked, our speaker said, when that two percent of the total farmland produced ninety percent of the produce grown in the country. Productivity flourished when farmers were allowed to reap the benefits of their labor. It was an experiment in capitalism, and it worked!

Very little of the Soviet Union's great wealth in a country with the greatest natural resources was spent to make the lives of its people better. Instead, the vast majority of revenues went toward the war machine, the race with America to develop defensive and offensive weapons and in keeping Communist agents posted in countries that had been invaded and occupied since World War II. The Soviet Union was still embroiled in an expensive war in Afghanistan as well as in insurgencies in Nicaragua and El Salvador in the Americas.

The diplomat posed the question, "How can a government that so totally ignores the needs of its people survive?" I had heard President Reagan pose the same question. The President had said further that the "evil empire" could not last.

When I heard Ronald Reagan predict the fall of the Soviet Union, I thought that our President was expressing wishful thinking. The terrible Communist empire was here to stay. After all, for as long as I could remember, Communism was the greatest threat we all feared – despite former President Jimmy Carter's assertion that it was an "inordinate fear."

Communism was too powerful and too dominant in the world, I believed, to ever lose its stranglehold on Eastern Europe, much of Asia and Africa, and even some parts of the Americas. The "Iron Curtain," a descriptive term first coined by British Prime Minister Winston Churchill, had divided continents, nations, and families for decades. An estimated sixty million to three hundred million people worldwide had died as a result of Communist oppression.

President Reagan, with a strategy of "we win, they lose" increased the military budget to six percent of the GDP. "He got Europe to accept nuclear weapons in their soil, despite the Nuclear Freeze movement…He provided arms to Afghan freedom fighters. He supported the Contras against the Sandinistas in Nicaragua. He invaded Granada."

Additionally, President Reagan pushed the Strategic Defense Initiative, fighting Congress for funding. Later, in arms limitation talks with Soviet leaders he would not bargain with "Star Wars," leaving our sworn enemy no choice but to pour all its resources into its own military space programs.

Little did I understand that the "evil empire" would soon bankrupt herself in a fatal attempt to compete with America's advanced system to detect and eliminate missile threats, while at the same time funding insurgencies in the Americas and fighting a costly war in Afghanistan.

In 1988 the Soviet Union retreated from Afghanistan, a war being lost to Stinger shoulder-fired-missiles that had been provided by America. Its economy in ruin, the totalitarian regime could not continue funding that war, nor could it continue supporting Soviet contingencies posted in so many Eastern European nations. As a result, one by one, those countries were able to break free of the domination they had been under for more than forty years.

Less than a year after Soviet troops left Afghanistan, the Berlin Wall came down!

"Freedom is breaking out all over the world," my husband said. "The Cold War is being won without the shedding of one drop of American blood."

*   *   *

The Mujahadeen, the "freedom-fighters," and the Arab jihadists were jubilant and emboldened by their impressive defeat of the second greatest power in the world. Now, anything was possible. Radical clerics throughout the world, including America's heartland, began calling for the return of Mohammed's army in triumph over the "Infidel." The defeat of the Soviet Union had convinced Islamists that their religious belief would empower them to defeat any enemy, large or small.

Never had I dreamed that the threat posed by the Soviet Union would disappear, only to be replaced by that of a well-funded network of terrorists led by a Saudi Arabian who desired to do just as Russian President Nikita Khrushchev had threatened, while angrily pounding his shoe on his desk.

"We will bury you," he had said. Osama bin Laden, in his hatred for the West, desires to do no less.

PART THREE
HONOR AVENGED

17
DEATH FOR APOSTASY

The Kingdom of Saudi Arabia has always been ruled under Islamic law. Believed to be the law of God, Shari'a is enforced with relentless and unyielding rigidity. Principles of "Judge not, lest you be judged," "Forgive others as you have been forgiven," and "Love your neighbor as yourself" are anomalies in the Kingdom that requires every citizen to be Muslim. To speak against Islam or its Prophet or to convert to another religion constitutes apostasy. Punishment for this unforgivable offense is death. Executioners, using their long swords, enact the prescribed retribution against apostates and those convicted of other serious crimes: beheading in the public square.

Executions in Riyadh took place on Fridays. Crowds of people crammed into the downtown square to witness the gruesome punishments. Men, veiled women, and even children, all in agreement with Islamic and Saudi Arabian justice, filled the air with chants in Arabic. *Allahu Akbar! Alhamdulillah!* "Allah is great. Praise belongs to Allah." The newsreader on the evening televised program announced the executions with solemn words to the effect, "Let this be a warning to our guests in the Kingdom."

There were many public beheadings during my two years in the Kingdom. While all were tragic, one of the most publicized was the execution of four laborers from the Philippine Islands. A robbery had taken place in a Riyadh business, and four young Filipino men were identified as suspects in the crime. Saudi Arabian police quickly located the four who had fled to the desert outside Riyadh. The terrified men were searched, and one of them was found to have a small knife. It had not been used in the robbery nor had it left his pocket prior to his arrest. However, having a knife in his possession during the robbery was considered proof of intent. The judge found all four men guilty of armed robbery with the potential of using the knife to commit murder.

The Filipino men were sentenced to death. The Western expatriate community sought help from embassies and home governments to stop the executions, but the punishments went forward as decried. Considered just retribution for their crime, the men were killed in the barbaric manner of an ancient system inconsistent with a modern civilized world. They were beheaded with the executioner's sword.

In 2000, one year before the terrorist attack on America, there were one hundred twenty-one public beheadings in Saudi Arabia. All were carried out in the name of Allah.

*　　*　　*

Islam is the only religion allowed of its citizens, but Saudi Arabia in the 1980s was filled with expatriates from all over the world, and many of them were Christian. Families such as ours, though not required to be Muslim, were not allowed to practice our faith in any open way. We became underground Christians, meeting surreptitiously in homes as did first century Believers.

Prior to our arrival in the Kingdom, several expatriate men from differing religious denominations formed a Christian council. Working together in secret, they organized a fellowship through which interested families could meet for worship. Using an underground network, word, often coded, was spread orally to those who expressed an interest in worship or who displayed an active faith. A resident of our compound told us about the gatherings and introduced us to the fellowship.

We gathered on Fridays, which we called "Desert Sundays," under the guise of a potluck dinner. Divided into small, flexible groups so that no crowd would be large enough to attract the attention of Mutaween, we met in designated homes across the city. Within the walls of private villas, we sang, shared concerns, had devotionals, prayer, and Bible studies. The leadership coordinated the weekly program so that each of the many groups received the same Scripture lesson in a given week.

It was a great opportunity, not only for Christian worship, but to meet other expatriates whom we would otherwise never know. The gatherings were multi-national; participants were from America, Europe, Asia, and even countries of the Middle East. Backgrounds were varied and interesting. We met families who were in the country with companies such as Merrill Lynch, Bell Canada, and Aramco. One fellow had been on NASA's astronaut list. Another was a graduate of the Citadel where he was a classmate of Pat Conroy, author of *Lords of Discipline*. Of course, I asked our new friend if the author had used literary license to exaggerate the hazing described in his novel. As the mother of sons in a military family, I hoped his answer would be in the affirmative. He assured me Mr. Conroy had not!

Some families were wealthy and accustomed to servants. Others, like ours, had never had a houseboy or a driver before coming to the Kingdom. Our Christian faith was often the only thing we had in common, but it was the basis for immediate kinship.

Western advisors tended to bring their families to live in the Kingdom, but Middle-Eastern men were more likely to be there without their wives and children. One Lebanese man with whom we became good friends frequently commented that I looked much like his sister and that visiting with us made him feel closer to the home and family he so missed.

During the 1980s, Lebanon was involved in a struggle over control of its government to determine whether it would remain a democracy with elections or become an Islamic state. Radicals were attempting to remove America's influence and the so-called "Christian" government in order to establish Shari'a in that nation. Both Sunni and Shi'a factions sought control.

Only a few years earlier, the government of Iran had fallen to extremists. The American Embassy in Tehran had been stormed and hostages taken. Emboldened by that "success," Shi'a militia groups formed, including the Iranian proxy Hezbollah, with the intent of spreading Islamic law to neighboring states. The method chosen was terrorism not evangelism, and the attacks on America, which began in Tehran, continued.

The American Embassy in Beirut was bombed. A few months later, the United States Marine barracks in Beirut was destroyed with a car bomb, resulting in the deaths of two-hundred forty-one Marines. And then, Malcolm Kerr, a brilliant scholar of the Middle East and President of the American University of Beirut was gunned down on his way to his office. In a few short years, radical Islam's war against America had spread from Iran to Lebanon.

* * *

Ziad Samir Jarrah, a privileged only son, was from Mazraa, Lebanon, a suburb of Beirut. His Muslim parents sent their son to a Catholic school where they believed he would get a superior education. Indifferent to politics or religion, Jarrah rarely attended Friday mosque prayers.

In 1996 he moved to Germany where he studied at the University of Greifswald. There, he met and eventually married an attractive, intelligent, and Westernized Turkish woman who was studying to be a physician.

While in Germany, Jarrah became acquainted with Mohammed Atta, the Egyptian who was disillusioned with the nepotism and squalor in his native country and with Marwan Al-Shehhi, who was from the United Arab Emirates. Together, the three attended the Al Quds Mosque in Hamburg, Germany, where radical Islam was taught. Each man subsequently swore his allegiance to Al Qaeda and to Osama bin Laden.

Mohammed Atta flew American Airlines Flight 11 into the North Tower of the World Trade Center, and his cousin Marwan Al-Shehhi flew United Airlines Flight 175 into the South Tower.

Ziad Samir Jarrah, the privileged only son from Lebanon, the young man who, until he attended a radical mosque in Hamburg, Germany, had not been interested in politics or religion flew United Airlines Flight 93 into the countryside of Pennsylvania.

Just before the crash, the cockpit recorder captured the words screamed by one of the hijackers, "Allah is the greatest!" In the perverted logic of jihadists, the attack on America was Death for Apostasy.

* * *

It was in the underground Christian fellowship that we met Waleed, the Palestinian young man who spent time in a Saudi jail. His friends had delivered food to him during his time of incarceration after a Saudi youngster crashed his bicycle into the side of Waleed's automobile. A single man, Waleed had lived and worked in the Kingdom for many years. As an Arab, it was particularly important that he keep his Christian faith secret outside our group.

We had been in the country less than a year when we received urgent calls for prayer. Each of the men who served in leadership roles on the Christian council had been arrested in a late night round up. They were being held in jail and interrogated.

It was rumored that surveillance cameras had been installed near some of the homes in an effort to document the groups who gathered each Friday. Perhaps Saudi residents had become suspicious of the unusual gatherings and alerted authorities. More likely, Mutaween, who were always looking for infractions of Islamic law, had become aware of groups of expatriates coming together each Friday.

No one knew how widespread the arrests would become. We all wondered if our door might be next to be crashed – if we, too, would face a Saudi jail. I hoped my husband's position as an advisor to the Kingdom's Air Force would provide a crucial measure of protection for our family.

While the arrested men were held in jail, their families were given one week to leave the Kingdom. Losing their lucrative jobs, the men were ultimately deported and barred from returning to Saudi Arabia.

We admired and appreciated the courage of the organizers who, at great personal risk, developed a way for Christians to meet and worship in a country that not only forbids organizations but also prohibits any religion other than the "one true religion," Islam.

From that time on, we met only within our compounds. We still had Bible study, prayer, and a potluck meal, but we were limited to a few interested families and the occasional AWACS "morale officer" visit.

I had always heard about the "godless" Soviet Union where religious worship was not allowed. Now I lived in a "god-filled" Arabia in which every rule of life was governed by Allah and his messenger Mohammed. But just as in the "godless" Soviet Union, all worship was prohibited in this "god-filled" state – unless it was Islamic.

* * *

We knew an Arab couple who were neither Muslim nor part of the Christian fellowship. Leyla, lovely and statuesque, could have been a fashion model. Her porcelain skin, gleaming black hair, and artful makeup made her noticeable in any gathering. She dressed tastefully and always modestly, but very stylishly as well.

The couple lived in a comfortable villa with servants for every task. Leyla was known for her gracious dinner parties. It was common for her to entertain twenty to thirty people, all seated at a formal, beautifully set table. As a wealthy woman, she enjoyed a measure of luxury in the Kingdom.

However, the Mutaween seemed particularly offended by Arab women who were not Muslim. Leyla endured frequent harassment by the religious police who scolded her for not wearing a veil and abaya. It was not only Mutaween who scorned her. Some Saudi men who could see her attractive face treated her with disrespect as well.

Leyla's Ethiopian driver delivered her to the city's newest boutique in a modern building. She entered the women's shopping area, which even in new buildings was secluded; partitions kept passing males from catching a glimpse of female shoppers. Safely inside the segregated area, Leyla waited for a friend whose driver had not yet delivered her. A woman alone in any market is a rarity in the country.

As Leyla looked at expensive designer gowns, a Saudi man entered the partitioned area, eased up behind her and groped her across her breast. Without flinching, Leyla, who was taller than he, spun around and with a right fist to the jaw decked the intruder.

As the stunned and humiliated man scrambled to gather his thobe and get to his feet, Leyla's friend entered the shopping area. After cursing her attacker in Arabic, Leyla warned her friend to stand back as the "scum" got out of their way. He slunk away without a word.

"Vermin," Leyla's husband muttered indignantly, after telling us of her experience.

The need to protect honor was bound intrinsically to the culture, but it was not restricted to matters of religion, family, or sexuality. We repeatedly saw the importance of preserving honor in everyday life. Just as we might argue over who will pay the restaurant bill, there was the same kind of back and forth exchange in almost everything: who would go through the door first; who would receive the best seat; who would serve tea. Each of the contenders knew, because of his status, which person would ultimately be afforded the position of honor. Nevertheless, the exchange took place so as not to humiliate the 'lesser" man.

In general, it was difficult, if not impossible, for Saudi Arabian men to admit error. Like the Iranian flight students had been, they simply could not suffer the loss of face by admitting they were wrong. Allah's will was the explanation for any mishap. Further, the spoken word was all that was necessary. If something was said to have been done, it was done. Finished. No discussion. One never contradicted or changed the spoken word, particularly when it came from an Islamic leader or a member of the Royal Family, the guardians of Islam. Honor had to be preserved.

An acquaintance who was an officer in the Army Corps of Engineers told of a dramatic instance in which the spoken word carried more weight than visible evidence. As an advisor to the Department of Transportation, he worked with a Saudi counterpart who was not a member of the Royal Family.

An oil tanker had overturned on a narrow pass through a hillside west of the city, resulting in a significant oil spill. The tanker lay on its side on the precipice, completely blocking the roadway. Our friend and his Saudi counterpart went to the site to decide how to clear the pass. A number of scenarios were discussed, and they were all difficult: attempt to upright the tanker and tow it out; push the tanker over the side of the hill; dismantle and haul it out piece by piece. Then, what was to be done about the spilled oil? The two men decided upon recommendations to be made to the prince who headed the department. Western advisors formulated plans and made recommendations, but decisions were always made by a member of the Royal Family. He alone had the authority to direct any action to be taken. After a week with no response or directive from the prince, our American friend asked his Saudi co-worker what action had been decided.

"It is finished. All done." The Saudi replied.

"What has been done?" asked the American in amazement. It was inconceivable to him that such a major transportation issue had been resolved so effortlessly and without his knowledge. "Was the tanker pushed over the side? How was the road repaired so quickly? Can traffic safely use the pass?"

"Yes, yes, all finished. No problem," again was the response.

Puzzled, our friend returned to the site to see how the tanker had been removed and the oil cleaned. To his shock, the scene remained exactly as before. No effort had been made to clear the wreck and resultant oil spill.

After returning to his office and receiving the same response, he insisted the Saudi accompany him on a return trip to the hillside pass. As they approached the tanker, the Saudi said, "It is fixed. No problem. All done."

Even in the face of obvious contradiction, the spoken word, especially from a member of the Royal Family, was absolute. After stating something as truth, it was impossible to admit error. The need to "save-face," the reliance on the spoken word, the enforcement of Shari'a, the prohibition of other religions, the scorn of non-believers, and death for apostasy were all means of protecting and avenging honor.

18
IN THE NAME OF HONOR

I never doubted his sincerity. Ahmed believed his words were true and honest and, well, even honorable. From birth he had been taught his role as a man – the preferred gender. He was an Arab for whom "saving face" was practiced as an art; a proud Saudi Arabian whose birthplace was also the birthplace of Islam; a Muslim whose death for Allah would secure Paradise.

His was a culture of honor, as defined by the seventh century traditions of the Prophet. Ahmed understood well that women were carriers of the honor – both for the family and the culture. Honor was more important than life. It had to be protected. It had to be avenged when damaged.

Murder is unlawful in Islam. In Saudi Arabia, the taking of another's life is punishable with death. Nevertheless, honor killings are still tolerated in much of the Muslim world, including the traditional families of Saudi Arabia. Killing in the name of honor is justified. It is excused, and any penalty for it is severely reduced.

Honor killings avenge the shame felt by men of the birth family. Perceived immorality is the most common trigger for this form of violence against women. A husband might kill his wife in a fit of rage, but it is more often her father or brothers who enact the ultimate punishment for an accused fault. Her actions, whether real or imagined, stain their reputations not that of her husband's, and the spilling of her "tainted" blood restores their family honor and that of the larger culture.

The United Nations Commission of Human Rights condemned the practice of honor killings in November 1998. One can reasonably conclude that the Commission's edict has done little toward ending the murder of women in the name of honor.

*   *   *

A tale of honor killing circulated in the Kingdom. It was one of many that gave example to the importance of preserving honor in the male-dominated Islamic state. Honor was determined not by a man's behavior but by the perceived behavior of females in his family.

The story told of Bedouins – desert nomads – who gave lodging for several days to men from a passing caravan. After being refreshed with food and drink in the Arabian tradition of hospitality, the men of the caravan prepared to resume their journey.

Before departing, however, the owner of the caravan suggested a marriage between his son and the Bedouin's daughter. It was not unusual for men away from home for long periods – on caravan trips, jihads, or tribal wars – to marry wives of convenience and then divorce them when they were no longer needed. The temporary marriages differed from ordinary ones only in that there was a set time limit – usually three nights, though the contract could be lengthened if desired.

The Bedouin refused the marriage proposal, and the caravan continued its trek across the desert without the requested bride. Later in the day, the Bedouin observed his daughter standing in the opening of the tent watching the slow moving caravan as it continued its journey across the flat Arabian Desert. Surely her only interest in the now distant travelers stemmed from a desire to have been allowed to marry the man from the caravan, the father concluded. How dare she long for any man and especially one whom he had refused? Such dishonor could not be tolerated.

The Bedouin killed his daughter. Spilling her blood avenged her behavior and restored his honor. It was an honor killing.

*   *   *

Honor killings are not restricted to the Bedouin of the desert or to past centuries. An alarming number of accounts have reached our media. We have been appalled by the senseless murders of females whose families immigrated to the West, presumably for a better life – a life of freedom. We read of a father in Dallas who murdered his daughters because they had boyfriends, a husband who killed his wife because she had become too much like her American neighbors, and men who killed their sisters for perceived immorality.

Possibly the most disconcerting case in America is that of Muzzammil Hassan, who lived with his wife in an affluent suburb of Buffalo, New York. The couple had established a television network, *Bridges,* with the stated purpose of countering stereotypes Westerners have of Muslim cultures.

In February 2009, Hassan's wife filed for divorce and requested an order of protection from her estranged husband. Only days later, she was discovered lying dead in the hallway outside the offices of *Bridges.* She had been decapitated! Hassan was arrested and charged with second degree murder.

How does our justice system determine whether a murder is an honor killing, an act of terrorism or, as some defendants have claimed, a domestic violence case that got terribly out of hand? And should it really matter when it comes to sentencing the perpetrator for the death of another person?

In general, honor killings have several characteristics that differentiate them from ordinary domestic violence. The victims of honor killings are Muslim females. The motivation is almost always a charge of immoral behavior. The perpetrator may be a husband, but more likely he will be a father or brothers.

Honor killings are often particularly brutal. The murder rarely happens in a fit of rage. Honor killings are planned and often have the support of family members. The killer claims to be the real victim, and his family does not shun him after the murder.

*   *   *

"Morsal liked hip-hop music and Afghan pop. She tried to live the kind of life she believed was correct, the life other girls in her school led…she was a girl who wanted nothing more than to be free."

Her family had fled Afghanistan and the repressive rule of the Taliban when she was only three. Settling in a large community of Afghan immigrants, the little girl had no memory of the life before, and by junior high school she had adapted well to her new country and her school – one that had students from eighteen different countries. The pretty girl was described as outspoken and spirited; she was even awarded a certificate as a "conflict mediator."

Her father and her older brother, Ahmad, did not adjust so well. A military fighter pilot for the Soviets in his old country, the proud father, struggling to find work as an immigrant, became a bus driver. But at home he was still in charge, still the master of the home. His family was the source of his pride and his honor. He determined that no one should be able to say that his children brought shame to him.

One of his most valued traditions was to defend his family's property and that included both his gold and his women. Clinging to the concept of honor, he resorted to the one advantage he had over females – brute strength. His son, Ahmad, learned his role as a man from his father.

"You are bringing shame to the family," the father and his son told Morsal.

The sixteen year old girl was sent back to Afghanistan to be reeducated in a Koran school taught in a language she did not understand. She claimed she had been taken to Afghanistan to be forced into a marriage but was allowed to return to her parents when she promised to obey them.

Shortly after Morsal returned to Hamburg, Germany, she was outside a McDonald's restaurant talking with a male cousin when her brother approached. Instantly sensing danger, she tried to run but stumbled and fell. Ahmad, seven years her senior, stood over his sister and stabbed her twenty times.

Spilling her tainted blood avenged her rebellious behavior – her desire to be like other girls – that had brought shame to his family. It was a murder for the sake of his honor and that of his father. It was an honor killing. It was May 2008.

During Ahmad Obeidi's sentencing for his sister's murder, he claimed that *he* was the real victim and that if the trial had taken place in Afghanistan, he would have been released long ago! The murdered girl's parents, in their son's defense, claimed Morsal bore some of the responsibility for her death.

* * *

A man of Kurdish descent, also living in Germany, killed his twenty year old sister, Gulsum. The family had attempted to force her into an arranged marriage, only to discover she was no longer a virgin. She was choked to unconsciousness and then clubbed to death. It was an honor killing. It was March 2009

* * *

In Saint Petersburg, Russia, a father hired two men to murder his twenty-one year old daughter, Rashida. Her crime: She wore short skirts. "The father's Muslim friends...started reproaching him for being negligent and allowing his daughter to walk around dressed like a fallen woman. They said the insult could only be washed away by blood." Rashida's lifeless body was discarded on a trash heap, but her father's honor was restored.

* * *

Her husband suspected she was having an affair. It was reason enough for his honor to be damaged. A charge of immorality did not have to be proved. The Jordanian court initially sentenced the man to fifteen years for the 2006 strangulation of his wife but immediately cut that sentence in half to give him a "chance to repent" though it is worth noting, the accused wife was given no such opportunity.

* * *

Of all the nations in the Middle East where honor killings are prevalent, only Jordan has raised a voice of condemnation. Saudi Arabia has been noticeably silent on the subject. Three members of the Jordanian Royal Family have spoken in opposition to this murderous practice: Queen Noor, wife of the deceased King Hussein, King Abdullah, Hussein's son and current monarch, and his wife, Queen Rania.

In 1998 both CNN and ABC began working on a story of honor killings in Jordan. Queen Noor, cooperating with the reports, is quoted as saying, "...this type of violence against

women is not consistent with Islam or with our constitution."
The queen, born in America of Arab descent, said that she has
"...very strong personal feelings as a Muslim, as a woman, as a
wife, and as a mother about this form of violence and every
form of violence against women."

Despite the work of the Royal Family and Queen Noor's
assertion, the Jordanian constitution still allows this archaic and
brutal practice:

> "...he who discovers his wife or one of
> his female relatives committing adultery and
> kills, wounds, or injures one of them, is
> exempted from penalty."... "He who
> commits a crime in a fit of fury caused by an
> unrightful and dangerous act on the part of
> the victim benefits from a reduction of
> penalty."

"[Jordanian] Parliament has refused to reform the penal
code in order to ensure harsher sentences." In 2008 seventeen
honor killings were recorded in that country. One can only
speculate the actual number of women murdered in countries
that tolerate the deplorable spilling of blood in the name of
honor. There are, undoubtedly, countless instances of which we
will never hear.

* * *

Veiling, seclusion in the harem, forced marriages of child
brides, punishment of "disobedient" wives, and prohibitions
against driving and employment are all part of the Islamic
culture of Saudi Arabia. They are, however, not the only
measures imposed on females in the name of honor.
Circumcision of young girls, the removal of all genitalia, is still
widely practiced. Estimates claim that ninety-seven percent of
Arab women have suffered this procedure, often by the age of
seven.

I have read that this mutilation is performed most
barbarically in some African States. I can only wonder how it is

accomplished in the remote Bedouin areas of the Arabian Desert and in the traditional settlements such as Khamis Mushayt and Hofuf.

An article published in the Arab News describes the practice as less common in Saudi Arabia than in African nations, but still prevalent, particularly in Southern Arabia:

> Most often this procedure is done without the care of medically trained people and the use of anesthesia is rare. The girl is held down by older women to prevent her from moving around. The instruments used by the midwife will vary and could include broken glass, a tin lid, razor blades, knives, scissors or any other sharp object. These items usually are not sterilized before or after usage and often the same instrument is used on several girls at the same time. Once the genital area for removal is gone, the child is stitched up and her legs are bound for up to 40 days.

Many years ago I watched a televised program that told of a French Catholic nun who had lived and worked for decades with the "trash people" of Egypt. Families who were garbage collectors for cities actually made their homes among the piles of refuse they collected, hauled, and dumped. The nun was said to have tried, unsuccessfully, to teach women how dangerous such a brutal act as female circumcision could be. Without benefit of sterile cutting implements, clean bandages, or trained professionals to perform the "surgery," the results could be horrific: massive infection, uncontrolled bleeding, emotional scarring, and even death. Botched female circumcisions leave tremendous disfigurement. With all the surrounding genitalia removed, there is nothing left to repair.

Many cultures believe the procedure is necessary in order for girls to maintain proper cleanliness and to be accepted as appropriate wives; no man would want a wife who had not been given this altered anatomy. Female circumcision can have only one ultimate purpose and that is to protect the honor of male family members. If a woman has no sexual desire, she is more likely to remain chaste.

Virginity of the bride is the standard for honor to the new husband. In Bedouin tribal life, not only was virginity required, the wife was expected to fight her husband on the wedding night in order to prove her virtue. The more she resisted, greater was the proof of her chastity.

Older women of the tribe displayed the bloodied bed sheet after consummation to demonstrate the virginity of the bride. Her husband was honored, both in having married a virgin and in overpowering his resisting wife into submission.

Affluent women throughout the Muslim world, knowing the life and death necessity to prove their virginity at marriage, have subjected themselves to surgical stitching called a hymenoplasty in order to ensure a blood-stained sheet when their marriages are consummated. One can only guess at the desperate measures taken by women without financial means who do not have access to the surgical procedure.

*   *   *

The radical interpretation of Islam, the enforcement of Shari'a, the culture of domestic violence, and the emphasis placed on family honor bred both wife-beaters and terrorists. Men who believed it was their right to punish women were more likely to embrace other extremist views.

A jihad, a holy war to rid the world of "evil" and establish a global Islamic Caliphate, would have been considered a noble endeavor by many who engaged in the physical abuse of females. Both honor killings and death to Infidels were justified in the name of honor.

Islam is the religion that is prominent in the Middle East. It claims roots, as do Judaism and Christianity, from Abraham, a man of faith who lived four thousand years ago.

19

THE PATRIARCH

He was the first patriarch of Judaism, a revered prophet in Islam, and the father of faith in Christianity. His descendants are the people whose Ten Commandments became the framework of Western law, whose Ark of the Covenant has been immortalized in film, whose lives have been portrayed in epic dramas and countless books. His offspring have both triumphed over their enemies and been held in captivity as slaves. They have suffered unspeakable discrimination and monstrous persecution. For centuries they have struggled to inhabit a specific geographic area, a piece of land that has come to be known as the Holy Land.

How much do we know about this man named Abraham who lived four thousand years ago and whose life still impacts three major religions coming out of the Middle East? The Biblical record of Abraham places him ten generations after Noah and about five centuries before Moses. He was a man with all the frailties of human-kind, but about him Scripture says, "Abraham believed God and it was accounted to him for righteousness."

Abram and his wife, Sarai, lived with many members of his birth family in the *Ur of the Chaldeans*, a land thought to be modern day Iraq. He was seventy-five years old when in an act of faith he left his home to become a nomad who spent the remainder of his life in tents.

Initially he moved with his father to a land called Haran before settling in Canaan. God had spoken to him, saying:

> "Get out of your country, from your family and from your father's house, to a land that I will show you. I will make you a great nation; I will bless you and make your name great; and you shall be a blessing. I will bless those who bless you and I will

curse him who curses you; and in you all the
families of the earth shall be blessed."

In time, Canaan suffered a severe famine, forcing Abram to
move to Egypt where food was available. As he approached the
land of the Pharaohs, he became concerned for his safety. Sarai
was a very beautiful woman. Abram feared that when the
princes of Pharaoh saw her, he would be killed so that she could
be taken into Pharaoh's house. Oddly, the Egyptians respected
marriage, but they did not respect life. The murder of a husband
so that a desired woman would be available was acceptable.

"Please say you are my sister, that it may be well with me
for your sake, and that I may live because of you," he asked of
his wife, who complied with his request.

Sarai was taken into the house of Pharaoh. In return, the
Egyptian ruler "treated Abram well for her sake." But it did not
go so well for Pharaoh. Great plagues came upon him and his
house, causing him to say to Abram, "What is this you have
done to me? Why did you not tell me that she was your wife?
Why did you say, 'She is my sister?' I might have taken her as
my wife. Now therefore, here is your wife; take her and go your
way."

Abram was a man of great wealth; he possessed large herds
of livestock, gold and silver, and many slaves. Because his wife
was barren, there was no heir to whom he would leave any of
his wealth. Sarai devised a solution to ease her disgrace in not
having borne children for her husband and to the problem of
who would inherit Abram's wealth.

She offered her Egyptian maidservant, Hagar, to her
husband, so that Abram would produce an heir. Sarai soon
regretted that decision. When Hagar saw that she had conceived
a child by Abram, she began to despise her mistress and to taunt
her. Sarai, grieved by the taunting, punished Hagar, who then
fled for her safety.

According to the Bible, an angel of the Lord found Hagar
and said to her, "Return to your mistress and submit yourself
under her hand...I will multiply your descendants

exceedingly…" Hagar did return to her place of servitude, and in time she gave birth to a son, Ishmael.

Abram was ninety-nine years old when God reiterated the covenant He had made. Abram's name was changed to Abraham and his wife's name to Sarah. The covenant was affirmed as an everlasting one; it included a promise that Abraham would be the father of many generations, of many nations, and of kings. It also gave all the land of Canaan to Abraham's descendants as an everlasting possession.

Abraham undoubtedly thought the generations of descendants God promised would come through Ishmael, his son by Hagar. Sarah was, by that time, well past the normal age of bearing a child. Scripture tells us that Abraham fell on his face and laughed, saying, "Shall a child be born to a man who is one hundred years old? And shall Sarah, who is ninety years old, bear a child? Oh that Ishmael might live before you." But God made clear that the "Son of the Promise" would be born of Sarah:

> "No, Sarah your wife shall bear you a son, and you shall call his name Isaac. I will establish My covenant with him for an everlasting covenant and with his descendants after him.
>
> And as for Ishmael, I have heard you. Behold, I have blessed him, and will make him fruitful, and will multiply him exceedingly. He shall beget twelve princes, and I will make him a great nation.
>
> But My covenant I will establish with Isaac, whom Sarah shall bear to you at this set time next year."

Isaac was born to Abraham and Sarah the following year. "God has made me laugh, and all who hear will laugh with me," Sarah said. She marveled, not only that she had borne a child in her old age, but also that she was able to nurse him. Isaac grew, and on the day he was weaned, Abraham made a great celebratory feast.

During the festivities, Sarah observed Ishmael, who was about thirteen years old, scoffing at Isaac. Insisting that her husband remove both Hagar and Ishmael, Sarah said, "Cast out this bondwoman and her son; for the son of this bondwoman shall not be heir with my son, namely with Isaac."

So, Abraham sent Hagar and Ishmael away after giving them bread and water. They departed and wandered in the Wilderness of Beersheba. Spared death in the harsh desert, Ishmael and his mother settled in the Wilderness of Paran, which is today's Arabia.

Many years after Hagar and Ishmael left, according to the Bible, God tested Abraham's faith by telling him, "Take now your son, your only son, Isaac, whom you love, and go to the land of Moriah, and offer him there as a burnt offering on one of the mountains of which I shall tell you."

Abraham and Isaac, who was likely a young adult by then, traveled along with two men to the mountain as directed by God. The journey lasted three days.

As Abraham prepared the burnt offering, Isaac said, "My father!...Look, the fire and the wood, but where is the lamb for a burnt offering?"

"My son, God will provide for Himself the lamb for a burnt offering," Abraham replied.

And so it was. As Abraham readied his son on the altar, an angel of the Lord called out to him, saying, "Abraham, Abraham. Do not lay your hand on the lad, or do anything to him; for now I know that you fear God since you have not withheld your son, your only son, from Me." Abraham took a ram, caught by its horn in a nearby thicket, and offered it as a burnt offering instead of his son.

*   *   *

Sarah died at the age of one hundred twenty-seven years. After her death, Abraham married again and fathered six more sons. Little about them or his sons by concubines is recorded in Scripture, except that they settled in countries to the east.

Only Isaac remained as Abraham's son, and it was to him that all of his father's inheritance was given when Abraham died at the age of one hundred seventy-five. The familiar names recorded in Scripture are all from the family of Abraham through his son Isaac: Joseph, Moses, Samuel, David, Solomon, and Elijah. Two thousand years after Abraham, Jesus Christ was born in the lineage of Isaac, the "Son of the Promise."

Abraham was a mortal whose imperfect life proved him, nonetheless, to be a man of faith. God told Abraham, "In your seed all the nations of the earth shall be blessed, because you have obeyed My voice."

*   *   *

Abraham is the father, or first patriarch, of Judaism. His son Isaac married Rebecca, who produced twin sons: Jacob and Esau. Jacob, whose name was changed to Israel, had twelve sons from whom the twelve tribes of Israel were formed. In Judaism, the people of Israel are chosen to keep the laws of God as recorded in the Torah.

The rite of circumcision was established as a sign of the covenant God made with Abraham and with his descendants through the "Son of the Promise." Mount Moriah, the place of Abraham's willingness to offer his son Isaac became, a thousand years later, the site of the Temple of the Jews in Jerusalem.

*   *   *

Abraham is called the Father of Faith in Christianity. Christians believe Abraham's willingness to offer his only son Isaac, the "Son of the Promise," is a foreshadowing of God's willingness to offer His only son so that the world would not perish but have everlasting life.

Further, the sacrificial ram is a representation of the Christ who became the sacrificial Lamb of God, providing atonement and redemption for all who believe. The crucifixion of Christ was on Golgotha, a hill near the Jewish Temple on Mount Moriah.

*   *   *

Abraham is an immensely important prophet in Islam, which teaches that he left the land of his father to establish a monotheistic religion. Muslims believe that God's covenant with Abraham is fulfilled in the descendants of Ishmael. Circumcision, which is not required in the Koran, is a semi-religious practice and not a sign of the covenant. Most importantly, Islam teaches that Ishmael was the son offered and that the sacrificial event took place in Mecca.

Arabia, the land in which Abraham's son Ishmael is believed to have settled, became, twenty-seven centuries later, the birthplace of Islam. The new religion was taught by a prophet named Mohammed who declared that he was Allah's Messenger.

20
ALLAH'S MESSENGER

The national flag of Saudi Arabia is the color of
Mohammed's cloak. It is a field of green on which the
Prophet's declaration of faith is inscribed in Arabic: *There is no
god but Allah and Mohammed is his messenger.* A long sword,
symbolizing the victories of Abdul Aziz ibn Sa'ud, the first
king of Saudi Arabia, stretches beneath the inscription. The old
king, thirteen centuries after the birth of Islam, united the
Arabian Peninsula as an Islamic state. It is one that adheres to
the teachings and traditions of Allah's Messenger.

The childhood of the Prophet Mohammed was traumatic.
Born in Mecca, Arabia, in about 570 AD, he was orphaned and
lived in poverty. His father, a poor merchant, died either before
Mohammed's birth or shortly afterwards, and his mother died
when the boy was six years old. After the death of his mother,
Mohammed was adopted by his grandfather who died two years
later. The boy was then taken in and cared for by an uncle who
was also quite poor.

Mohammed's family was of the tribe of Koreish, which was
a significant tribe in Arabia. However, his immediate family
was a side branch and had no prestige, power, importance, or
wealth. They lived very humbly, probably in a house built of
mud walls with a roof thatched of date-palm leaves. There was,
undoubtedly, a shortage of food. Mohammed spent his
childhood as a shepherd and as an attendant of caravans.
Neither would have been a position of honor.

His adoptive uncle, Abu Talib, who became Mohammed's
best friend and protector, occasionally made caravans or trading
trips to southern Arabia, to Syria, and probably to Palestine as
well. The young Mohammed accompanied his uncle on these
long merchant trips where he had exposure to both Christians
and Jews and to their oral traditions.

The men of Arabia had a long oral history. Few could read,
but all loved the beauty of the spoken word. At night, men

gathered around campfires and shared their stories, their poetry, legends, and religious beliefs. Memorized, embellished, and most likely altered, the oral traditions continued. Each raconteur repeated the stories, adding his own zeal and fervor for the enjoyment of all.

So strong is the power of the oral tradition, to this day Saudi Arabian men love the spoken word in general and poetry in particular. It is said that recitation of poetry can bring tears to the eyes of men who have heard the same verses all their lives.

When he was twenty-five, Mohammed began service for an older, wealthy widow named Khadijah, who was also a descendant of the Koreish tribe. He accompanied her caravans to trade fairs in Mecca. Caravans were always at great risk from marauding raiders and thieves who waited for the chance to steal camels and plunder goods meant for trade. Tribal warfare was common. Men lived and died by the sword. *He who smites with the spear and wields the sword will inherit* had long been the Arab tradition.

Travelers were afforded hospitality and lodging along the way, even by enemy tribes. Strangers were taken in and given rest, food, and drink for three days before being asked their names. Desert life was so harsh that without this code of hospitality many travelers would have died. One could rest in the protection of his host and be refreshed with dates, dried bread, and a bit of camel's milk before continuing his journey across the stark Arabian Desert.

Once his travel resumed, however, there was no expectation of protection from his host, who then might become the plunderer. Camel raids were almost a game. Stolen camels were recaptured, stolen again, and recaptured with the zeal of team sport.

Tribal and family idols offered the best hope of protection for caravans traversing the desert. The polytheistic Arabia, before Islam, had hundreds of different gods and goddesses. Allah was one of many named gods, but he was not worshipped, ritualized, or believed to be involved in human affairs.

Hundreds of gods were brought to Mecca, which was the site of trading fairs and the central shrine of idol worship. Tucked into camel bags for the journey, various family idols offered needed protection, as well as hope for trading success. Additionally, 360 idols were housed in the cube-shaped shrine, the Ka'aba. A specific idol for use in the Ka'aba was provided for each calendar day of the year.

Some of the idols required the sacrificing of children. Idols had to be appeased, and the deaths of children provided surety of the idols' favor. Female infanticide was a common practice, both in idol sacrifice and as the unwanted gender at birth. Baby girls were buried in the desert sand and left to die.

After two years of service to her, the twice-widowed Khadijah proposed marriage to Mohammed. As the husband of a wealthy woman, he continued the merchant caravans to trading fairs in Mecca but without much enthusiasm. Mohammed gradually became more reclusive, preferring to spend his time in reflection and solitary contemplation.

Khadijah had a relative named Waraka, who had embraced Judaism. From Waraka, Mohammed learned of *Adonai,* the God of Israel, the creator and sustainer of life. He heard stories of the Patriarchs of Israel: Abraham, Isaac, and Jacob. He learned of Joseph, Moses, and David.

At age forty, Mohammed is said to have received his first divine communication from the Angel Gabriel, who commanded him to teach the "true religion" that came to be known as Islam.

The religion teaches that Mohammed made a miraculous night journey from the Ka'aba in Mecca to Jerusalem on a white, flying horse called *El-Buraq.* (Jerusalem is not specifically named in the Koran as the holy city of Mohammed's night flight.) It was during his time spent in the holy city that Mohammed stopped to pray at the rock – the remains of the Jewish temple on Mount Moriah. From that point, he climbed to heaven on a suspended stairway that alternated between golden and silver steps. After personal tutelage by Allah, Mohammed returned to Mecca aboard the same flying steed and arrived at his home before dawn.

Six years after Mohammed's death, his followers captured the city of Jerusalem. Later that century, Muslims built the Dome of the Rock on the very site where the Jewish Temple had stood. The spectacular edifice of Islam was, in part, meant to commemorate the miraculous night journey of its prophet.

*   *   *

The new religion Mohammed taught had two basic doctrines that were in direct contradiction to polytheistic Arabia. He declared there is no God but Allah and, therefore, the hundreds of idols being worshipped were meaningless. He taught that while Jewish prophets had received some word from God and Christians some also, the final revelation had been given to him and that he was Allah's Messenger.

Mohammed's teachings were revolutionary in the day in which he lived. He forbade usury, the charging of interest. He condemned the giving of false witness against a brother Muslim, although false witness could be given to save one's life or reputation or if telling the truth would cause financial ruin. He elevated the status of the poor and taught that alms should be given to help them. Brotherly love, however, was confined to other Muslims. He taught that all sons born to a man had equal inheritance. There were no illegitimate sons, whether born of wives, concubines, mistresses, or slaves. Mohammed taught that parents should be obeyed and revered. Slaves, wives, and orphans should be treated with kindness. The eating of pork, the drinking of wine or other intoxicants, and gambling were forbidden. Any form of apostasy was not allowed and all apostates were to be punished.

Mohammed condemned infanticide. Pre-Islamic Arabs practiced infanticide for multiple purposes: idol sacrifice, gender preference, and to avoid the possibility of dishonor to the family, caused by a daughter's perceived scandalous behavior. We were told in our cultural training course, prior to moving to the Kingdom, that the practice of female infanticide still existed in some parts of the remote desert of Arabia. I have no way of confirming if, in fact, unwanted infant girls are still buried alive in the desert sand.

Though Mohammed forbade the practice of sacrificing children to idols, he did not condemn the selling of one's children into slavery. The slave trade flourished in Mecca with traders and pilgrims, primarily from Africa, selling humans into a lifetime of bondage. Mohammed's descendants, the Shareef, continued the slave trade after the establishment of Islam and profited financially from it for hundreds of years. Hajjis, pilgrims performing the religious journey of their lifetime, sold their children into slavery in order to finance their trips home.

Mohammed did not condemn plural marriages, the keeping of concubines, or the forced marriages of child brides. Following his example, Islam allowed a man to have four wives at a time. Concubines and slave mistresses were permitted in any number, though most Muslim cultures no longer sanction the keeping of concubines or slaves. Mohammed taught that women should be covered to preserve their modesty and to protect them from being molested.

Because Mohammed was illiterate, all of his teachings were given orally. Others wrote them in Arabic and put them into a collection that formed the Koran. According to some Islamic scholars, the fact that the Prophet was illiterate underscores the miraculous nature of the revelation to him.

In the beginning, Mohammed had very few followers, called Mohammedans or Muslims; most were either members of his family or his slaves. Merchants feared that his teachings against usury and idol worship would ruin them financially. He was despised as a madman, an imposter, and a liar. Arabians rejected his new religion and rose up against the Messenger of Allah.

In the year 622, Mohammed sought refuge in the city of Medina when he learned that the Koreish tribe, the tribe of his family in Mecca, planned to kill him. His flight to safety is known as the *Hijra* and it marks the beginning of the Muslim calendar. In Medina, Mohammed assumed leadership of the two most powerful tribes. Gradually the number of his followers increased, and eventually he was ready to go to war with the Meccans who had rejected him and his teachings.

Calling the battle a jihad, a holy war, he fought the enemies of Islam in the name of Allah. The Arab tradition that "He who smites with the spear and effectively wields the sword would inherit" prevailed. Against incredible odds, the battle of 314 Muslims against 600 Meccans was won by Mohammed's men. The conquering by sword validated the religion. His followers began to spread Islamic teachings both by word and by the sword.

In the Christian tradition, in matters of personal relationships, Jesus taught that if someone strikes one of your cheeks, you must turn the other. In Islam, according to a young Palestinian interviewed for a televised PBS program I watched, Christians turn the other cheek. Muslims hit back twice.

* * *

Mohammed's wife Khadijah bore him six children, but his sons died in infancy, leaving him with four daughters. Khadijah, too, died several years into their marriage. Mohammed, who was forty-eight, was encouraged by his friends to take another wife. His friend and associate Abu Bakr who had embraced Islam had a six year old daughter, Aisha.

The little girl had already been betrothed to a man from another tribe, a man who was not yet a Muslim. By mutual agreement that betrothal was voided, clearing the way for her to become the Prophet's wife. Three years later the marriage was consummated after she had what was believed to be her first menses. While the onset of menstruation is indeed rare at that age, the likelihood of an impoverished child with a lack of nutrition developing so early seems even more remote.

Aisha remained one of Mohammed's wives until his death when she was eighteen years old, but she bore him no children. Many of the revelations the Prophet received from Allah were said to have been given when he was in the company of this favored wife.

The original designation of the four great women of Islam was made before Aisha reached her supreme position within the faith. Scholars of the Hadith have said about her, "The virtue of Aisha...over all the women of the world is like the virtue of [a meat dish] over all other food." While Sunni Muslims consider Aisha an exemplary Muslim woman, many Shi'a Muslims do not hold her in the same high regard. Instead, Shi'a exalt Fatimah, the youngest daughter of the Prophet and wife of Ali whom they believe is the first legitimate Imam to follow Mohammed.

In addition to Khadijah and Aisha, Mohammed's other wives were:

Sawda bint Zam'a was a widow and sixty-five years old at the time of her marriage to Mohammed.

Hafsah bint U'mar was married to the Prophet after several other men refused her father's offer of his daughter.

Zaynab bint Khuzayma died three months after her marriage to Mohammed.

Salama bint Umayya was a widow with many children when she married the Prophet.

Zaynab bint Jahsh was the daughter of Mohammed's aunt, Omameh. Zaynab was married to Zayed, but the Prophet received a verse in the Koran that stated if the marriage of Zaynab and Zayed did not last, the Prophet must marry her. So, he did.

Juwayriya bint Al-Harith became a prisoner after her tribe lost a battle with the Muslims; her father offered Mohammed a payment for her release, but after negotiations, she became the Prophet's wife instead of being returned to the tent of her father.

Safiyya bint Huyayy was said to be of the tribe of Beni Nadir, descendents of Levi of Israel.

Ummu Habiba bint Sufyan's first husband was the son of Mohammed's aunt. After his death in Ethiopia, the king of that African nation arranged the marriage between the widowed Ummu and Mohammed.

Mayamuna bint Al-Harith was from Mecca and accepted Islam early in her life.

Maria Al-Qabtiyya and three other women were slaves who were given to Mohammed as a gift from the King of Egypt. Maria Al-Qabtiyya bore the Prophet a son, and she was the only one of his wives, other than Khadijah, to do so.

Rayhana was taken captive as part of the spoils after Mohammed and his men attacked her tribe. She did not embrace Islam but was said to have had a respectable position in the home of the Prophet as one of his wives.

Mohammed died in 632, ten years after the Hijra – his escape to Medina when his life was threatened. None of his widows remarried. A passage in the Koran forbade the marriage of any Muslim to a widow of the Prophet.

Following his death, his converts had many questions about the practice of Islam that had not been spelled out in the Koran. It was decided that, in addition to his teachings, the example of the Prophet's life and that of his closest companions would serve as a holy guide. The subsequent collection of writings about the earliest patriarchs of the religion comprise the *Hadith* or *the traditions*. At least one-third of the Hadith is attributed to the words of Aisha, the youngest and favorite of the Prophet's wives.

The combination of the Koran and the Hadith became the basis of Shari'a, the social code of Islam. Shari'a is considered "the straight path." It governs every aspect of life in the Islamic state of Saudi Arabia.

Mohammed's teachings incorporated the Old Testament Patriarchs of Israel about whom Waraka, his wife's relative, had taught him. Surely his teachings were influenced by the oral traditions of both Judaism and Christianity to which Mohammed had been exposed during trading caravans into Syria and Palestine. Additionally, the new religion, "the final revelation" given by the Angel Gabriel retained many of the practices of old, polytheistic Arabia.

Arabians practiced prayer to plural gods and they made an annual pilgrimage to the Ka'aba, the shrine of worship in Mecca even before Mohammed's establishment of Islam. Both the practice of prayer and the annual pilgrimage were continued in

Islam with changes made to fit the new monotheistic teachings of Mohammed.

During the annual pilgrimage, a day is set aside for visiting Arafat, the mountain where, according to Islam, "the final revelation [of the Koran] was sent." Burak Sansal in "Hajj and Eid" explains the importance of the annual pilgrimage:

> "Hajj is also an act of renunciation. Muslims from every corner of the globe wear their coffins – two cotton sheets – to represent their deaths to this life and head to their Primordial Home. They pay their debts, ask forgiveness of everyone, bid farewell to one and all, and prepare to die to this world to live in Him."

Mohammed, born in the sixth century after Christ, proclaimed that he was the Messenger of Allah. He taught the stories of Judaism and Christianity, the stories of the Bible, but he taught them differently. He taught that the black rock that became the cornerstone of the Ka'aba had fallen from Heaven as God's sign of reconciliation with Adam and Eve. He taught that Abraham left the land of his father because of disagreement over plural gods. He taught that God's covenant with Abraham would be fulfilled through Ishmael. He said it was Ishmael, Abraham's son by Hagar the Egyptian servant of Sarah, who was offered in sacrifice and not Isaac. He taught that Jesus Christ was born in a miraculous event but was no more than a prophet. He taught that God had revealed some truths to the Jewish prophets and some to Christians, but the final revelation from God had been given to him by the Angel Gabriel.

The Prophet's teaching about Paradise is described by Wollaston in *Mohammed, His Life and Doctrines:*

> The pleasures of Paradise will be so overwhelming that God will give to everyone the potentialities of a hundred individuals. To each individual a large mansion will be assigned, and the very

meanest will have at his disposal at least 80,000 servants and seventy-two wives of the girls of paradise.

While eating they will be waited on by 300 attendants, the food being served in dishes of gold, whereof 300 shall be set before him at once, containing each a different kind of food and an inexhaustible supply of wine and liquors.

The magnificence of the garments and gems is conformable to the delicacy of their diet. For they will be clothed in the richest silks and brocades, and adorned with bracelets of gold and silver and crowns set with pearls, and will make use of silken carpets, couches, pillows....God will grant them perpetual youth, beauty and vigour.

There are three divisions of Muslims. Each claims to represent the true teachings of the Prophet Mohammed:

Shi'a Muslims believe that Mohammed's cousin and son-in-law, Ali, was the legitimate successor to the Prophet. Imams, religious leaders, were to be direct descendants of Ali. Since the disappearance of the twelfth descendant, Muhammad al Mahdi, and until his messianic-like return, representatives not descendants of Mohammed serve as Imams.

Sunni Muslims believe that leadership within the religion should come from community consensus. Sunnis comprise 85% of the Muslim population. Saudi Arabians, for the most part, are Sunni and hold to the teachings of a religious leader, Muhammad ibn Abd al-Wahhab, who believed Islam should not stray from the traditions of the patriarchs.

Sufism is a form of Islamic mysticism. Muhammad ibn Abd al-Wahhab repudiated all vestiges of Sufism.

The five tenets of Islam came from Mohammed's teachings and from the example of his life. Some of the tenets are a continuation of pre-Islamic practice:

THE PROFESSION OF FAITH: "There is no God but Allah and Mohammed is his messenger."

PRAYER: All Muslims must pray five times a day facing the central shrine of worship, the Ka'aba in the Grand Mosque in Mecca.

ALMSGIVING: All Muslims who are financially able have a social responsibility to pay an annual alms tax to the poor.

RAMADHAN: During the ninth lunar month, fasting is meant to provide a time of reflection, empathy for the poor, and giving thanks for the Koran.

HAJJ: Adult Muslims who are financially and physically able are expected to make the annual pilgrimage to the Ka'aba in Mecca at least once in their lifetime.

* * *

One can get extremely divergent views of the Prophet Mohammed depending upon the source used. A favorable biographer will describe him as a gentle man who elevated the status of the weak, the poor, and women. He is known as a servant of Allah. A different biographer will describe him as one who lived violently by the sword and a man who was an abuser of females and slaves. He is known by some as an apostate.

Whatever the accurate description, the Prophet Mohammed established Islam in the seventh century, and it has become the fastest growing religion in the world.

21
THE LION OF THE NEJD

He kept in his bedroom the seven foot spear that he carried on the night he recaptured the desert city of Riyadh. The daring conquest had restored honor to his family, the Al Sa'ud. He united Arabia under a single religion – the religion that had governed his life. He financed the building of mosques and madrasahs throughout the Middle East, making Islam the fastest growing religion in the world. He gave each of his forty-five sons, born of his many wives, a personal slave, an *akhiwiya* or little brother. His sons both revered and feared their father. They marveled at his sexual prowess, even to the end of his life. He was called The Lion of the Nejd. He was Abdul Aziz ibn Sa'ud, the first king of Saudi Arabia.

The Kingdom known as Saudi Arabia is less than one hundred years old. Abdul Aziz united the Arabian Peninsula into a country so committed to the rules of Islam that even he at times chaffed at the "severities which were imposed on his community in the name of religion." From the beginning of his Islamic state, "Singing and musical instruments were taboo. There was not a single plant or flowerpot in Riyadh's terraces and courtyards, and there were quarters of the town where you could not laugh inside your own home without risking a knock on the door and a reprimand for levity from a passing zealot."

By the 1980s, Americans, as a whole, knew little about the Middle-Eastern desert kingdom that, by virtue of its oil reserves, held great sway over our economy. There were few books chronicling the history of the Islamic state and even fewer televised documentaries.

One broadcast entitled *Death of a Princess* piqued my interest when it was televised in the early 1980s. The story of a female member of the Royal Family and her young lover could have been a scene copied from the movie *The King and I.* However, in this tragic story the princess and her lover, who had planned an escape from the Kingdom, were publicly executed. The controversial report was based on a British filmmaker's dramatization. It was one that had infuriated the House of Sa'ud.

The British dramatization told the story of Princess Misha'il, a granddaughter of Prince Muhammad and great-granddaughter of King Abdul Aziz. The princess, who had been married at an early age to a much older relative, engaged in a romance with a younger man. When their illegal affair was discovered, the princess was executed. Her grandfather, a first generation prince, had the power to spare her life had he chosen to do so. Instead, Princess Misha'il was forced to kneel in front of a pile of sand and was shot. Her lover, who witnessed her execution, was then beheaded.

While I lived in the Kingdom, it was commonly rumored among expatriates that young, single princesses habitually cruised the desert and the beaches in their chauffeured limousines looking to pick up men for sexual escapades. The rumor was most likely untrue. The British filmmaker of *Death of a Princess,* in order to make his dramatization more colorful and without any evidence to support his characterization, included a scene in his film depicting "cruising princesses." That unsupported notion came to be accepted by viewers as truth and became part of the oft-repeated folk-lore about women of the Royal Family.

Not only was King Khalid infuriated by the world's shock and criticism of the executions of the princess and her lover, considered a rightful and just sentence for adultery under Islamic law, it is said that he was particularly outraged at the depiction of cruising princesses. That undocumented and unproven representation of Saudi life within the Royal Family was seen as a slur against women in the House of Sa'ud.

Another film about Saudi Arabia, this one a documentary explaining the Kingdom's roots in Islam, was aired in America at about the same time. It chronicled the history of Abdul Aziz's conquest of Arabia in the early 1900s and his renewed alliance with the Wahhabi interpretation of the religion. Prior to viewing the documentary, my husband and I had attended a cultural training course taught at Hurlbert Field in Florida. Life in Saudi Arabia, described to us in that intensive course, was consistent with the documentary that I later watched. I considered the televised film not to be at all controversial. I asked my friend Ahmed if he had seen the documentary while he was a student in the United States.

"I watched for a few minutes," he responded. "It was full of lies. I would not watch more."

Puzzled, I asked him to explain.

"It was a lie from the very beginning," he said. "Abdul Aziz was a hero. He was not a thief and a liar."

I had not remembered any such claim of dishonesty in the film I viewed. I wondered if we were talking about the same documentary.

"The film said Abdul Aziz put Arabia under the umbrella of Islam. That is a lie."

"But Arabia is an Islamic state," I responded. "Wasn't Abdul Aziz the one who united your country in Islam?"

"Or course, of course!" Ahmed answered, impatient with my questioning.

Now I was really puzzled. "Ahmed," I said. "What was it about the film that made you angry?"

"Under!" he snorted. "Under the umbrella! It was not under!"

As I struggled to discern the distinction he was making, Ahmed was eager to make his point.

"Under means to lie, to cheat. It means to steal, to hide. Like, you know, to sweep the dirt under the rug."

How easily language can create misunderstanding! I understood "under the umbrella" to mean unification. Ahmed understood it to mean deceit. The founder of Saudi Arabia, in my friend's mind, was being dishonored by the film. Obviously, this film was banned from his country, as were the film *The Death of a Princess* and most of the books I had read.

I tried to explain the term "under the umbrella." I told Ahmed the film had not meant to convey any disrespect. I said that the way the expression was used did not mean that unification was done in a dishonest way. Ahmed would have none of it. Words are powerful in the Arab tradition. A man's honor can be besmirched with the use of the wrong word.

"They should have used a better word. Not *under!*"

* * *

Abdul Aziz ibn Sa'ud was the first king of Saudi Arabia. It was he who united Arabia as an Islamic state and named the Kingdom for his family, the House of Sa'ud. A deeply religious Muslim of the Wahhabi tradition, Abdul Aziz proclaimed himself the protector and defender of Islam and of its holy places, Mecca and Medina.

Abdul Aziz was born in 1880 in Riyadh, Arabia. He was the son of Abdul Rahman bin Faysal bin Turki Al Sa'ud and Sara bint Ahmad al-Kabir Sudairi. (Abdul Aziz was the son of Rahman, who was the son of Faysal, who was the son of Turki from the family of Sa'ud. His mother, Sara, was the daughter of Ahmad of the family of Kabir Sudairi.) Abdul Aziz is known by several abbreviated forms of his name including Ibn Sa'ud, which means *the son of* Sa'ud.

When Abdul Aziz was about ten years old, a rival tribe, the *Al Rasheed,* forcibly took his family's land and governing authority. The terrified boy and his older sister, Nura, clung together on the same camel as they fled for their lives, barely escaping the swords of their enemy. Their flight to safety from Riyadh eventually led them into forced exile in Kuwait.

Humiliated by the devastating defeat at the hands of the Rasheed, the old patriarch of the Sa'ud family was said to have sulked in his tents. He was penniless and powerless as he spent his days brooding in his humiliation. However, his son Abdul Aziz plotted the time he would return to Arabia to reclaim family lands and restore his father's honor. The younger member of the House of Sa'ud spent the next decade honing his raiding skills and filling family coffers by pillaging from trading caravans and Hajj pilgrims. Raiding expeditions in Arabia were almost as much for sport as they were for financial gain. Stealing camels and plundering caravans, even those of religious travelers, were common endeavors. Any young Arabian male would have enjoyed the thrill of the adventure.

Still living in exile in 1902, the twenty-one year old Abdul Aziz and some of his relatives set out on a raiding expedition that would bring extraordinary change to the exiled family of Saud. Among the men joining the group were Abdul Aziz's half-brother Muhammad and their cousin Abdullah bin Jaluwi.

Targeting mainly the tribe of his old nemesis, the Al Rasheed, Abdul Aziz and his men stole camels and increased their ranks with tribesmen loyal to the family of Sa'ud. The success of their raids convinced Abdul Aziz that Allah's blessing was upon him. With his confidence bolstered and his bravado invigorated, the young Bedouin decided to attack the Mismak Fortress of governmental offices in Riyadh. About forty men accompanied him as he set off for Riyadh, while others stayed behind to guard the booty of camels that had been stolen in previous nights, primarily from the Al Rasheed.

Under the cover of darkness, the men used the trunk of a palm tree as a ladder to scale the mud wall and gain entry into the fortress. With little light to aid them, they moved stealthily through the residences in search of the Rasheed ruler. The sleeping occupants in each home were tied and gagged to ensure none would be able to alert guards. The governor's wife and her sister were found asleep, but the governor, Ajlan, whom the invaders expected to be in his bed, was instead spending the night in his government office that was enclosed in a gated conclave within the fortress. For the remainder of the night, Abdul Aziz and his men readied themselves outside that gate, praying to Allah and nervously waiting for daybreak.

At the first light of morning, Ajlan emerged from his sleeping quarters through the small gate and into the open court, expecting only his usual early morning horseback ride. Abdul Aziz and his men, waiting for just such an opportunity, immediately attacked the unsuspecting and vulnerable governor.

Abdullah bin Jaluwi, the cousin of Abdul Aziz, threw his spear in the initial assault, but his aim missed the Rasheed. The point of that spear lodged in the mud wall to the side of the gate where it remained a tangible reminder to future generations of the battle that took place there.

The governor desperately attempted to retreat into safety within the enclosure from which he had come, but Abdul Aziz and his men pursued him to his death. In the melee that followed, there is uncertainty about whose spear actually struck the fatal blow, but Abdul Aziz, as leader of the jihad, was declared victor. It was a monumental triumph for him and his family. The jihad was successful. Allah had prevailed. Honor was avenged.

With the assassination of the Rasheed governor, the family of Sa'ud reclaimed governmental control of the city of Riyadh. Abdul Aziz, the emboldened jihadist, continued his quest to recover lands that his family had lost to the Al Rasheed and consolidate control over others. One can imagine the sight of hundreds of men, their swords outstretched as they raced across the desert on camels galloping at full speed. Over the next two years, Abdul Aziz laid claim to nearly half of the entire desert plateau, known as the Nejd, which surrounded Riyadh. The fearless Bedouin warrior became known as the Lion of the Nejd.

Abdul Aziz founded a militant religious organization that assisted in his conquests. He revived the traditional alliance of his family with the teachings of Wahhab, a reformer who had attempted to return the religion to its purest interpretation and away from the more mystical Sufism. The centuries-old alliance had given the Sa'ud family governing authority in exchange for adherence to the teachings of the reformer.

The Rasheed did not give up without a fight. With help from an old ally, the Ottoman Empire, they were able to put Ibn Sa'ud on the defensive and in June 1904 delivered him a humiliating defeat. The Rasheed-Ottoman victory was short-lived, however. Supply problems diminished the effectiveness of Turkish troops, forcing them to leave the Arabian Peninsula. The warriors of Sa'ud were able once again to take the offensive against the Rasheed.

Abdul Aziz gained control of the entire Nejd by 1912. Continuing his jihad to unite Arabia under the Wahhabi interpretation of Islam, he captured the city of Mecca, including the Grand Mosque, in 1925. The birthplace of Mohammed and

Islam's holiest site had been under Hashemite tutelage for seven hundred years.

The Hashemite are descendants of Hashim ibn Abd al-Manaf, the great-grandfather of both the Prophet Mohammed and his cousin Ali. Mohammed's uncle and Ali's father, Abu Talib, was chief of the Hashemites. Today's Hashemites generally claim to be Sunni nobility as descendants of the Prophet's daughter Fatimah.

When the Hashemite in Mecca lost their position of leadership to the Al Sa'ud, British support resulted in them being installed as monarchs in both Iraq and Jordan. Hashemite blood line can be traced to the former Jordanian King Hussein, whose son King Abdullah retains power to this day.

"The Iraqi Hashemite branch, though, was strongly opposed by the local Shi'a Ayatollahs from the beginning. So in 1922 the Iraqi Shi'a religious leaders in Najaf issued a *fatwa* forbidding observant Shi'a from supporting the Hashemites."

The Shi'at Ali of Iraq remained the minority sect and in response to the fatwa continued to resist the authority and rule of the Sunni Hashemites. Until the fall of Saddam Hussein, Iraqi Shi'a did not participate in government and were not allowed to make pilgrimages to the shrines of Kufa and Karbala, the places of "martyrdom" for Ali and his son Hussein. The former President of Iraq undoubtedly viewed the presence of Shi'at Ali in his country a threat. Just a few years earlier, the Shi'a Ayatollahs had generated an Islamic Revolution in Iran, forcing the exile of the Shah.

The Royal Family of Saudi Arabia is also reportedly concerned by the number of Shi'a militants who are now flooding the border of Iraq, a border shared with the Kingdom.

* * *

Abdul Aziz ibn Sa'ud was proclaimed king in the Grand Mosque at Mecca in 1926. His name was given to the country when Arabia officially became *Saudi Arabia* and began to be recognized by other nations in 1932.

Six years later, deep reserves of "black gold" were discovered in the eastern provinces of the Arabian Peninsula – an area largely inhabited by Shi'a who are said to identify more closely with the Iranian Ayatollahs than with the House of Sa'ud. If Abdul Aziz ibn Sa'ud had stopped his jihad after capturing the Nejd, those oil-rich eastern provinces would not be part of Saudi Arabia. The Shi'at Ali who live there would be among the richest people in the world, while Saudi Arabia, without control of the deep oil reserves, would likely still be a desert Bedouin people living in squalor.

*   *   *

He who smites with the spear and effectively wields the sword shall inherit had long been the Arab tradition. The Prophet Mohammed had used the sword to defeat the opposing Meccans and, in doing so, validated the religion he taught. Centuries later, Abdul Aziz used the sword to unite Arabia as an Islamic state.

The national flag of Saudi Arabia bears witness to the feats of both men. Below the inscription of the first tenet of Islam, *There is no God but Allah, and Mohammed is his Messenger,* believed by Muslims to be the words of God, stretches the conquering sword of Abdul Aziz.

The sword remains a powerful symbol in Saudi Arabia. Two curved swords surmounted by a date palm form the common civil symbol of the Kingdom. Old Saudi men, turbaned and bearded, wear jewel encrusted curved daggers in ornate sheaths on belts outside their flowing robes. And, the sword is the tool of the executioner for crimes against Islam in Saudi Arabia.

The sword was not the only means Abdul Aziz used to unite Arabia. As he moved into each area, he married the daughter of the tribal chief, which allowed him to build alliances that he believed would endure for many generations. Men could obtain a divorce easily by merely speaking their intent three times, and they could engage in temporary marriages. These practices allowed Abdul Aziz to maintain the standard of four wives while fathering sons from diverse tribes throughout the Arabian Peninsula. Historians vary on the number of his wives who produced at least forty-five sons and about twenty daughters for the Lion of the Nejd.

During our time in the Kingdom, there were an estimated 5000 princes who were all direct descendants of Abdul Aziz. Current estimates of the Royal Family number in the 30,000s. The princes fill important offices of the government, the military, and much of business. Saudi law requires that the country be ruled by a son or grandson of Abdul Aziz ibn Sa'ud, and there are plenty from whom to choose.

* * *

Abdul Aziz "seldom allowed himself to get sentimental about women – at least not in front of other men. He discussed the bodies of his slave girls freely. Siesta time was when he liked to dally with them and when he had finished with a girl he might pass her over to his friends." But, there was another side to the man who would "lash out and beat men, including his own sons, when he was offended with them." His favored wives described an Abdul Aziz who in private was remarkably gentle and affectionate.

The king fell deeply in love with one of his wives, whose name was Jauhara. She gave him two healthy sons, one of whom, Khalid, became the fourth king of Saudi Arabia. When Jauhara died of an illness, the king was said to have grieved inconsolably, as did her little sons.

The king remained, throughout his life, extremely close to his sister Nura who was not only his confidant but his best friend as well. The two of them had shared a camel, clinging to one another as they escaped the swords of the Al Rasheed. When the telephone finally came to the Kingdom, it was to his sister's home that the first line was installed.

After many years of rule, Abdul Aziz's son Sa'ud, whose mother was Wadhba, succeeded him as king. It was commonly rumored in the Kingdom that Sa'ud lived lavishly and lasciviously. He had great wealth at his disposal, which he squandered. He was said to be more interested in wine and women than in governing. The Saudi Council of Ministers eventually deposed him.

Each subsequent king has been a son of Abdul Aziz. Sa'ud's half brother Faisal, whose mother was Tarfah, followed him as the third ruler of the Kingdom. It was King Faisal who announced an oil embargo against America after the Arab-Israeli War of 1973. Faisal ruled the Kingdom until 1975 when he was assassinated by a nephew. American newspaper accounts at the time suggested that the nephew was mentally deranged.

Living in the Kingdom, I learned that news in Saudi Arabia is so censored, it is unlikely our news-gatherers were told anything other than what the House of Sa'ud wished known. For whatever reason, the nephew entered the king's private room and shot Faisal at close range, killing him.

Khalid, Abdul Aziz's son by Jauhara, then assumed power and was king for seven years until his death from heart disease, a malady that continues to plague the Royal Family.

Crown Prince Fahd, "The Leopard," (His father was said to have called him "The Fox.") made significant decisions for his country and moved it closer in alliance with America even before he became king in June 1982. King Fahd ruled during a time of incredible wealth, modernization, and aggressive military development.

While we were in the Kingdom, we often heard of the powerful Sudairi Seven, the seven sons of Abdul Aziz by Hussah. King Fahd was the eldest of her seven sons. His brother Sultan is the current Crown Prince, and his brothers Prince Nayef and Prince Salman are likely to become kings in the future. Fahd's sons, who were educated in America, are potential kings as well.

Abdullah became ruling monarch in 2005 after Fahd's death from heart disease. King Abdullah, whose mother was Fahda, is considered more religious and conservative than his half-brother who preceded him as ruler of the Islamic state

*　*　*

A deeply religious Muslim, King Abdul Aziz ibn Sa'ud was convinced that Communism, along with Zionism, sought to destroy Islam. He refused to align with the Soviet Union, saying that he could not trust any nation that did not believe in God. His newly-formed nation, the Kingdom of Saudi Arabia, became America's best friend among Arab nations.

But now the very religion of the old Saudi king, the religion that had governed his life and led him to unite Arabia under its veil, the religion that had caused him to ally with the United States instead of the godless Soviet Union, was the same religion being used by radical Islamists to wage a holy war against America. It was a jihad few of us saw coming.

22
JIHAD

I could not have imagined the end of the Soviet Union or that the threat of Communism would cease to be our greatest fear. Neither could I have guessed that radical Islam using the weapon of terrorism would become the new threat to America in the twenty-first century.

American soldiers had fought and died in distant lands, and many were buried in cemeteries half a world away. Our battleships had been attacked in Hawaii, and several outer Aleutian Island had been briefly occupied by the Japanese before either territory became a state, but we had never been attacked on our own soil – not until a jihad was waged against the United States by a group known as The Base for Islamic Jihad. All of the terrorists who struck America on September 11, 2001, had been schooled in radical Islam, and most were from the Middle-Eastern country in which I had lived and my husband had advised, the Kingdom of Saudi Arabia.

Saudi Arabia was considered America's best friend among Arab nations. Their kings visited our presidents. We bought their oil and sold them our finest fighter aircraft. We trained their military pilots at our bases, and their princes were educated in America's most prestigious universities.

The Kingdom was a moderate state politically. It was not moderate in its adherence to Islam. Religious police relentlessly enforced the strictest interpretation of Islamic law. There was no separation between religion, government, or culture. The old Saudi king, Abdul Aziz ibn Sa'ud, had established a country so committed to the rules of Islam that even he felt the burden of the restrictions it imposed.

A devout Muslim, Abdul Aziz used the oil wealth of Saudi Arabia to fund madrasahs and mosques throughout the Muslim world. Each taught Salafism, an interpretation of Islam that places great emphasis on the traditions of the religion's patriarchs. Schooled in those madrasahs, vulnerable young men were impassioned by a promise of Paradise. Many believed there was no greater sacrifice than to die for Allah in a jihad against the "enemies of Islam." Among radicals, an enemy of Islam was increasingly defined as anyone who did not share the same interpretation and practice of the religion.

Saudi Arabians are a proud, some would say arrogant, people. They are proud that their country is both the birthplace of Islam and the guardian of its two holiest sites. They are proud that they speak Arabic, the language of the Koran. There is immense pride in their belief that God, having revealed some of His truths to Jewish prophets and some to Christians, gave his final and complete revelation to the Prophet Mohammed, a man who was one of them. For Saudi Arabians, Islam is not merely a religion; it is their life; it is their identity.

In a culture where the religion and the traditions of the Prophet Mohammed provide answers to all of life's questions, and apostates are beheaded; where Mutaween use cane poles to enforce Shari'a, and honor killings are tolerated; where every plan is conditioned with Insh'allah; where saving face is practiced as an art; where honor trumps truth, humiliation can lead to desperate acts.

Ambassador Marc Ginsberg, appointed to Morocco by President Carter, is an expert in the Arabic language and the Arab culture. According to Ambassador Ginsberg who made televised remarks after the execution of former Iraqi President Saddam Hussein, "Humiliation is the most powerful driving force in the Arab world." The Ambassador explained that Arabs who may be divided on important issues are brought together when one, even from an opposing group, is humiliated. Arabs unite behind that man and join forces against the person or government causing humiliation to a brother Arab. Arab honor and humiliation have influenced the Middle East for a very long time.

The Prophet Mohammed was humiliated as Arabians rejected him and his teachings. He was called an imposter, a liar, and a madman by members of his own tribe. Forced from his home in Mecca, he fled to Medina in 622 A.D. Years later in a victorious jihad against the Meccans, he was personally vindicated and his honor avenged. His triumph by sword gave credence to the new religion he taught.

Abdul Aziz ibn Sa'ud was humiliated when his family lost governing power and tribal lands to the Al Rasheed. Exiled to Kuwait, his humiliation festered until at the age of twenty-one he pronounced a jihad and returned to the peninsula to reclaim by sword his family's honor. His triumph over the governor of Riyadh – killing him in front of the fortress gate – is lauded in poetry.

The Arab world has a long history of humiliation and the compulsion to restore its honor. Countries of the Middle East, including Saudi Arabia, have repeatedly endured humiliation in conflicts with Israel, the Jewish state most Arab nations refuse to recognize. Jihads were called against Israel in 1957, 1967, and 1973. Each war ended, some as quickly as in six days, with Arab defeat and devastating humiliation.

Terrorists whose actions ultimately led to the attack of 9-11 were humiliated when Arab lands were conquered by Israel and when Egypt signed a peace treaty with the Jewish state. Among the men who were dramatically influenced and personally humiliated were Ramzi Yousef, the terrorist who planted a bomb in the World Trade Center in 1993 and Abdullah Azzam, a radical cleric from Palestine who created Al Qaeda.

* * *

Soviet troops retreated from Afghanistan in 1988, ending their nine year war with the Mujahadeen. Finally, a holy war had been won by the Muslim brothers. Honor was avenged. Not only had the warriors of Allah been victorious, they had defeated the second greatest power in the world – the mighty Soviet Union. Now anything was possible.

Impassioned by the victory in Afghanistan, radical clerics in mosques around the world began to preach that Islam could reclaim its position of prestige and power that had long been held by nations of the West. The means of achieving their goal would be terrorism. The clerics proclaimed that Islam would "liberate" Palestine and conquer the governments of the world –

not with democracy or Marxism but with the power of the belief.

Terrorism cells had, by the end of the Afghan war, been established in thirty-five nations and in at least forty United States cities – an astounding fact given that Al Qaeda had been in existence only four years!

In the year the Mujahadeen were victorious in Afghanistan, the creator of Al Qaeda traveled to America's heartland where he preached radical Islamic jihad to American Muslim youth. After defeating the Soviet Union, Abdullah Azzam proclaimed that nothing was impossible any more. Mohammed's army would return!

Back in Pakistan later that same year, Abdullah Azzam was traveling with two of his sons to an Al Qaeda meeting in a local mosque when a car bomb exploded and killed them. This assassination, which was never solved, cleared the way for Osama bin Laden, the Saudi Arabian multi-millionaire, to assume full leadership of the terrorist organization he had funded and Abdullah Azzam had created. Osama bin Laden could now direct "The Base for Islamic Jihad" in any direction he chose.

* * *

All of my life I had known that Communism, as it spread like a cancer following World War II, was the greatest threat to freedom-loving people. The Mujahadeen of Afghanistan fought to expel the Soviet invaders from their homeland, and America, along with Saudi Arabia, had assisted in their fight for freedom. But freedom is relative.

In the days following 9-11, Americans were stunned by nightly newscasts describing the plight of women in Afghanistan, now under the repressive rule of the militant Islamic group known as the Taliban. We learned that Afghan women were required to wear the burqa and were largely confined to their homes. They were restricted from work and denied education. Those accused of an infraction of Islamic law were subject to beatings and honor killings, including stoning. Basic health care was not available to them without male permission. Most pleasures were forbidden. All music, singing, whistling, and even kite flying, a long Afghan tradition, were banned. An Afghan Pashto saying sums up the subjugation women faced: *A woman belongs in the house – or in the grave.* Afghanistan was being ruled by strict Islamic law that was very similar to the Sala, also known as Wahhabi, interpretation under which Saudi Arabia had been united a century earlier. There was very little difference in the enforcement of Shari'a in the two countries, except that most Saudis no longer lived in poverty.

After having lived in Saudi Arabia and being aware of the subjugation faced by women living under Shari'a, I came to the sobering and disconcerting realization that Communism under the evil empire of the Soviet Union would have allowed more freedom to Afghan females than did the repressive rule of the Taliban. Rather than being forced into marriages as child brides, veiled, secluded, and subjected to honor killings, women under Communism were schooled and expected to work alongside men for the good of the socialist state. For Americans and most of the world, Communism represented an intolerable loss of freedom. For women under the Taliban, it would have been a gain.

*   *   *

At first our nation was stunned. Then we grieved the terrible loss of life. And then we were angry. Resolve soon followed. Previous attacks on American interests had been treated as individual criminal acts. After 9-11, we finally understood that a different kind of war had been waged against our country. The enemy was not a specific government – one with armies, uniformed soldiers, and space-age missiles. Instead, terrorism, the weapon of radical Islamists, was the means used to conquer lands and spread a religious dogma to the "Infidels" of the world. Jihadists were willing to die in a holy war, an Armageddon, to rid the entire world of "evil" and bring all people into agreement with the first tenet of their religion: *There is no god but Allah and Mohammed is his messenger.*

The War against Terror for the first time included states that sponsor terrorism. Our President announced changes in the Intelligence community that would help prevent another attack. The military, including one of my former students, was sent into battle against the Taliban in Afghanistan. Osama bin Laden became the most wanted man in the world – dead or alive!

Just as I had wondered why the American Embassy in Iran was attacked and hostages taken in 1979, now I wondered how America had become an enemy of Al Qaeda, a terrorism group whose name I had never before heard.

There were many widely reported theories for why we were attacked. A preacher in Chicago told his congregation, "The chickens have come home to roost." The West's oppression of less developed nations, our demand for oil, and poverty in the home countries of terrorists were all tossed about to explain the murderous attack. But Saudi Arabia was one of the richest per-capita nations in the world. Its male citizens had only to ask to receive all the money they needed from their oil-rich government. America certainly did not oppress the Kingdom. Neither poverty nor oppression by the West was a reasonable explanation for the fifteen Saudi Arabian terrorists.

Just as during the Six Day War in 1967, I now heard that the terrorist attack stemmed from control over the vast oil fields of the Middle East. There is no doubt that oil funds terrorism. Without oil revenue, Al Qaeda, Hamas, Hezbollah, and other terrorism groups would not have the means to fund their attacks. But oil is not the *motivation* for their acts of terrorism.

I heard U.S. Congresswoman Patty Murray from Washington quoted from a speech she made to high school students as she spoke of Osama bin Laden. "He's been out in those countries for decades, building schools, building roads, building infrastructure, building day care facilities, building health care facilities, and the people are extremely grateful. He's made their lives better."

I was speechless. If accurately reported, the Congresswoman's lack of understanding of an Islamic state was astounding. A Wahhabi Muslim like Osama bin Laden would *never* build day care centers. To do so would be totally contradictory to everything Islamic cultures require of women. Females in Saudi Arabia, Afghanistan, and the Sudan, countries where he had lived, had very little access to schools or hospitals and absolutely no day care centers. The idea of leaving one's children in any facility was preposterous. A woman could not work, shop alone, have lunch out with friends, attend a club meeting, or even leave her home without male escort. Why would she ever need a day care center? Even if she were to leave her home for a rare excursion with her husband, there were plenty of women remaining in the harem to care for children. Day care center, indeed! An absurd notion!

Osama bin Laden funded refugee camps in Pakistan and supported the war-wounded during the Soviet invasion of Afghanistan, but there is no likelihood he built any of the facilities the Congresswoman attributed to him in either Pakistan or Afghanistan or in the Sudan during his exile there.

He paid the government of Sudan to allow him safe-haven in that Islamic country that still enslaves humans, and he supported the repressive rule of the Taliban in Afghanistan, the country to which he returned after being expelled from the Sudan. He certainly did nothing to make lives better for the citizens of Saudi Arabia.

Osama bin Laden's father was in the business of construction and largely because he was favored by early kings became a billionaire through his work in the Kingdom. Is that what the Congresswoman was referring to? I wondered. It was hardly a charitable enterprise. Further, Osama was only thirteen when his father died. Certainly none of the building enterprises would have been attributed to the young Osama who was born after his mother had been divorced by Muhammad Awad bin Laden.

It was reported that "The Champ," Mohammed Ali, offered to make a film explaining to his Muslim brothers in the Middle East the wonderful freedoms we have in America. Again I was struck by the lack of understanding of what freedom means in an Islamic state. Western freedoms are considered satanic by many of the religious leaders in Saudi Arabia. We are not envied for our freedoms. We are reviled because of them.

Freedom of speech is considered an attack on Islam. No other religion is allowed in the birthplace of Islam. The total control of citizens under Islamic law is the glue that holds the Kingdom together.

* * *

The attack on America was not caused by oppression by the West, poverty, oil, or the lack of infrastructure in the home countries of jihadists. It had far more to do with the desire of radical Islamists to spread their religion and to establish an Islamic Caliphate throughout the world.

Perhaps some believed they could hasten the return of the messianic-like ruler, The Mahdi, by ridding the world of "evil." Others who revered the traditions of the Prophet Mohammed may have viewed the attack on America as an honor killing – the spilling of "tainted blood" to restore honor to men who were conflicted by temptations in the West.

Some had likely accepted without question their religious leaders' denouncement of America as the "enemy of Islam." The Ayatollah Khomeini had, years earlier, falsely accused Americans and Israelis of defiling the Grand Mosque in Mecca. His followers who believed the words of their religious leader attacked an American Embassy and killed United States Marines.

After the stunning defeat of the Soviet Union in Afghanistan, radical clerics taught that anything was now possible; that even America could be brought under the veil of Islam, just as were Saudi Arabia, the Sudan, Afghanistan, and Iran.

The attack of 9-11, most of all, was the result of devastating personal humiliation Osama bin Laden faced when he was rejected in 1990 by the Saudi Arabian ruler, King Fahd bin Abdul Aziz.

* * *

Two years after Soviet troops retreated from Afghanistan, Kuwait, having refused to forgive a ten billion dollar war debt, was invaded by Iraq and plundered of its wealth. Fellow

Muslims were raped and murdered in the invasion and occupation by its neighbor Arab state. Saudi Arabia with its vast oil fields was clearly next to be attacked. If undeterred, Saddam Hussein would gain control of the two greatest oil reserves in the world, effectively giving him a stranglehold over every industrialized nation that depended on oil. That was a chilling scenario. But the threat to Saudi Arabia had enormous religious significance as well.

The birthplace of Islam and its two holiest sites, Mecca and Medina, were in danger of being seized by "The Butcher of Baghdad." To a radical Islamist whose religion governed every aspect of life, the loss of those shrines would have been even more intolerable than the Soviet invasion of Afghanistan had been. Saudi Arabia had to be protected. The birthplace of Islam could not be invaded, raped, and plundered, as was Kuwait. The Kingdom's holiest shrines of Islam could not be desecrated.

Osama bin Laden left Afghanistan and returned to his home country where he offered the services of the victorious Mujahadeen to King Fahd. Who better to protect the birthplace of Islam than holy warriors who had just proven that Allah was with them in Afghanistan? Allah would give the holy warriors of Islam victory over Iraq as well.

"*Alhamdulillah*," Osama surely would have said. "Praise belongs to Allah."

King Fahd rejected Osama's offer. Prince Turki, the Saudi Arabian Minister of Intelligence who had suggested to Osama in 1979 that he go to Afghanistan and use his finances to aid in the relief efforts, summed up the rejection of Osama and his offer of the Mujahadeen this way.

"King Fahd's reply was, '...Kuwait is not Afghanistan. No thank you. Don't call us, we'll call you.'"

Osama bin Laden had to have been deeply humiliated. He was the proven holy warrior; the victorious one over the Soviet Union. (There is little evidence to support the notion that he actually fought in Afghanistan.) He was the native son of Saudi Arabia, the one who had Allah's power with him. Who better to defend Islam's two holiest places of Mecca and Medina?

King Fahd's rejection of Osama bin Laden as the defender of Saudi Arabia was only the beginning of his humiliation. President George H. W. Bush and the powerful military of the United States of America, along with a coalition of nations, were chosen to defend the birthplace of Islam. The holiest places were to be protected by the "Infidel." America, the "Great Satan," the friend of Israel, was chosen in his place!

Humiliated and incensed, Osama bin Laden began calling for the overthrow of the House of Sa'ud. Forced to leave Saudi Arabia in 1991 and stripped of his citizenship, Osama bin Laden was exiled with his wives and children to the Sudan where he paid the government to give him sanctuary. His terrorist acts against Saudi Arabia and the "Infidel" chosen in his place resulted in bombings of Arabian residential communities and in the deaths of Americans. Eighteen U.S. soldiers died in a gunfight in Somalia in 1993. A car bombing of the United States-operated Saudi National Guard Training Center in Riyadh killed five American military servicemen in 1995. A year later, a car bomb exploded outside Khobar Towers, A U.S. military complex in Dhahran. Nineteen U.S. servicemen died and hundreds were injured in that deadly attack.

In time, Sudan, too, forced him to leave. Osama bin Laden returned to Afghanistan, which was by then ruled by the oppressive Taliban. Leaders of the militant Islamic group had been schooled in the religious madrasahs and mosques where a strict interpretation of Islamic law and hatred for the "Infidel" of the West were taught. With his similar views, Osama bin Laden was welcomed into the repressive world of the war lords. His training camps for terrorism grew with aggressive recruitment.

Our media reported that Osama resented the presence of American troops in the Kingdom. That is surely only part of the explanation for his hatred for the West. Our military advisors wearing the uniforms of their branches of service in the United States had been in the Kingdom for decades. It was when Osama bin Laden was personally rebuffed as the holy warrior who could protect Islam's holiest places from Iraq and he suffered the humiliation of seeing the "Infidel" chosen in his place that he began calling for the destruction of America.

Osama bin Laden reportedly was convinced that the 9-11 attack would force America into a war in Afghanistan, a war he wanted, a war he believed his holy warriors could win. It would be fought on the same battleground where the Mujahadeen had already proven their ability to defeat the Soviet Union.

Had he totally ignored the impact of the C.I.A., the missiles supplied by America, the drain on the Soviet economy and Russia's inability to continue the costly war? Apparently, Osama bin Laden was driven by only one "truth." His holy warriors had prevailed, and that meant Allah was with them. Now, anything was possible.

* * *

The murder of Rabbi Meir Kahane in November 1990 by El Sayyid Nosair is believed to be the first Al Qaeda attack within America's borders. Rabbi Kahane had just concluded a speech in a New York hotel when Nosair, wearing a Jewish garment, entered the room and shot the Rabbi at close range. At the time, the murder was treated by our media as "One crazy Arab killing one crazy Jew." I was reminded of the attitude my father had held and expressed so long ago: "Jews and Arabs are the same. They are like brothers in the same family who fight all the time."

We could not have been more mistaken about the murder of Rabbi Kahane. The Al Farouq Mosque in Brooklyn raised money for the legal defense fund of Nosair, and Osama bin Laden contributed $20,000. Represented by attorney William Kuntsler, Nosair was convicted only of a minor weapons charge, despite many witnesses to the murder.

Ramzi Yousef, a nephew of Khalid Sheik Mohammed, was in the apartment of El Sayyid Nosair on the night of Rabbi Kahane's murder. Yousef, born in Kuwait of Pakistani descent, was fluent in seven languages and held degrees in chemistry and electrical engineering. He is quoted as saying, "Yes, I am a terrorist and proud of it as long as it is against the U.S. government."

Humiliated by the Arab defeat by Israel in 1967 and again in 1979 when Egypt's President Anwar Sadat signed the Camp David Accords, a peace treaty with Israel, Ramzi Yousef had an expressed desire to kill as many Jews as possible. Ahmed Murad, his childhood friend, suggested to him that a lot of Jews live in New York and that many of them work in the World Trade Center. With permission from the cleric of the Al Farouq Mosque in Brooklyn, New York, Ramzi Yousef built a bomb in hopes of bringing down the World Trade Center.

Among the terrorists who assisted Yousef in building the bomb were the cleric of the Al Farouq Mosque and El Sayyid Nosair, the Egyptian who had murdered Rabbi Kahane only three years earlier. Funding came from Ramzi Yousef's uncle, Al Qaeda's Khalid Sheikh Mohammed, the former engineering student whose shoes were thrown into the campus lake at the Baptist College he attended in America.

Detonated on February 26, 1993, the bomb failed to topple the North Tower and cause its collapse onto the South Tower releasing a cloud of cyanide gas, as Yousef had hoped. Humiliated by his failure to bring carnage of Biblical proportion in the deaths of tens of thousands of Americans, Yousef vowed to be successful the next time.

The next time was September 11, 2001. Among those who formed the plot to use airplanes to attack America were Ahmed Murad, Ramzi Yousef, and Yousef's uncle, Khalid Sheikh Mohammed. Funding came from the Saudi Arabian Osama bin Laden and his Al Qaeda global network of Islamic jihad.

*   *   *

The USS Cole had moored in the Yemeni port of Aden for a routine refueling. A small craft armed with explosives and manned by two persons approached the port side of the American destroyer. In the explosion that ensued, seventeen United States sailors were killed and thirty-nine others were injured.

Eight months later, an "Al Qaeda recruitment video featuring [Osama] bin Laden boasted about the attack and encouraged similar attacks." The celebrated murder of American servicemen was used to recruit future jihadists. The attack on America of 9-11 was only three months away.

* * *

A jihad, a holy war, is not an ordinary war. A jihad is a fight for Allah. It is a fight for Islam. A religious war is a sacred duty whenever there is a chance of success against the "Infidel." According to Abdullah Azzam, the creator of Al Qaeda, the jihad not only means fighting with the sword, it is an obligatory duty.

The Iraq / Iran War of 1980 was not a jihad. The Egyptian / Israeli War of 1967 was a jihad. The invasion of Kuwait in 1990 by Iraq was not a jihad. The attack on America was a jihad.

The zeal of spreading radical Islam, along with humiliation suffered when "Infidels" of the West prevail over servants of Allah can, in the hands of radical clerics, lead to enormous anger in vulnerable young men who have been taught that there is no greater service than to die in a jihad for Allah.

The terrorists who planned and funded the attack on America and those who carried out the hijacking of commercial airplanes all had a history of radical Islam. Most of them, including Osama bin Laden, one of the "pilots," and fourteen of the muscle men were from the Kingdom of Saudi Arabia.

Al Qaeda aggressively recruited young men for Islamic jihad, and Saudi Arabians were obviously vulnerable to the recruitment. Men, schooled in madrasahs and radical mosques, faced demoralizing incongruity between opportunities made possible by the new wealth and the revered traditions of Mohammed. Their honor conflicted, young Muslims responded to the promise of Paradise as a reward for their deaths in service to Allah.

The muscle hijackers trained in terrorist camps in Afghanistan where they practiced for 9-11 by slitting the throats of camels. Believing it was their duty to serve Allah in a jihad against America, they were prepared to die.

Some Americans dismiss the threat of radical Islam as exaggerated for political purposes. The terrorists, thought to be relatively few in number, are viewed after all as cowards who hide in caves. They wear rag/tag clothing – not the military uniforms of a powerful government. They do not fight with conventional warfare. Rather, young men and on occasion women strap explosives to their bodies in suicide attacks.

How can such persons pose a serious threat to America, the country with the most powerful military in the world? Alerting the nation to the threat we face is fear mongering and done to garner votes, the critics say.

Steven Emerson, an expert on terrorism and head of The Investigative Project on Terrorism, documents a chilling picture of how widespread the network of radical Islamic terrorism really is and the proliferation of cities within the United States with active terror cells. In spite of death threats against him and the resultant necessity of not maintaining a home address, Emerson continues to warn our government and its people of the magnitude of the threat.

It has been reported that the growth rate of Muslims worldwide exceeds the world's birthrate, placing the estimated number of Muslims at as many as 1.2 billion. My friend Ahmed proudly told me that Islam is the fastest growing religion in the world.

Polled after the terrorist attack on London's public transport system in July 2005, twenty-four per-cent of the local Muslim community expressed agreement, if not support, for the attack. If representative of world-wide sentiment, twenty-four percent of 1.2 billion is two hundred eighty-eight million who would be supportive of or at least sympathetic to a terrorist attack on a Western city in which they live!

The majority of Muslims are, no doubt, peaceful adherents of the teachings of their Prophet. Certainly I have known and worked with many Muslims in Saudi Arabia and in America who would not desire harm to our country. I regard them as my friends. Further, I do not believe that former King Fahd or his nephews the Ambassadors Prince Bandar or Prince Faisal would have supported a terrorist attack on our country.

Perhaps only ten percent of Muslims worldwide are jihadists. That would be 120 million radicals who consider America the Great Satan. Or, fewer still, only five percent would be sixty million who hate America. Even one percent of the 1.2 billion comes to a staggering twelve million!

In contrast, the combined forces of the United States active duty military in May 2007 numbered less than one and a half million, with an approximate equal number in reserve components. The number of law enforcement agents, deemed by some critics of the War on Terrorism as the appropriate vehicle to deal with isolated "criminals" who threaten America, is much smaller still.

Other Americans insist that to call 9-11 terrorists "Islamic terrorists" is as wrong as calling domestic terrorists like Timothy McVeigh, Eric Rudolph, or the Unabomber Ted Kaczynski "Christian terrorists." Our war on terrorism is religious bigotry, they say.

To equate the two types of terrorists is to totally ignore the motivation, organization, training, and funding of Islamic terrorism. Our domestic terrorists were not part of a global network with training and funding provided by an organization with the expressed purpose of destroying our government. They did not have a common goal, religion, or dogma. Their acts were those of isolated, fanatic, misguided, and crazed individuals and had nothing to do with any religious background they might have once had. Each man acted from his own twisted perspective.

The terrorists who attacked America on 9-11 were part of a funded global jihad network. They prepared for their jihad in well-organized training camps. From different countries and with differing incomes and levels of education, they had all been schooled in the madrasahs or mosques of radical Islam, leaving them vulnerable to recruitment by Al Qaeda.

*　　*　　*

Janet Napolitano, Secretary of Homeland Security, has warned our nation of a new variety of homegrown terrorists, and our news media have confirmed the threat. Abdul Hakim Mujahid Muhammad, a recent convert to Islam, is accused of having "political and religious motives" in the shooting of United States soldiers. An American citizen whose name was Carlos Bledsoe before he embraced Islam, Abdul Hakim was arrested and charged with first degree murder and sixteen counts of terrorist acts.

Less than two weeks earlier, in May 2009, four American homegrown terrorists were arrested in New York. The four were charged with plotting to bomb synagogues and use Stinger surface to air guided missiles to shoot down military planes. "They stated they wanted to commit jihad," New York Police Commissioner Raymond Kelly told congregants inside the targeted Jewish Temple.

At least three of the four men converted to Islam while serving time in American prisons. It was not immediately clear if their subsequent radicalization took place inside those prisons or in mosques after their release, but it is clear that radical clerics, making use of our freedoms of religion and speech, are recruiting Americans to become jihadists willing to die to bring an end to those same freedoms. For decades, terrorism groups have recruited jihadists from madrasahs and mosques of the Middle East. America's prisons have become the alarming new source of recruitment.

In his message delivered in November 2001, Osama bin Laden said, "We love death. The United States loves life. That is the big difference between us." His message of hatred for the "Infidel" and his call for a holy war – a jihad against America – has undeniable support in radical mosques throughout the world.

* * *

An Islamic extremist group, the *Hizb Ut-Tahrir,* held a conference in America's heartland on July 19, 2009. Meeting in the Oaklawn Hilton Hotel in Chicago, the very symbol of capitalism, the group of about three hundred zealots called for the fall of capitalism and the rise of Islam in its place. Freely using the liberties they denounced and spewing hateful rhetoric, the group specifically espoused an end to Western governments and a return by force to a Caliphate, a worldwide United Muslim State ruled by Shari'a. The stated goal of Hizb Ut-Tahrir is to have the green flag of Islam fly over the White House declaring in Arabic, *There is no god but Allah and Mohammed is his messenger.*

*　*　*

Khalid Sheik Mohammed, the engineer of 9-11, was associated with the *Hizb Ut-Tahrir* before he aligned with Al Qaeda.

*　*　*

The world heard the hateful, demagogic rhetoric of Adolph Hitler and for too long ignored it as the ranting of a lunatic. We dare not make the same mistake with the venomous and violent speech of Islamic radicals who are now calling for the return of Mohammed's army and the destruction of Israel and Western civilization.

The voices of freedom-loving Christians, Jews, and Muslims must unite in the repudiation of extremists who seek to bring carnage of Biblical proportion to the religions and civilizations of those who choose to live differently.

23
VEILED HONOR

The Saudi Arabia I lived in was on a collision course
between the traditional and the modern. It was a country so
dedicated to the teachings of Islam that even the king who
established it as an Islamic state had at times chaffed at the
restrictions it imposed. Some predicted the Kingdom could not
survive another fifty years with its dual personality. There were
contradictions in every part of the culture.

The Royal Family had the duty to enforce Islamic law
following the example of Mohammed, but there were persistent
rumors of drug and alcohol abuse, sexual indulgences, and a
"playboy" lifestyle within the House of Sa'ud.

Phenomenal wealth had brought rapid modernization to the
oil-rich nation, though women were still diminished and
obscured beneath thick black veils in the archaic practice that
pre-dates Islam.

Arabian males studied abroad, often engaging in forbidden
lifestyles, while religious police in their homeland wielded cane
poles enforcing the strictest interpretation of seventh century
Islamic law.

Only the religion of Islam was allowed and apostasy was
punished with death, but the Kingdom hired "Infidels" to serve
as advisors in every facet of business and the military.

Official slavery had ended in the Kingdom, but Third World
laborers lived in squalor and did the work Saudis themselves
would never do.

There was a constant call for Arab unity against Israel, but it
was Iraq not the Jewish state who invaded Kuwait and
threatened Saudi Arabia.

It was the Royal Family's duty to protect and defend Islam's
holiest sites, but the U.S. military was needed to prevent the
plunder of the Islamic state from another Muslim state.

King Abdul Aziz ibn Sa'ud was a deeply religious Muslim,
but it was the radical interpretation of the old king's religion in

the hands of terrorists that replaced the Soviet Union as America's greatest threat.

Saudi Arabia was considered the best friend America had among Arab nations, but on September 11, 2001, fifteen terrorists from that country struck with deliberate murderous intent. Nearly three thousand Americans died.

* * *

It has been said that the measure of a people is how they react to tragedy in another culture. When disaster hits in Mexico, South America, Asia, or the Middle-East, Americans are quick to send aid. When the tsunami struck South-East Asia on December 26, 2004, and a horrific cyclone devastated Burma on May 7, 2008, America offered millions of dollars and kept increasing the generous aid as the extent of each disaster was known. We were anxious to save the lives of Muslims, Buddhists, and Hindus. We collectively grieved for their loss.

Who can forget, in contrast, news clips of women rejoicing in the streets singing the Arab song of joy, *"La, La, La, La, La"* and chanting, *Allahu Akbar!* "Allah is great!" when news of the 9-11 attack on America and horrible loss of life reached the Middle East?

* * *

When terrorists, most of them from Saudi Arabia, attacked America, I thought of Fahda the Arabian woman who was ready for change and of Haifa the woman who offered me her dresses and of Lea the young bride who hoped her husband loved her. I thought of the giggling teen-agers at Lea's party who were so curious about America, whose questions about forbidden freedoms produced embarrassed titillation. I thought of the Bedouin women living in squalor in Hofuf, the ones with desperate, haunting eyes. I wondered if any of these women of the Kingdom sang the Arab song of joy at the deaths of Americans.

I thought, too, of Ahmed and Khalid. Both had been educated in America where they enjoyed our freedoms. They were kind and anxious to share their culture. They proudly opened their homes and introduced me to their mothers and sisters. They invited me to share in family and religious holiday celebrations. They were open and surprisingly candid in answering my endless questions. They endured the embarrassments I unwittingly caused them, saying, "No problem. I can handle it."

Moreover, they were unswervingly fervent in defending Islamic law. I had asked Ahmed if he envisioned a day in the future, perhaps in fifty years, when the rules might change. Could there come a day when his sisters and daughters would be allowed basic freedoms such as to drive an automobile or remove the veil.

"No, no, never! I would fight to the death to prevent this....We must protect our families....We must protect our honor....It is our duty to protect Islam!" he had answered.

Is it possible that Ahmed and Khalid could have become terrorists? Could their Islamic Wahhabi fervor have led them to hatred and the murder of "Infidels?" Had they become teachers of radical Islam in the madrasahs and mosques of the Middle East recruiting young men to fight in a jihad against America? Had they been persuaded that terrorism is Allah's will...a way to protect Islamic law in their beloved kingdom and to spread their religion to other countries?

"Islam is the fastest growing religion in the world," Ahmed never tired of proudly proclaiming to me.

And, what had become of the baby boys I held and complimented – the baby boys for whom I had asked Allah's protection. Had they become terrorists, years later, who desired most of all to kill Americans?

AFTERWORD

With the fall of Iran in 1979 a new threat emerged. The country once known as Persia became an Islamic Republic ruled by Ayatollahs who pursue the development of nuclear weapons and the destruction of Israel. Radical Islam experienced a resurgence as a political force, resulting in the proliferation of terrorism cells throughout the world.

Thirty years later in June 2009, Senator Joseph Lieberman spoke of the Islamic revolution in Iran, saying, "The revolution was meant to free the people. Unfortunately, it ended up as revolutions often do enslaving them in a different way."

The world watched as Iranians once again flooded the streets – this time protesting questionable election results. Demanding that their votes be counted and their voices heard, men and women risked injury and imprisonment, even death.

In a culture that gives few rights and even less honor to females, one young woman in her death became the standard bearer for the cause of freedom in Iran. Neda Agha-Soltan, whose name means "voice" in Farsi, died in a Tehran street after being shot by a sniper. Her death from "the shot heard around the world" became the rallying cry for the reform opposition movement in Iran.

Another young woman, one in Saudi Arabia, shared Neda's elusive dream of freedom. She said wistfully, "I like to be free. All people want to be free."

GLOSSARY

abaya The black, cape-like garment worn by women in Saudi Arabia to cover their clothing

Abu "The father of" Saudi Arabian men are generally identified by their eldest son. Khalid abu Abdullah means, Khalid, the father of Abdullah. Abu Abdullah is the shortened version and has the same meaning.

aghal The black cord, doubled and worn on top of the headdress for men

Akhiwiya "Little Brother" the title given by Abdul Aziz to the personal slave purchased for each of his sons

Al-Aqsa Mosque Located in Jerusalem; built alongside the Dome of the Rock as a place of prayer for Muslims

Al Haram Al Sharif The Islamic compound in Jerusalem, which includes the Dome of the Rock and the Al-Aqsa Mosque; the third holiest site in Islam

Al Qaeda "The Base for Islamic Jihad" established by Abdullah Azzam and funded by Osama bin Laden to fight the "enemies of Islam"

Al Rasheed "The family of Rasheed" a rival family of the Al Sa'ud in the nineteenth and twentieth centuries

Al Sa'ud "The family of Sa'ud"

AWACS Acronym for Advanced Warning and Control System; surveillance aircraft provided by America to Saudi Arabia

baksheesh A tip, gratuity, or bribe

Bedouin Nomads of the desert

bin Son of as in Ali *bin* Faisal; Ali *the son of* Faisal

bint Daughter of as in Nura *bint* Ahmed; Nura *the daughter of* Ahmed

Burqa An ankle-length tent-like garment worn by females in Afghanistan; it is typically blue and has a tightly woven mesh slit for the eyes

Caliph A cleric of the Sunni sect of Islam

Caliphate A government ruled under Islamic law

Chador A loose covering worn by Iranian females; it is typically black and drapes over the head and under the chin

Dhahran The Saudi Arabian city located at the coast of the Persian or Arabian Gulf

Dome of the Rock Third holiest shrine in Islam; built on the Temple Mount in Jerusalem

Eed al Adha The feast to celebrate the end of the annual Hajj to Mecca. Pilgrims offer animal sacrifices on this day.

Eed al Fitr The feast to celebrate the end of the month-long fast of Ramadhan. A time of family celebration and gifts, it is sometimes likened to Christmas.

El-Buraq "Lightning" a winged horse-like creature on which the Prophet Mohammed claimed to have been taken from Mecca to the Holy City (believed to be Jerusalem) during a mystic night flight

Fatwa An Islamic legal opinion

Fedayeen "One who sacrifices himself" Arab terrorism group, equipped by Egyptian intelligence for the purpose of conducting hostile actions on Israel's borders and infiltrating Israel with acts of terrorism

ghutra The headdress worn by Saudi males; usually red and white, but may be solid white in summer

Grand Mosque Located in Mecca; the holiest site in Islam and destination of the annual Islamic pilgrimage

Hadith The collection of sayings and actions of the Prophet Mohammed and his closest associates; compiled after

Mohammed's death to answer questions about the faith that were not addressed in the Koran

Hajj The annual pilgrimage to Mecca; required of all Muslims who are physically and financially able to make the journey, at least once in their lives

Hajji A pilgrim who is performing the Hajj, the annual pilgrimage to Mecca

Hamas "Islamic Resistance Movement" A Sunni Muslim extremist group based in the Gaza Strip

harem The separate part of the home in which the women of a Saudi Arabian household reside; females include wives, concubines, relatives, and servants; harem can also refer to the sexual partners of one man

Hezbollah "Party of God" An Iranian Shi'a movement formed at the time of the Iranian Islamic Revolution

Hijab A common scarf-like covering used by women throughout the Muslim world; it generally drapes over the head and under the chin without covering one's face

Hofuf The Bedouin settlement located inland from Dhahran, known as the date capital of the world; the site of the world's largest camel market and the legendary Arab Market; one of the world's oldest, continually inhabited settlements

ibn The son of, as in Sultan *ibn* Fahd; if the given name is omitted, ibn is capitalized: Ibn Fahd

Imam A cleric of the Shi'a sect of Islam; originally a descendant of the Prophet Mohammed; now representatives of Mohammed serve as Imams

Infidel An unbeliever; one who does not hold to the same interpretation of Islam

Insh'allah Allah willing

Jeddah The Saudi Arabian city located on the coast of the Red Sea that most closely resembles a resort location; most foreign embassies are located in Jeddah

jihad A holy war; a jihad reflects the combined effort of the Muslim community to achieve a religiously selected objective; it can include military or terrorist actions, boycotts, embargoes, and economic sanctions

Ka'aba The focal point of the Grand Mosque in Mecca; a cube shaped monument toward which all Muslims must pray; Islam teaches that the cornerstone of the Ka'aba was cast down by God as a sign that He was no longer displeased with Earth's first couple

Khamis Mushayt A Bedouin settlement located in southern Arabia near the Yemen border

Koran The Book of Islam; contains Allah's revelation to Mohammed and is comprised of 114 chapters

maarhaba A greeting, as in "hello"

madrasah An Islamic School

Mahdi Muhammad al-Mahdi, who would have been the twelfth Imam of Shi'a Islam; since his disappearance in 873, Shi'a Muslims have awaited his messianic-like return.

majlis A reception or sitting room

Masha'allah Allah's will

Mismak Fortress The mud garrison in the center of Riyadh that once housed government offices; site of the beginning of Abdul Aziz's jihad to reclaim control and unite Arabia under the umbrella of Islam

Mujahadeen The Afghan rebels who resisted the Soviet invasion of Afghanistan

Mutawa (S) **Mutaween** (Pl) "High commissary for the propagation of virtue and the prevention of vice" Religious police who enforce Islamic law

Niqab Worn by women who follow the Sala, or Wahhabi school of Sunni Islam in Saudi Arabia and other Gulf states; a black covering that has only a narrow opening for eyes

nouveaux riche The new rich

quais Good

Ramadhan The Muslim month of fasting; a time of reflection and thanksgiving for the Koran; also meant to foster empathy for the poor.

Riyadh The capital city of Saudi Arabia, centrally located in the Arabian Peninsula

RSAF Acronym for the Royal Saudi Air Force

sabkhas Sandy, salty marshland, inland from the Persian Gulf; they are known for the formation of sand roses

Salafism The fathers or early generations; Salafism is a generic term, depicting a Sunni Islamic school of thought that holds the pious ancestors, the Salaf, of the patristic period of early Islam as exemplary models; Saudis prefer the term Salafism to Wahhabi Islam

Savak Secret police of the Shah of Iran

shamal A desert dust storm, usually formed by wind blowing across Syria and Iraq

Shareefs Descendants of the Prophet Mohammed

Shari'a Islamic law; considered the law of God and the straight path

Shi'a The minority sect of Islam; comprised of about fifteen percent of Muslims, worldwide; religious leaders were to be direct descendents of Ali, the nephew and son-in-law of the Prophet Mohammed

Shi'at Ali "Partisans of Ali," or followers of Ali, the cousin and son-in-law of the Prophet Mohammed; Shi'a Muslims believe that only a descendant of the Prophet is a legitimate ruler of Islam.

shokran Thank you

shwarma A sandwich, usually made of thin pieces of roasted goat and yogurt sauce inside flat bread

souq A traditional market in Arabia

Sunni The majority, about 85 percent, of Muslims worldwide; religious leaders are chosen by consensus.

Taliban A militant Sunni Islamist militia, driven by an extremely harsh Medieval interpretation of Sunni Islam; followers are predominantly the Pashtun of Afghanistan and Pakistan

thobe The long, shirt-like robe worn by Saudi males; usually white but may be gray or brown in cool months

USMTM Acronym for the United States Military Training Mission

wadi A gully or streambed that is dry except during the rainy season when water collects

Wahhabi Named for Muhammad ibn Abdul Wahhab, who in the mid-eighteenth century formulated an austere, literal interpretation of the Koran; Islamic rule subsequently sought to refuse "all pleasant things" and unite all of life in the worship of Allah.

zanjero (Spanish) A manager of irrigation water who controls its distribution to farmers or homeowners who subscribe to the irrigation system

SOURCES

"Abdul Aziz bin Abu Rahman ibn Faisal Al Saud Ibn Saud," (1880-1953) *Jewish Virtual Library* jewishvirtuallibrary.org/jsource/biography/AlSaud.html

AccessIslam,thirteen.org/edonline/accessislam/glossaryhtml

Akeel, Maha, "Female Circumcision: Weight of Tradition Perpetuates a Dangerous Practice," *Arab News,* Jeddah, Saudi Arabia, March 20, 2005

"Al Aqsa Mosque, Jerusalem," *Atlas Tours,* http://www.atlas tours.net/holyland/al-aqsa-mosque.html, 2008

Alireza, Marianne, *At the Drop of a Veil,* Boston, Houghton Mifflin, 1971

Al-Misri, (April 12, 1954), quoted by Mitchell Bard, in "Myths and Facts Online," http://www.jewishvirtuallibrary.org, 2007

Amanpour, Christiane, "God's Warriors," *CNN Presents,* August 26, 2007

Amrani, Nora H., "Honor Killings and Women's Rights," vibrani.com/honorkillings2.htm, 2007

"Ancient Egyptian Papyrus," mnsu.edu/emuseum/prehistory/egypt/dailylife/ papyrus.html, 2007

Arab News, Comments make by Prince Turki, September 18, 2002, reported in "Prince Turki bin Faisal ibn Abdul Aziz Al Saud," global security.com

"The Ark of the Covenant," National Geographic Channel, February 21, 2009

Baier, Bret, *Special Report with Brit Hume,* Fox News Channel, November 16, 2007

"Bangladesh," *Country profiles*, ftp://ftp.fao.org/docrep/fao/oo8/a0205m/Bangladesh.pdf, 2007

Bard, Mitchell, "The Arab Boycott," *Jerusalem Post*, June 22, 2006, jewishvirtuallibrary.org/jsource/History/Arab-boycott.html

Bard, Mitchell, quoted in *Middle Eastern Affairs*, (December 1956) p. 461, http://www.jewishvirtuallibrary.org, 2007

Bard, Mitchell, "Myths and Facts Online, The 1956 War," http://www.jewishvirtuallibrary.org, 2007

Bettelheim, Judith, quoted in "The Lantern Festival in Senegambia," *African Arts*, Vol. 18, No.2 (Feb., 1985 pp. 50-102, Wikipedia, the Free Encyclopedia.

Blandford, Linda, *Oil Sheikhs*, London, Weidenfeld and Nicolson, 1979

"Blind Student Killed by Religious Teacher," from correspondents in Pakistan, May 30, 2008, www.news.com au/story

Bush, Laura, First Lady, interviewed by Greta Van Susteren, *On The Record*, Fox News Channel, October 29, 2007

Carter, Jimmy, President, "Human Rights and Foreign Policy," commencement speech given at Notre Dame University, June 1977

Cheney, Lynne, during television interview on The Fox News Channel about her book *Blue Skies, No Fences: A Memoir of Childhood and Family*, Threshold Editions, October 2007

Chesler, Phyllis, *Middle East Quarterly*, reprinted in ACT Northern Virginia/Richmond/DC Metro Chapter, May 3, 2009, http://actdcmetro.wordpress.com/category/honor-killings and *Pajamas Media*, www.phyllischesler.com

Colby, Jamie and Eric Shawn, Fox News Channel, July 19, 2009

Coll, Steve, "Who is Osama bin Laden?" *The Washington Post*, July 19, 1992, Global Research.com

"Dome of the Rock," Wikipedia, the free Encyclopedia, en.wikipedia.org/wiki/DomeoftheRock

Eltahawy, Mona and Kalpana, Sharma, "U.S. Should Heed How Our Allies Treat Women," October 24, 2001 womennews.org/article.cfm/dyn/aid/696/contect/archive

Emerson, Steven, *American Jihad The Terrorists Living Among Us*, New York, The Free Press, Simon and Shuster, 2002

Fox News.com, February 5, 2007

Gaouette, Nicole, "Voices From Behind the Veil," *The Christian Science Monitor*, December 19, 2001, csmonitor.com/2001/1219/pls3-w ogi.html

Ginsberg, Mark, Ambassador, Fox News Channel, December 30, 2006

"The Good Wife's Guide," *Housekeeping Monthly*, May 1955, reprinted in *Reminisce,* April/May 2008

The Great Women of Islam, http://jannah.org/madina/index.php?topic=1024, retrieved July, 2009

"Hagia Sophia, Wikipedia, the free encyclopedia, Retrieved July 2009

"Hajj" and "Festival of Sacrifice," Islamset-Islamic Pilgrimate, islamset.com/islam/festiv/hajj.html

Hashemite Royal Court of Jordan, Queen Noor, noor.gov/jo./main/honorcrm.htm

Hashim, Khadijah, "Khadijah," March 10, 2007, posted by aymenmdinBlogrool.trackbackhttp://www.islamfortoday.com/Khadijah.html

Hemmer, Bill, *America's Newsroom*, Fox News Channel, November 27, 2007

Historical Perspectives on Islamic Dress," http://www.womeninworldhistory.com/essay-01.html, retrieved July 2009

Holy Bible: Scripture taken from the New King James Version, copyright 1979, 1980, 1982 by Thomas Nelson, Inc. Used by permission. All rights reserved

"Honor Killing Victim Wanted to Live Like Other German Girls," *The High Price of Freedom,* Spiegel Online, http://www.spiegel.de/international/germany,0,1518,druck-555667,00, May 27, 2008

Hoven, Randall, "Inordinate Fear?" November 07, 2007, *American Thinker,* May 23, 2008, http://www.americanthinker.com/2007/11/inordinate-fear.html

"How Ahmed Chalabi Conned the Neocons," dir.salon.com/story/news/feature/2004/05/04/chalabi/index2.html

"How Many Muslims are in the United States and the Rest of the World," Ontario Consultants on Religious Tolerance, reliiousstolerance.org/isl_numb.htm, retrieved 2008

"Human Rights in Saudi Arabia: A Deafening Silence," reprinted from *Business World,* (Manila) December 2001, hrw.org/backgrounder/mena/Saudi

Imm, Jeffrey, Source: 9NEWS, Posted in Honor Killings, Ideology…, reprinted in *ACT*, April 21, 2009,

Immigration Hearing, UPI, March 9, 1993

"Introduction to Islam," and "Women in Islamic Cultures," skidmore.edu/academics/arthistory/ah369/intro.html, retrieved 2008

Jensen, J.R., *Six Years in Hell: A Returned Vietnam POW Views Captivity, Country, and the Future,* available from Amazon.com, prices vary for collectible copies

Jordanian penal code article 340, no.16, 1960; Article 98

"Kaaba," Wikipedia, the free encyclopedia, en.wikipedia.org/wiki/Kaaba, 2008

"Khadijah" by Khadijah Al Hashim, March 10, 2007, posted by aymenmd in Blogrool.trackback http://www.islamfor today.com/ khadijah. html

Kelly, Megyn, *America's Newsroom,* Fox News Channel, August 22, 2007

Kelly, Raymond, New York Police Commissioner, "Homegrown Terrorists Bent On Carrying Out Jihad," May 21, 2009, wcbstv.com

"King Abdullah," Saudi – U.S. Relations Information Service, February 12, 2007, www.saudi-us-relations.org

"The Kingdom in the Closet," www.theatlantic.com/doc/200705/gay-saudi-arabia

The Koran: Various passages

Lacey, Robert, *The Kingdom,* New York and London, Harcourt, Brace, Jovanovich, 1981: Excerpts from THE KINGDOM: Arabia and the House of Sa'ud, copyright 1981 by Robert Lacey, reprinted by permission of Houghton Mifflin Harcourt Publishing Company

Lieberman, Joseph, United States Senator, interviewed by Shepard Smith, Fox News Channel, June 15, 2009

Massey, Ray, *Liberty Post*.org, July 28, 2007

"Military of the United States," May 23, 2008, Wikipedia, the free encyclopedia, http://en.wikipedia.org/wiki/Military-of-the-United-States

"Muhammad, Aisha, Islam, and Child Brides,"
http://www.answering islam.org/Silas/childbrides.htm, retrieved
2008

Murray, Patty, Congresswoman, WA, quoted after 9-11,
"Hannity and Colmes," Fox News Channel

Owen, Richard L., "Yom Kippur War," June 2007,
Wikipedia, the free Encyclopedia

Queen Rania of Jordan, Interviewed by Wolf Blitzer, "The
Situation Room," CNN, April 22, 2009

Payton, Joanne, "Stop the Honor Killings," *Sayidaty
Magazine*, sister publication of *Arab News,"* January 7, 2007,
stophonorkillings.com/indes.php?name

Prince Bandar bin Sultan bin Abdul Aziz, Ambassador to
the U.S., *Al-Watan*, and reprinted in "Who's Who in the House
of Saud?" *The Saudi Question*, June 1, 2004

Prince Mohammed Al Abdullah Al Faisal, Former Saudi
Minister of Education, in a phone call to *Al Arabiya,* the Saudi
Arabian Television Channel, January 24, 2008

"Prince Turki bin Faisal ibn Abdul Aziz Al Sa'ud,"
globalsecurity.org/military/world/gulf/Turki-bin-faisal.htm, July
21, 2005

"Ramzi Yousef," quoted from CNN.com, January 8, 1998,
and reprinted in "Ramzi Yousef," Wikipedia,
http://en.wikipedia.org/wiki/ramzi-yousef

"Recruiting Center Shooting Suspect Pleads Not Guilty,
Held Without Bail," Fox News.com, June 2, 2009

"Religious Police in Saudi Arabia Arrest Mother for Sitting
with a Man," *The Times,* February 7, 2008,
www.timesonline.co.uk/tol/news/wold/middle-east

Risnor, Robinson, *The Passing of the Night: My Seven
Years as a Prisoner of the North Vietnamese,* available at
Amazon.com, $12.95

Robinson, Adam, "Bin Laden: Behind the Mask of the Terrorist," *Arcade Books*, New York, 2002, Review by Goertzel, Ted, PhD, http://arcadepub.com

Royal Inquest, Investigative Discovery Channel, June 12, 2009

Rusin, David J., "New Honor Killings Follow Same Old Template," *Islamist Watch*, ACT, May, 3, 2009

Sansal, Burak, "The Hajj and Eid," 1996-2008, www.allaboutturkey.com

"Saudi Arabia," Cultural Training Course, Hurlbert Field, Florida, 1981

"Saudi Arabia," *Freedom House*, freedomhouse.org/template

"Saudi Arabia Islamic Politics," atheism.about.com/library//FAQs/islam/countries/bl-SaudiIslamPolitics.htm

"Saudi Cleric Favours One Eye Veil," http://news.bbc.co.uk/2/hi/middle_east/7651231.stm

Saudi-U.S. Relations Information Service, February 12, 2007, www.saudi-us-relations.org

Sixty Minutes: Power to the People (Women Speak Out in Saudi Arabia) March 24, 2005, www.cbsnews.com/stories/2005/03/23/60minutes, Excerpts reprinted by permission of CBS News Archives

"The Story of Ziad Jarrah," *The Fifth Estate, the Pilot,* originally aired October 10, 2001, Updated January 19, 2005, http://www.cbc.ca/fifth/thepilot/story.html

"USS Cole Bombing," Wikipedia, the free encyclopedia, retrieved 2009

"War on America," Part One, *Inside 9-11*, National Geographic Channel, nationalgeographic.com/channel

The Weekly Standard, http://theweeklystandard.com/Content/Public/Articles/000/000/016/745nkkhz.asp, July 2009

Wehner, Peter, "Why they fight," *The Wall Street Journal Opinion Journal Federation*, January 9, 2007 www.opinionjournal.com

Whitaker, Brian, "Sex and Shopping in Israel and Saudi Arabia, April 19, 2006, commentisfree.guardian.co.uk/brian_whitaker/profile.html

Wright, The Reverend Jeremiah, quoted on CNN, Fox News Channel, 2008

Wollston, "Mohammed His Life and Doctrines," *The Catholic Encyclopedia*, newadvent.org/cathen/10424a.html

"Women and Islam," various books and pamphlets written by Muslim clerics and provided by Ahmed

Wright, Robin, "Saudi Ambassador Abruptly Resigns, Leaves Washington," *The Washington Post*, December 12, 2006, P. A23

News coverage and analysis presented on CBS, CNN, Fox News Channel, The History Channel, MSNBC, The National Geographic Channel, and PBS

SOURCE NOTES

Chapter One: Under the Veil of Islam

p. 4 *I remembered the Biblical account ...*, *The Holy Bible*, Genesis 24: 64-65

Chapter Two: Festering Humiliation

p. 9 *"Break off all links...,"* Robert Lacey, *The Kingdom*, p. 289

p. 10 *"and his militant younger brothers...,"* Ibid

p. 14 *"Over the cooler months..."* "The Good Wife's Guide," *Housekeeping Monthly*, May 1955, reprinted in *Reminisce,* April/May 2008

p. 15 *"The Arab people...,"* *Al-Misri*, (April 12, 1954), quoted by Mitchell Bard, in "Myths and Facts Online, The 1956 War"

p. 15 *"Egypt has decided...,"* *Middle Eastern Affairs*, (December 1956) p. 461, quoted by Mitchell Bard, Ibid

p. 17 *"My mother would kill me,"* *"It would break my mother's heart ...,"* quotes attributed to Mrs. Lynne Cheney while discussing her book *Blue Skies, No Fences: A Memoir of Childhood and Family,* Threshold Editions, October 2007

p. 20 *Years later, another young Muslim...,* "War on America," *Inside 9/11,* National Geographic Channel

p. 23 *Muslim cleric, Abdullah Azzam...,* "War on America," *Inside 9/11*, National Geographic Channel

Chapter Three: An Emerging Threat

p. 25 *..."most powerful driving force...,"* Marc Ginsberg, Ambassador, Fox News Channel, December 30, 2006

p. 27 *"Two Weeks That Changed The World,"* Robert Lacey, *The Kingdom,* p. 397

p. 28 *..."set into motion...,"* "The October War," The History Channel, December 2008

p. 28 *... "psychological vindication" "Egypt began to leave...,"* Major Richard L. Owen, "Yom Kipper War," Wikipedia, June 2007

p. 29 *Ramzi Yousef...*, "War on America," *Inside 9-11,* National Geographic Channel

p. 29 *An underground movement...*, Christiane Amanpour, "God's Warriors," CNN Presents, August 26, 2007

p. 30 *"We were here first," "We are here now,"* "The October War," The History Channel, December 2008

p. 30 *According to Islamic teachings...,* Atlas Tours, "Al Aqsa Mosque, Jerusalem," http://www.atlas tours.net/holyland/al-aqsa-mosque.html.2008

p. 30 *"more spectacular edifice...,"* "Dome of the Rock," wikipedia.org/wiki/DomeoftheRock, retrieved 2008

p. 30 *"The site chosen...,"* Ibid

p. 33 *As partisans of Ali...,* Chronology of Shi'a and Sunni sects taken from Peter Wehner, "Why they fight," *The Wall Street Journal Opinion Journal Federation,* January 9, 2007 www.opinionjournal.com

p. 33 *"A popular Shi'a..." "Day of Ashura,"* Wikipedia, the Free Encyclopedia, quoting Judith Bettelheim, "The Lantern Festival in Senegambia." *African Arts,* Vol. 18, No. 2. (Feb., 1985) pp.50-102

p. 34 *...*"seemed to hope*...,"* Robert Lacey, *The Kingdom,* p. 452

p. 37 *...*"he had finally to agree*...,"* Ibid, p. 452

p. 37 *"President Carter was...,"* Ibid, p. 452

p. 38 *...*"only son, Isaac*...,"* The Holy Bible, Genesis 21:10, Genesis 22: 2-13

p. 39 *"We love death..."* quote attributed to Osama bin Laden, televised news coverage, November 2001

p. 41 Historical context for attack on the Grand Mosque, Robert Lacey, *The Kingdom,* p. 480

p. 42 *...*"defiled Islam's most sacred shrine.*"* Ibid, p.480

p. 42 *...*"tyranny oppressing them,*"* Historical context for Shi'a uprising, Ibid, p. 489

p. 44 *The former engineering student...,* "War on America," *Inside 9-11,* National Geographic Channel

p. 44 *Under Islamic law...,* Adam Robinson, *Bin Laden: Behind the Mask of the Terrorist,* book review by Ted Goertzel, PhD, http://arcadepub.com

p. 45 *Infuriated by the Soviet invasion...*, "Prince Turki bin Faisal ibn Abdul Aziz Al Sa'ud," globalsecurity.org, 2007

p. 46 *Abdullah Azzam and Osama became partners...*, "War on America," *Inside 9-11*, National Geographic Channel

p. 48 *Among the many groups...*, Steven Emerson, *American Jihad: The Terrorists Living Among Us*, pp.131-133

Chapter Five: Compounds of Walled Seclusion

p. 64 *"to receive lashes...,"* Fox News.com, February 5, 2007

p. 69 *"Sodomy is punishable...,"* "The Kingdom in the Closet," theatlantic.com, 2007

p. 75 *More than two decades later...*, First Lady Laura Bush, interviewed by Greta Van Susteren during a Breast Cancer Awareness Tour in the Middle East, *On the Record*, Fox News Channel, October 29, 2007

Chapter Six: Sa'eed

p. 82 *The annual per capita...,* "Bangladesh," *Country Profiles*, bangladesh. pdf

p. 85 *..."the Saudi ambassador...,"* Mitchell Bard, "The Arab Boycott," *Jerusalem Post*, June 22, 2006, jewishvirtuallibrary.org/jsource/History/Arab-boycott.html

p. 90 *I had read...*, "Bangladesh," *Country Profiles*, bangladesh. pdf

p. 91 *Hajj, the annual...*, Access Islam, thirteen.org/edonline/accessislam/glossary_a html

p. 92 *"For the pilgrims...,"* Robert Lacey, *The Kingdom*, p. 515, 516

p. 93 *The Ka'aba is described...*, Ibid, p. 18

p. 93 *When the Prophet Mohammed conquered...*, "Kaaba," Wikipedia, the free encyclopedia, en.wikipedia.org/wiki/Kaaba

p. 94 *Eed al Adha...*, Islamset-Islamic Pilgrimage, "Hajj and Festival Sacrifice," islamset.com/islam/festiv/hajj.html

p. 95 *"Neither their meat...,"* *The Koran*, Chapter 22:37

p. 95 *"And he shall...,"* *The Holy Bible,*, Leviticus 6: 6-7

p. 95 *..."Lamb of God...,"* *The Holy Bible*, John 1: 9

Chapter Eight: Shari'a

p.117 *"I like to drive..."* "Women Speak Out in Saudi Arabia," Ed Bradley Reports on Women's Rights In Islamic Kingdom, ABC *Sixty Minutes,* March 24, 2005

p.117 *"The most important change...,"* *"It was the pattern...,"* Khaled al Dakheel, Professor at King Saud University, quoted by Ed Bradley, Ibid

p.118 *"The state's duty...,"* King Abdullah, "Saudi – U.S. Relations Information Service," February 12, 2007, www.saudi-us-relations.org

p.118 *"It's not important...,"* Prince Sultan bin Salman, "Women Speak Out in Saudi Arabia," Ed Bradley Reports on Women's Rights In Islamic Kingdom, ABC *Sixty Minutes,* March 24, 2005

p.120 Marianne Alireza, At *the Drop of a Veil*

p.121 *"I believe in...,"* "Women Speak Out in Saudi Arabia," Ed Bradley Reports on Women's Rights In Islamic Kingdom, ABC *Sixty Minutes,* March 24, 2005

p.122 Linda Blandford, *Oil Sheikhs*

p.122 *Her depiction of the newly wealthy...,* Robert Lacey, *The Kingdom,* p. 461

p.126 *Considered property...,* Nora H. Amrani, "Honor Killings and Women's Rights," vibrani.com, 2007

p.126 *Aisha was only six...,* "Muhammad, Aisha, Islam, andChildBrides," http://www.answeringislam.org/Silas/childbrides.htm, October, 2007

p.126 ..."no use for women older...," Robert Lacey, *The Kingdom,* p. 90

p.126 *Enchanted by her...,"* "The Tale of Abdul Aziz and Hussah," *Robert* Lacey, *The Kingdom,* p.174, 175

p.128 *"When it comes to marriage...,"* *"I did not ask my* daughter...," Joanne Payton, "Stop the honor killings," from *Sayidaty Magazine,* sister publication of *Arab News,* January 7, 2007

p.128 ...*a Saudi Arabian court refused...,* Fox News Channel, December 21, 2008 p.131 *It was a culture of honor...*, Unidentified female guest responding to recent honor killings, Fox News Channel, July 10, 2008

p.131 *"Domestic violence and marital rape...,"* "Saudi Arabia," freedomhouse.com

p.131 *...a Saudi princess...,* Phyllis Chesler, "Let's Rescue the Heroes: Free Asma'a al-Ghoul," *Pajamas Media* July 20, 2009 http://www.phyllis-chesler.com/590/rescue-the-heroes-asmaa-al-ghoul

p.132 *..."foreign women who are victims...,"* Phyllis Chesler, "Battered Women, Si; American-Haters, No," *Pajamas Media,* July 16, 2009

p.132 *A rare but much publicized report...,* "Saudi Arabia," freedomhouse.com

p. 132 *Punishment ranging from...,* Nora H. Amrani, "Honor Killings and Women's Rights," vibrani.com

p.133 *Four male witnesses to the crime of rape...,* Mona Eltahawy, and Kalpana Sharma, "U.S. Should Heed How Our Allies Treat Women," women'snews.org, October 24, 2001

p.133 *...the revelation from Allah...,* The Koran 24:12

p.133 *...a nineteen year old...,* Reported by Bret Baier, *Special Report with Brit Hume,* Fox News, November 16, 2007

p.134 *"It's practically impossible for us to understand..."* Senator Jon Kyl, quoted by Phyllis Chesler, "Child Barbarians in Phoenix: Obama Extends Their Stay Liberian Boys Gang-Rape an Eight-Year-Old; Just Like Old Times," *Pajamas Media,* July 31, 2009, http://www.phyllis-chesler.com/595/child-barbarians-in-phoenix

p.135 *A charge of adultery...,* Robert Lacey, *The Kingdom,* footnote, p. 97

p.135 *"...forcedly subjected to poor...,"* "Human Rights in Saudi Arabia: A deafening Silence," reprinted from *Business World* (Manila), 2001

p.136 *...if one woman erred...,* The Koran: Al Baqarah 2:282

p.138 *Each generation has passed on...,"* Robert Lacey, *The Kingdom,* p. 176

p.138 *Queen Rania of Jordan...,* Interview with Wolf Blitzer, *The Situation Room,* CNN, April 22, 2009 p.138 *"Where do girls go…,"* Nicole Gaouette, "Voices From Behind the Veil," *The Christian Science Monitor,* December 19, 2001

p.139 … *"was bruised and crying…,"* "Religious Police in Saudi Arabia Arrest Mother for Sitting with a Man," *The Times,* February 7, 2008, www.timesonline.co.uk/tol/news/wold/middle-east

p.140 …*"minimize the opportunities…,"* Brian Whitaker, "Sex and Shopping in Israel and Saudi Arabia," commentisfree.guardian, April 19, 2006

p.140 *After a three-hour spectacle…,* Ray Massey, *Liberty Post*.org, July 28, 2007

p.142 *Sheikh Muhammad al-Habad…,* "Saudi cleric favours one eye Veil," http://news.bbc.co.uk/2/hi/middle_east/7651231.stm

p.142 *A woman wearing a burqa…, The Weekly Standard,* http://theweeklystandard.com/Content/Public/Articles, July 2009

p.142 *"This is not a religious issue…,"* French President Sarkozy, *The Weekly Standard,* Ibid

p.142 *"O Prophet, tell your wives and daughters…,"* The *Koran* 33:59

Chapter Nine: Phenomenal Wealth

p.149 *whose people eked…,* Robert Lacey, *The Kingdom,* p. 280

p.149 *"medieval walled city…,"* Ibid, p. 281

p.149 *"hordes of Bedouin…,"* Visitors to Riyadh, Ibid p.280

p.149 *"The airport…,"* Ibid, p. 281

p.159 *Prince Nayef bin Sultan Al Shaalan, Royal Inquest,* Investigative Discovery Channel, June 12, 2009

p.161 *"Little Brother,"* Ibid, p. 177

p.161 *"When Prince Faisal ibn Abdul Aziz…,"* Ibid, p. 177

p.162 *The slave market…,* Ibid, p. 177

p 162 *A UPI article…,* UPI, March 9, 1993

p 166 …*Abdul Aziz did not trust…,* Robert Lacey, *The Kingdom,* p. 141

p.169 *The little boy, Muhammad Atif...*, "Blind Student Killed by Religious Teacher," From correspondents in Pakistan, May 30, 2008, www.news.com.au/story

Chapter Ten: From Camels To Mercedes

p.173 *A group of forty-seven...*, "Saudi Arabia Islamic Politics," saudiislampolitics.htm

p.173 *"The previously unofficial...,"* Ibid

Chapter Thirteen: A World of Travel

p.228 *Papyrus making was...*, "Ancient Egyptian Papyrus," mnsu.edu/emuseum/prehistory/egypt/dailylife/papyrus.htmlwww.touregypt.net/featurestories/papyrusmuseum. html

p.230 *Mohamed Atta...*, "War on America," *Inside 9-11*, National Geographic Channel"

p.244 *"...the greatest surviving example of...,"* "Hagia Sophia," Wikipedia, the free encyclopedia, Retrieved July, 2009

Chapter Fourteen: Ahmed

p.253 *Khadijah was the first convert...,"* "Khadijah" by Khadijah Al Hashim, March 10, 2007, posted by aymenmd in Blogrool.trackback http://www.islamfor today.com/ khadijah. html

p.254 *...estimates of Muslims...*, "How Many Muslims are in the United States and the Rest of the World," Ontario Consultants on Religious Tolerance, 2002, religioustolerance.org/isl_numb.html

p.255 *Hagar and Ishmael, The Holy Bible,* Genesis 21:9-14

Chapter Sixteen: Advising the Royal Saudi Air Force

p.279 *"The Saudi ambassador...,"* "Saudi Ambassador Abruptly Resigns, Leaves Washington," Robin Wright, *The Washington Post,* December 12, 2006, P. A23

p.280 *"Remember that we face...,"* Comments make by Prince Turki to the *Arab News,* September 18, 2002, reported in "Prince Turki bin Faisal ibn Abdul Aziz Al Saud," global security.com p.280 *"The editorial...,"* Prince Bandar bin Sultan bin Abdul Aziz, Ambassador to the U.S., in an editorial published by the Saudi Arabian Newspaper, *Al-Watan*, and reprinted in "Who's Who in the House of Saud?" *The Saudi Question,* June 1, 2004

p.280 *In 2004 the government of Saudi Arabia...,* Megyn Kelly, *America's Newsroom,* Fox News Channel, August 22, 2007

p.280 *Three years later...,* Bill Hemmer, *America's Newsroom,* Fox News Channel, November 27, 2007

p.281 *"Education in Saudi Arabia suffers...,"* Prince Mohammed Al Abdullah Al Faisal, former Saudi Minister of Education, speaking to *Al Arabiya,* Saudi Arabian Television Channel, January 2008

p.290 *"inordinate fear,"* President Jimmy Carter in a commencement speech entitled "Human Rights and Foreign Policy," given at Notre Dame University, June, 1977 Randall Hoven, "Inordinate Fear?" November 07, 2007, *American Thinker,* May 23, 2008, http://www.americanthinker.com/2007/11/inordinate-fear.html

p.291 *"He got Europe...,"* Ibid

Chapter Seventeen: Death for Apostasy

p.298 *Ziad Samir Jarrah...,* "The Story of Ziad Jarrah," *The Fifth Estate, the Pilot,* originally aired October 10, 2001, Updated January 19, 2005, http://www.cbc.ca/fifth/thepilot/story.html

Chapter Eighteen: In the Name of Honor

p.304 *A tale of honor killing...,* I first heard this story in the Saudi Arabian cultural training class, Hurlbert Field, Florida, and then again while living in the Kingdom; its original source is unknown to this author.

p.304 *...the temporary marriages...,* The Koran 4:24

p.305 *In general, honor killings...,* Phyllis Chesler, *Middle East Quarterly,* reprinted in *ACT* Northern Virginia/Richmond/DC Metro Chapter, May 3, 2009 p.305 *"Morsel liked hip-hop music…,"* and contextual information, "Honor Killing Victim Wanted to Live Like Other German Girls," *The High Price of Freedom,* Spiegel Online,http:www.spiegel.de/international/germany,0,1518druck "the High Price of Freedom"555667,00, May 27, 2008

p.306 *During Ahmad Obeidi's sentencing…,* David J. Rusin, *Islamist Watch,* "New Honor Killings Follow Same Old Template," *ACT,* May, 3, 2009

p.307 *A man of Kurdish descent…,Ibid*

p.307 *"The father's Muslim friends…, Ibid*

p.307 *Her husband suspected…,*Jeffrey Imm, Source: 9NEWS, Posted in Honor Killings, Ideology…, reprinted in *ACT,* April, 21, 2009

p.307 *Queen Noor, cooperating…,* The Hashemite Royal Court of Jordan

p.308 *"he who discovers…,"* Jordanian penal code article 340, no. 16, 1960; Article 98

p.308 *"Parliament has refused…,"*Jeffrey Imm, Source: 9NEWS, Posted in Honor Killings, Ideology, reprinted in *ACT,* April, 21, 2009

p.309 *"Most often this procedure…,"* Maha Akeel, "Female Circumcision: Weight of Tradition Perpetuates a Dangerous Practice," *Arab News,* Jeddah, March 20, 2005

Chapter Nineteen: The Patriarch

p.311 *"Abraham believed God…,"* The Holy Bible, New King James Version, Romans 4: 3

p.311 *Get out of your country…,"* Genesis 12:1-3

p.312 *"Please say you are my sister…,"* Genesis 12:13

p.312 *"What is this that you have done…,"* Genesis 12:18

p.312 *"Return to your mistress…,"* Genesis 16:9-10

p.313 *"No, Sarah your wife…,"* Genesis 17:2-21

p.313 *"God has made me laugh…,"* Genesis 21:6

p.314 *"Cast out this bondwoman…,"* Genesis 21:10

p.314 *"Take now your son…,"* Genesis 22:2

p.314 *"My father!…," "My son…," "Abraham, Abraham…,"* Genesis 22:7-8

p.315 *"In your seed…,"* Genesis 22:18

Chapter Twenty: Allah's Messenger

p.317 *The childhood of the Prophet...*, Information taught in Saudi Arabia: Cultural Training Course, Hurlbert Field, Florida, October 1981 and from various encyclopedia articles on Mohammed

p.321 *The slave trade flourished...*, Robert Lacey, *The Kingdom,* p. 177

p.322 *The little girl...*, Silas, "Muhammad, Aisha, Islam, and Child Brides," http://www.answering islam.org/Silas/childbrides.htm

p.322 *"The Virtue of Aisha...,"* "The Great Women of Islam," http://jannah.org/madina/index.php?topic=1024, retrieved July 11, 2009

p.324 *None of his widows remarried...,* The Koran 33.53

p.324 *"...the final revelation...,"* "The Hajj and Eid," Burak Sansal, 1996-2008, www.allaboutturkey.com

p.325 *"Hajj is also...,"* Ibid

p.325 *"The Pleasures of Paradise...,"* Wollaston, "Mohammed, His Life and Doctrines," *The Catholic Encyclopedia*

p.326 *There are three divisions...,* "Introduction to Islam," and "Women in Islamic Cultures," skidmore.edu

Chapter Twenty-One: The Lion of the Nejd

p.329 *He kept in his bedroom...,* Robert Lacey, *The Kingdom,* p. 174

p.329 *He gave each of his...,* Ibid, p. 177

p.329 *"...severities which were imposed...,"* Ibid, p. 178

p.329 *"Singing and musical...,* Ibid, p. 178

p.330 *The British filmmaker...,* Ibid, p. 462

p.330 *Not only was King Khalid...,* Ibid, p. 458

p.333 Historical context for the conquest of Mismak Fortress, Robert Lacey, *The Kingdom,* pp. 48-52 and Saudi Arabia: Cultural Training Class, Hurlbert Field, Florida, October, 1981 p.334　*The Rasheed did not give up...,* "Abdul Aziz bin Abdu Rahman ibn Faisal Al Saud Ibn Saud" (1880-1953) www.jewishvirtuallibrary.org/jsource/biography/AlSaud.htmlwww.

p.335　*"The Iraqi Hashemite...,"* "How Ahmed Chalabi conned the neocons," dir.salon.com/story/news/feature/2004/05/04/chalabi/index2.html

p.337　*Abdul Aziz "seldom allowed...,* Robert Lacey, *The Kingdom,* p. 90

p.337　*"...lash out and beat men...,"* Ibid, p. 90

p.337　*The king fell deeply ...,* , Ibid, p. 90

p.338　*"best friend and confidant"...,* When the telephone..., Ibid, p. 91

Chapter Twenty-Two: Jihad

p.342　*"Humiliation...,"* Ambassador Marc Ginsberg, Fox News Channel, December 30, 2006

p.343　Contextual perspective on the spread of terrorism, Steven Emerson, *American Jihad: The Terrorists Living Among Us*

p.343　*Back in Pakistan...,* "War on America," *Inside 9-11,* National Geographic Channel

p.345　*"A woman belongs in the house...,"* "Historical Perspectives on Islamic Dress," http://www.womeninworldhistory.com/essay-01.html, retrieved July 2009

p.346　*"The chickens have come home...,"* The Reverend Jeremiah Wright, speaking after 9-11 and quoted by Fox New Channel and CNN, 2008

p.346　*"He's been out in those countries...,"* Congresswoman Patty Murray, WA, quoted after 9-11 by Fox News Channel

p. 349　*Osama bin Laden left...,* "War on America," *Inside 9-11,* National Geographic Channel

p. 349　*"King Fahd's reply was...,"* Ibid, quoting Prince Turki bin Faisal, "War on America," *Inside 9-11,* National Geographic Channel

p. 351　*Osama bin Laden reportedly...,* Ibid

p.351 "One crazy Arab…" "War on America," *Inside 9-11*, quoting Steven Emerson, National Geographic Channel

p.351 *Ramzi Yousef…*, "War on America," *Inside 9-11*, National Geographic Channel

p.351 *"Yes, I am a terrorist…*," quoted from CNN.com, January 8, 1998, and reprinted in "Ramzi Yousef," Wikipedia, the free encyclopedia, http://en.wikipedia.org/wiki/Ramzi-Yousef

p.352 *With permission from the cleric…*, "War on America," *Inside 9-11*, National Geographic Channel

p.352 *Yousef vowed to be successful…*, *Ibid*

p.352 *…"Al Qaeda recruitment video…*," "USS Cole Bombing," Wikipedia, the free encyclopedia, retrieved 2009

p.353 *The muscle hijackers…*, "War on America," *Inside 9-11*, National Geographic Channel

p.354 *…how widespread the network…*, Steven Emerson, *American Jihad: The Terrorists Living Among Us*, Appendices A,B

p.355 *In contrast, the combined…*, "Military of the United States," May 23, 2008, Wikipedia, the free encyclopedia, http://en.wikipedia.org/wiki/Military-of-the-United-States

p.356 *Abdul Hakim Mujahid Muhammad…*, "Recruiting Center Shooting Suspect Pleads Not Guilty, Held Without Bail," Fox News.com, June 2, 2009

p.356 *"They stated they wanted to commit jihad."* New York Police Commissioner Raymond Kelly, "Homegrown Terrorists Bent On Carrying Out Jihad," May 21, 2009, wcbstv.com

p.356 *"We love death…"* quote attributed to Osama bin Laden, televised news coverage, November 2001

p.356 *An Islamic extremist group…*, Jamie Colby and Eric Shawn, Fox News Channel, July 19, 2009

Afterword

p. 363 *"The revolution was meant…"* Senator Joseph Lieberman, interviewed by Shepard Smith, Fox News Channel, June 15, 2009

ABOUT THE AUTHOR
Mary Laurel Ross

A graduate of Arizona State University, the author earned a
degree in Education, graduating with distinction among the top
ten percent of her class. Her professors nominated her for
inclusion in Who's Who Among America's Colleges and
Universities and in the Education Honorary, Kappa Delta Pi.
Recognized for her instructional skills, her teaching career
spanned twenty-seven years in five states as well as in an
international school in the Kingdom of Saudi Arabia.

Now retired, along with her husband of forty years, she finally
has time to put memories to pen. Her interests include adult
literacy, gardening, and her three grandchildren for whom she
writes children's stories.